GENDERED
JUSTICE

ISSUES IN CRIME & JUSTICE

Series Editor

Gregg Barak, Eastern Michigan University

As we embark upon the twentieth-first century, the meanings of crime continue to evolve and our approaches to justice are in flux. The contributions to this series focus their attention on crime and justice as well as on crime control and prevention in the context of a dynamically changing legal order. Across the series, there are books that consider the full range of crime and criminality and that engage a diverse set of topics related to the formal and informal workings of the administration of criminal justice. In an age of globalization, crime and criminality are no longer confined, if they ever were, to the boundaries of single nation-states. As a consequence, while many books in the series will address crime and justice in the United States, the scope of these books will accommodate a global perspective and they will consider such eminently global issues such as slavery, terrorism, or punishment. Books in the series are written to be used as supplements in standard undergraduate and graduate courses in criminology and criminal justice and related courses in sociology. Some of the standard courses in these areas include: introduction to criminal justice, introduction to law enforcement, introduction to corrections, juvenile justice, crime and delinquency, criminal law, white collar, corporate, and organized crime.

TITLES IN SERIES:

Effigy: Images of Capital Defendants, by Allison Cotton

The Prisoners' World: Portraits of Convicts Caught in the Incarceration Binge, by William Tregea and Marjorie Larmour

Perverts and Predators: The Making of Sexual Offending Laws, by Laura J. Zilney and Lisa Anne Zilney

Racial Profiling: Research, Racism, Resistance, by Karen S. Glover

State Criminality: The Crime of All Crimes, by Dawn L. Rothe

Punishment for Sale: Private Prisons and Big Business, by Donna Selman and Paul Leighton

Forensic Science in Court: Challenges in the Twenty-first Century, by Donald E. Shelton

Threat Perceptions: The Policing of Dangers from Eugenics to the War on Terrorism, by Saran Ghatak

Gendered Justice: Intimate Partner Violence and the Criminal Justice System, by Venessa Garcia and Patrick McManimon

GENDERED JUSTICE

INTIMATE PARTNER VIOLENCE
AND THE CRIMINAL JUSTICE SYSTEM

VENESSA GARCIA
AND PATRICK MCMANIMON

ROWMAN & LITTLEFIELD PUBLISHERS, INC.
Lanham • Boulder • New York • Toronto • Plymouth, UK

Published by Rowman & Littlefield Publishers, Inc.
A wholly owned subsidiary of The Rowman & Littlefield Publishing Group, Inc.
4501 Forbes Boulevard, Suite 200, Lanham, Maryland 20706
http://www.rowmanlittlefield.com

Estover Road, Plymouth PL6 7PY, United Kingdom

British Library Cataloguing in Publication Information Available

Library of Congress Cataloging-in-Publication Data

Garcia, Venessa.
 Gendered justice : intimate partner violence and the criminal justice system
/ Venessa Garcia and Patrick M. McManimon.
 p. cm. — (Issues in crime & justice)
 Includes bibliographical references and index.
 ISBN 978-0-7425-6643-9 (cloth : alk. paper) — ISBN 978-0-7425-6644-6 (pbk. :
alk. paper) — ISBN 978-0-7425-6645-3 (electronic)
 1. Intimate partner violence. 2. Women—Violence against. 3. Women—Crimes
against. 4. Criminal justice, Administration of—Social aspects. I. McManimon,
Patrick M. II. Title.
 HV6626.G36 2010
 364.15'553—dc22   2010032811

CONTENTS

1 Gendered Justice: The Social Construction of
  Womanhood and Intimate Partner Violence   1

2 Understanding the Scope of Intimate Partner Violence   19

3 Deconstructing Cultural Images and Myths of Intimate
  Partner Violence: Overcoming the Presence of the Past   45

4 Legal Jurisprudence and the History of Intimate
  Partner Violence   65

5 Policing Intimate Partner Violence   87

6 Intimate Partner Violence in the Courts   109

7 Correcting Intimate Partner Violence   139

8 Escaping Intimate Partner Violence: The Shelter Movement   161

9 Reality Reconsidered: Female Intimate Partner Violence
  Victim Images in Society   181

Appendix   197

Notes   199

References   201

CONTENTS

Index   221

About the Authors   235

1

GENDERED JUSTICE

The Social Construction of
Womanhood and Intimate Partner Violence

Intimate partner violence and sexual assault are the most common female-gendered victimizations to occur in any society. As official and self-report data have demonstrated, these crimes are most commonly male on female (Catalano, Smith, Snyder, & Rand, 2009; Federal Bureau of Investigation, 2008) and can involve physical and sexual violence, as well as financial and psychological abuse. While intimate partner violence undoubtedly involves a prior victim/ offender relationship, sexual assault may often involve a stranger attack. However, we have long learned that violence against women, including sexual assault and intimate partner violence, is more likely to involve men who are known to them, either as acquaintances, family, or current or former intimate partners.

National facts about intimate partner violence reveal that 4.3 per 1,000 females age twelve or older are victimized, over five times more than males (Catalano, et al., 2009). Additionally, 99 percent of all cases are committed by male offenders. Further, black females are more likely to be victims of intimate partner violence than white females and are twice as likely to be victims of intimate partner violence homicide. The nature of the intimate relationship is also not as dramatic a determinant of the violence. For example, spouses or ex-spouses were the perpetrators in 24 percent of female homicide victimizations; however, boyfriends or girlfriends were the perpetrators in 21 percent of female homicide victimizations. Interestingly, our social constructs paint a picture of the white, older female victim as a middle-income earner, a good mother, and an individual who has done all in her power to please her abuser and to secure protection via the criminal justice system.

Yet, for all of her efforts to stop the violence, social constructs tend to trump social status and make it nearly impossible to achieve victim status. First, it is important to note that our social constructs demand that victims of intimate partner violence experience extreme violence to be truly recognized as innocent. Second, though sexual assault is frequently involved (Belknap, 2007), victims of intimate partner violence who claim to have been raped by their abusers are often accused of lying in order to get even. Third, intimate partner violence victims are guilty (i.e., victim blaming) until proven innocent. Intimate partner violence victims are required to explain why the violence against them has occurred and why they did not stop it. While females who possess master statuses are more likely to be awarded the victim role, social constructs of the violence itself trump their master statuses.

Historical practices have allowed for the husband to chastise his wife and to expect, even force, conjugal relations. These traditional views place the blame on the wife for stepping out of place. Unfortunately, these historical gender ideologies still influence current gender ideologies. So, when we ask, "Why does she stay?" we place the blame on the victim. Current research finds that social constructs still hold women responsible for the dynamics within intimate relationships (Hust, Brown, & L'Engle, 2008).

Social constructions have created an *ideal victim* of intimate partner violence. In addition to requiring victims of intimate partner violence to express no blame, they must also display attempts to stop the violence. Intimate partner violence victims must be good women, passive women; however, they must also demonstrate a level of resistance, lest they be accused of liking the violence. Resisting the violence is necessary to show lack of consent, yet too much resistance reveals the victim to be aggressive, thereby redefining the crime as *mutual combat* (Grady, 2002; Straus, 1990; Straus & Gelles,

1986). Hence, the social construction of intimate partner violence creates paradoxes that make it difficult for victims to obtain help. The good woman is the deserving victim (i.e., deserving of justice and help). Good women are passive, yet intimate partner violence victims must resist. The good woman stands by her man for better or worse but must simultaneously try to escape the violence. However, if she stays with her man out of devotion or dependency, as is the expectation of the good woman, then she likes being abused.

INTIMATE PARTNER VIOLENCE:
A HISTORICAL PERSPECTIVE

Imagine you are a man or woman living in the United States of America of the 1780s. What does your life look like? As a man, what are your gender role expectations, what responsibilities do you have toward your family, and do you have the right to physically chastise your wife? As a woman, what are your gender role expectations and your familial responsibilities, and do you have the right to sue for physical violence perpetrated by your spouse? The legal history of the United States is premised in English common law. Some have claimed that in 1780s England Judge Sir Francis Buller stated that a husband can physically discipline his wife, even with a weapon; however, if he uses a stick, it cannot be thicker than his thumb. This became known as the *rule of thumb*. Many claim, however, that there is no written reference to this statement in English common law. Unfortunately, the English idea or social construct of the husband's rights was adopted into United States legal practice, thus shaping the approach to intimate partner violence within this country.

Now imagine it is 1824, and you have been physically abused by your husband. You seek legal recourse in order to protect yourself from the violence. However, the court rules that a husband has the right to physically chastise his wife, though in moderation (Boston Public Health Commission, 2009, as cited in *Bradley v. State*, 1824). Again, while one would be hard-pressed to find written reference to Sir Francis Buller's rule of thumb, it is nonetheless officially referenced in U.S. court decision making. Intimate partner violence at the hands of your husband is officially sanctioned.

Traveling forward fifty years in U.S. progression, you once again attempt to gain legal protection against physical abuse by your spouse. Fortunately, at least in one state, the courts now officially give women protection from spousal abuse (*Fulgham v. State*, 1871). Unfortunately, the criminal justice system refuses to enforce this ruling, because social constructs of the husband's rights and the woman's place are culturally ingrained. Stepping back to see the larger picture of intimate partner violence in the United States, one can travel eight years forward in time and find that North Carolina has ruled that a husband cannot be held criminally responsible for assaulting his wife, unless the violence was cruel in nature or caused permanent damage (*State v. Oliver*, 1879), reinforcing the rule of thumb doctrine.

One hundred years later you are still being abused, and the criminal justice system still refuses to recognize the violence as a crime, even when courts rule otherwise. Not until the 1970s does change start to take hold of the country in terms of recognizing women as victims of a social problem. How is such violence allowed to persist in a nation where "all men are created equal" and where everyone has the "inalienable right to life, liberty and the pursuit of happiness"? The answer, not so simply stated, is because our culture is based on social constructions of gender that result in inequality and that drive the processes of every institution within the nation. As a result, the United States has developed a *gendered justice* in which men have more rights and recognized agency than do women.

In this book we examine intimate partner violence within the context of gendered justice. We approach this subject through the social constructionist framework. This chapter will lay out the framework of social constructionism; define various important concepts; and place social constructionism in the current historical, legal, political, and social context. This chapter will outline gendered justice as a reflection of the larger U.S. culture. The first part of the book will examine the scope of intimate partner violence, legal reform surrounding responses to intimate partner violence, cultural myths, and victim blaming. In the second part of the book, the responses of law enforcement, courts, corrections, and communities are examined. The book concludes with a chapter that examines the implications of social constructs of intimate partner violence.

On February 9, 2009, pop star Rihanna (21) was brutally beaten by pop star Chris Brown (19) (Leonard, 2009). For days, the news media released pictures of a bruised and battered Rihanna, who was brutalized by her much stronger fiancé. Rihanna was hospitalized and Chris Brown was arrested. Both the victim and offender were African American and would typically not warrant newsworthy status; however, since both were famous cultural icons, the story was covered by the media for weeks. Initial reactions were shock and disappointment, but after a period of time, it was revealed by the media that Chris Brown had physically assaulted Rihanna in the past. People started to ask why she had stayed in the relationship. In fact, a survey of Boston youth revealed that almost 50 percent of the two hundred youth surveyed believed that violence was normal in relationships (Boston Public Health Commission., 2009). Newspapers reported that most of the youth blamed Rihanna for the violence (Boston Public Health Commission, 2009 as cited in Leonard, 2009). Over time, Rihanna was scrutinized for allowing the violence to escalate and for eventually going back to Chris Brown. According to *Good Morning America*, Hollywood was shocked that she returned to Chris Brown (Barsky, 2009). By returning and putting herself back into a violent situation, Rihanna lost a bit of sympathy. And while Chris Brown made a televised public apology, the news media continued to refer to the case as "the alleged" beating, providing a hint that perhaps Rihanna was not as innocent as she claimed.

GENDERED JUSTICE

Gendered justice is a form of justice within most societies that is structured by a patriarchal organization of society. *Patriarchy* is the organization of a society in which power and dominance run down the male line of the family. This results in male dominance over women in the society. Patriarchal societies vary in degree of dominance. In any given society at any given time, males may have total power and control over women, or their dominance may only be slight, approaching an equalitarian society. In any case of patriarchal structure, gender inequality persists and women are oppressed.

Legal, political, and social discourse have examined the status and treatment of racial, religious, and age groups and have concluded that, historically, these groups have been discriminated against. Additionally, discourses on gender inequalities have recognized the inequality of women. However, what has been lacking within these discourses is the recognition of cultural influences and social constructs as the ideological foundations of each institution within our society. Hence, while the United States Declaration of Independence claims that "all men are created equal," in recognizing the existence of a gendered justice, we must necessarily deconstruct what our founding fathers meant by "men."

In their use of written and spoken English language, many today still opt for the universal "male" to represent all individuals. However, legal language and cultural constructs tell us that the founding fathers were in fact referring only to men, and not to women or children. In addition, they were referring only to males eighteen years of age or older who were white landowners. Hence, social constructs of those individuals who had the "inalienable right to life, liberty, and the pursuit of happiness" did not include women, children, or racial, ethnic, religious, or economic minorities. Legal reform that finally recognized these groups as part of the "universal male" (i.e., the *law on the books*—as it is written) came as a result of cultural change, or changing social constructs. However, research shows that the *law in action* (i.e., as it is practiced) still socially constructs the "universal male" as an adult male, white, middle to upper income, and of a Christian religion.

Understanding the fact that there is no universal male, how do we interpret discourse within our criminal justice system? We must examine our hegemonic ideologies. *Ideology* is "a body of ideas reflecting the social needs and aspirations of an individual group, class, or culture" (Pincus, 2008, p. 19), while *hegemonic ideologies* are those ideologies that dominate within a society. Furthermore, hegemonic ideologies are necessarily held by the dominant members of any given society. Within the United States the dominant groups are male, white, middle to upper income, adult, heterosexual, and Christian (but mostly Protestant). These ideologies map out a society's ideas of work, family, culture, race, gender, and so on. Thus, in order to understand how and why a society functions the way it does, we must necessarily understand society's ideologies. As ideologies explain social behaviors and arrangements, we must examine race ideologies, income and work ideologies, age ideologies, religion ideologies and, most important to intimate partner violence, gender ideologies. As we see with the exclusion of so many groups with regard to equal rights throughout our history, it is also important to consider the *intersections* of these ideologies, as not all women are treated equally.

When examining any issue within our gendered justice system, we must understand our current ideologies and how they are influenced by the historical context. As stated earlier, racial, economic, and religious minorities were not considered to be part of the "universal male," and they were defined and treated as noncitizens or second-class citizens.[1] Women, on the other hand, have historically been defined as being an extension of their fathers or husbands. While the previous groups tended to be excluded and mistreated according to race, class, and religion ideologies that proclaimed their inferiority, women were treated as second-class citizens in order to protect them from the dreads of society, and even from themselves. And since women were not considered rational enough to make these decisions, especially legislative decisions, the legal system was governed by males holding gender ideologies and using a male lens.

Early gender ideologies affirmed that women's place was within the realm of the family, where they were to be docile but where they managed the household under the rule of the husband. Women's domain was the home, or the *private sphere*, while men's domain was the workforce, or the *public sphere*. While legal, financial, and disciplinary decisions were made by the husband, the woman was responsible for childbearing and child rearing. In order to enable the maximum functioning of this gender structure, American justice treated men and women differently.

Early American legal language was *gender specific*, in that laws were written specifically proscribing or prescribing the rights and responsibilities or the treatment of a specific gender. For example, early laws excluded women from various work industries, such as law enforcement and legal practice, from owning property or income, and from voting, and did not classify intimate partner violence as criminal assault. The legal system included mostly *gender-neutral laws*; that is, they were written without preferential treatment toward any specific gender. They were written to include both men and women. However, within a gendered justice system, the implementation of these laws was often gender specific, discriminating against women.

The gendered nature of justice is indisputable when examining American history. One can use the various examples of women's movements, which secured women's rights to vote, divorce, gain child custody, own property, work, and gain recognition as criminal victims of intimate partner violence, as evidence of a gender-specific justice. Many like to think that since activists succeeded in changing most gender-specific laws to gender-neutral laws, there is no more sexism in our society, especially not in our justice system. In other words, "the fight was won; now let's move on." However, this is far from the truth. Research has revealed that in the last several decades, gendered justice, which is based in gender ideologies, has become more egalitarian, yet patriarchy and sexism are still embedded in it today (Belknap, 2007; Garcia & Schweikert, 2010; Naffine, 1987). This persistence is revealed in the social construction of gender within our culture. This social construction drives our ideologies, which in turn drive our institutional functioning.

SOCIAL CONSTRUCTIONISM

Gendered justice is a reflection of culturally agreed-upon ideas of the roles of men and women in our society. These cultural ideas are known as social constructs and are defined in the social constructionism perspective. According to *social constructionism*, our reality, our society, and our culture are created in a continual process of interaction, *making*, and *doing* (Acker, 1992; Berger & Luckmann, 1966; Garcia & Schweikert, 2010; Grossberg, Wartella, & Whitney, 1998).

The social construction of reality is a process in which people give meaning to all interactions, behaviors, and conditions and claim them to be *essential* to reality (Garcia, 2008; Loseke, 1999; Surette, 1998).

Essentialism claims that statuses and situations are inherent in our reality. Thus, women make less money in the workforce because they are less capable by nature. Social constructionism, however, claims that through interaction we create the conditions of women in the workforce by socially constructing images of women as less capable, less competitive, and less rational. These constructs are then defined as essential, or inherent, in women. On the other hand, we socially construct images of men as more capable, more competitive, and more rational. The images we socially construct are generalized in order to gain a better understanding of the individuals who belong to the grouping under consideration. Thus, the images that are generalized to all men or all women are generalized and specifically applied to individuals in a given interaction.

In addition to generalizing, social constructs are also categorized and typified into groupings in order to simplify complex situations. Through interactions we internalize meaning, then act accordingly. According to Berger and Luckmann, the individual "simultaneously externalizes his *or her* own being into the social world and internalizes it as an objective reality" (1966, p. 129, italicized text added). So we internalize the categories and give meaning and value to these categorizations. It is important to understand that members of the categories do not have to be observed to be given meaning and value. The process of generalization via socialization can occur through hearsay or media exposure (Hust, et al., 2008; Kukkonen, 2008). One category becomes the basis for understanding a gender or a race or a class. This category becomes the standard for which behaviors, beliefs, and conditions are most preferable to society. This is the standard to which all different categories are held. If different categories do not equate with the standard, then they are seen as deviant. Over the course of time these standards become normal to society, or the norm.

Norms within our social constructs are significant to our interactions. Those social categories that become the standard for a social group become the norm, while different groups become *other* (Rosenblum & Travis, 1996). Thus, for gender the norm is male, for race the norm is white, for class the norm is wealth, and for age the norm is adult. We also extend these constructs to religion, setting the norm within the United States as Christianity; to nationality, with American as the norm; and to sexuality, with heterosexual as the norm. Within this analysis of interpersonal violence, heterosexuality is a primary concern of society.[2] To be *othered* is to be defined as wrong or as deviant. Among some social groupings it is the affiliation with the category itself that makes the members deviant. For example, Black and Hispanic males tend to be viewed as deviant in criminal and economic institutions. Muslims are assumed to be terrorists, and youth tend to be defined as deviant, i.e., as criminals in training.

Social constructs become ingrained into culture through the process of socialization and are reinforced via daily interaction. As a result, the *making* of constructs requires the *doing* of constructs and thus allows for changes of these same constructs over time (Acker, 1992; Garcia & Schweikert, 2010; Grossberg, et al., 1998). *Doing* requires that people behave according to the expectations of their gender, race, class, and so forth. Feminist theory has claimed that men and women must *do gender* on a day-to-day basis or face rejection (Acker, 1992; Belknap, 2007; Garcia, 2003; Garcia & Schweikert, 2010; West & Fenstermaker, 1993). As a result, women and men must behave according to culturally prescribed gender roles. Gender roles are so fundamental to culture that prescriptions (i.e., behavior and beliefs one shall engage in) and proscriptions (i.e., behavior and beliefs one shall not engage in) are codified by our legal system. People who do not *do gender* are not considered to be good men or good women. They may face social ostracism or an increased severity of criminal punishment when in violation of a law (Keitner, 2002).

It would be simplistic to believe that all that is expected is to *do gender*. As discussed above, society prescribes behaviors and beliefs for other master statuses, as well. Master statuses are positions one holds that define who the person is. They are important to one's self-identity and to how society defines a person. As a result, people must also *do race*, *do class*, and *do age*. Master statuses are also primary within our ideologies. Since any one person holds a master status in each of these social groups, we can then argue that we *do culture*.

The ideologies that drive our understandings of race, class, and age provide social constructs that place people within hierarchies, much like patriarchy does with gender. Unfortunately, the meanings we link to social constructs place the norm at the top of the hierarchy and the *other* below the norm, with some groups at the very bottom. Hierarchies are framed within systems of social difference and determine the distribution of power and resources. Those at the top of the hierarchy obtain and retain the most power and resources, while the *others* fight to possess what is left. These *others* become marginalized (the normative group being central) and are known as oppressed groups. However, people can possess more than one marginalized status. This is referred to as *multiple marginality*. For example, a female may be African-American, poor, and young. While a male represents the gendered norm, he may be a Hispanic immigrant. These social facts require that we examine how the intersections between master statuses (i.e., the multiple marginalities) and intimate partner violence affect these individuals.

Social Construction of Womanhood

Before we begin our discussion of intersections and intimate partner violence, we must examine the social construction of womanhood, whose formation began during the colonial era. Colonial America brought images of gender, work, and family, as well as common law, from Europe. Among the many constructs of gender was the ideology that a woman's place was with the family, while a man's place was to protect and financially provide for the family. This is referred to as the separate spheres ideology. This ideology places women in the private sphere (i.e., the home and family) and men in the public sphere (i.e., work and politics). In agricultural societies these duties were often fulfilled at home, with men taking the primary responsibility of interacting with the public sphere when needed while women remained home. Among the nonagricultural sects the same form of gendered structure existed. The notion of woman as wife and daughter solely was codified in laws that dictated their lack of voting rights and their lack of the right to own property and even to claim custody of children on the rare occasion that divorce occurred (Mason, 1994). Women who worked out of the home were most commonly located in lower economic classes and worked out of necessity.

With the advent of the Victorian era (1837–1901), a new image of womanhood was constructed that placed women on a higher moral pedestal. During this time, women came to be seen as too delicate and frail to engage in the hard labor that many women already knew. Women needed the protection of men in all instances, including shielding from the harshness of society. This social construction, which later came to be known as the *cult of domesticity* or the *cult of true womanhood*, could be accomplished only by the wealthier classes, who could afford not to have wives and daughters work outside of the home (Pascale, 2001; Schenone, 2003). Those who were less economically comfortable, including most immigrants, were unable to live on just the income of the husband. As a result, wives and daughters were required to join the paid workforce. Unfortunately, social constructions dictating the nature of women and work during the Victorian era were quickly adopted as the hegemonic gender ideology, and lower-income and immigrant women came to be defined as deviant, as not real women, and were not seen as delicate and frail.

Victorian era womanhood imposed a way of life on women that was oppressive while simultaneously defining women as better than men. Some of the revered attributes of womanhood included higher morality, passivity, delicacy, even frailty, and the need for protection (Garcia, 2003; Pascale, 2001). Since high morality (and only the morality viewed correct by the most powerful groups in society) is something that is desirable, it was determined that women needed to be protected in order to ensure that they maintained their morality and were able to pass it along to their children, as well as to other segments of society in need of direction. And, since women were also passive and delicate, further desirable traits in a good woman and good wife, they needed to be protected by the men in their lives. Social constructs of manhood dictated that good men were good husbands, strong, intelligent, and capable of protecting the women and children in their lives. So while men protected women from physical harm, they also protected them from social harm, which could work to destroy their higher morality.

Put together, this required that women be kept home as much as possible and chaperoned when traveling outside of the home. Women caught without a chaperone, especially in the presence of a man not closely related to them, were viewed as tainted. This also required that women not join the paid workforce. When women worked outside of the home, the only acceptable capacity was to volunteer their time for a good cause that needed their moral support.

Unfortunately, social constructs must be understood through *intersections*. And while women were viewed as having a higher morality than men, only white wealthy women were constructed with this image. Race, class, and immigrant ideologies intermingled with gender ideologies, enhancing marginality and transforming it into multiple marginality (Belknap, 2007; Della Giustina, 2010). Class ideologies, in part, focus on the morality and hard work of economic groups. When we examine these ideologies, society tends to focus on individual or cultural defects theories, claiming that poor people are poor because they lack the morality to engage in hard work and law-abiding behavior (Michalowski, 2009). Similarly, race ideologies construct racial and ethnic minorities as deviant, unintelligent, and lazy (Smith, 2009). These ideologies are often extended to immigrant groups (Doob, 2005; Fernandez & Alverez, 2009; Gerstenfeld, 2004; Perry, 2009; Perry, Fernandez, & Costelloe, 2009; Pincus, 2008). The consequences are that these groups are denied the same status and privilege as the dominant groups. Thus, while white wealthy women were kept home and were protected, minority women were often in the workforce and were not treated with the same respect and protection.

Fortunately, as society progressed, so did the ideologies of womanhood, as well as the laws regulating women's rights, work abilities, and movements. Though the Nineteenth Amendment to the U.S. Constitution gave women the right to vote in 1920, the women's suffrage movement began in 1848 with the first women's rights convention in Seneca Falls, New York (Mason, 1994). This was the beginning of social discontent with women's place in society on a large scale. The efforts of women such as Elizabeth Cady Stanton, Susan B. Anthony, Lucretia Mott, and Elizabeth Blackwell, among so many others, ushered in an era where women's acceptance into the workforce began to be a possibility. Unfortunately, much of this amounted to paper promises, and true equality was a long time coming.

During World War II, war factories enticed women to contribute to the war effort and work while their men were away. The mass media provided many advertisements revealing constructs of women as brave and capable employees. The famous Rosie the Riveter wore a red polka-dot bandana and a blue button-down shirt, revealing arm muscles (Yellin, 2004). Women finally had the opportunity to work at jobs that were otherwise closed to them and that provided higher wages. By 1943, fifteen million women were part of a workforce that demanded more women employees. During World War II, women were praised for their strength, commitment, work ethic, and competency; however, once the war ended, many women were laid off and were told to go home to care for their families or were demoted to lower-paying "women's jobs." While many women did rejoin the private sphere, many others stayed in the workforce. So while the social constructs of womanhood returned to a reformed Victorian ideology, the doors were open to possibilities for women. Women were enticed by the kind of freedom that one can attain only with some level of wealth.

The 1950s were a struggle to return to the good old days when men went to work and provided for their families and women stayed home and were said to be happy to run the household and raise the children. However, women's dissatisfaction with their status spread, and women increasingly rejected their "domestic cages" (Meyerowitz, 1994). Slowly, activism among women increased. Many women demanded their place in the workforce or at least the right to choose to join it. Title VII of the Civil Rights Act of 1964 banned any employer from basing the terms of employment on sex, race, religion, or national origin, and eight years later the Equal Employment Opportunity Act of 1972 was passed to enforce Title VII. While the category "sex" was added to Title VII in order to derail the passage of the amendment, and it took about ten years for the act to gain recognition, it opened the doors to the ideology of women in the workplace (Belknap, 2007).

This was a major turning point for the social construction of womanhood. While women did not immediately gain enforced rights, the sphere of women was legally recognized to encompass the public sphere. Earlier constructs of womanhood remained, such as women as nurturers, as natural mothers, and as passive, emotional, and needing protection. Many women still claimed the home as their domain; however, many women decided to step out of traditional gender roles.

Between 1940 and 2003 women's participation in the workforce and completion of four or more years of college increased from 4 percent to 26 percent (National Center for Education Statistics, 2003, as cited in Pincus, 2006, p. 86). In 1948, 32 percent of the female population participated in the paid labor force (U.S. Department of Labor, 2003, as cited in Pincus, 2006, p. 83). By 2003 the percentage of women participating in the paid labor force had increased to 61 percent. Between 1970 and 2003 white women's workforce participation increased from 42 percent to 60 percent, while black women's participation increased from 52 percent to 65 percent. However, the ideology of women's work was such that women had limited access to highly prestigious and highly paid jobs, evidence of continued inequality. For example, in 2009 women made up 47 percent of the workforce and 51 percent of professional employees (Bureau of Labor Statisics, 2009), but they were largely overrepresented in women's work. That year 99 percent of dental hygienists, 98 percent of preschool and kindergarten teachers, and 91 percent of licensed practical, vocational nurses were women. Overall, women make seventy-six cents for every dollar that equally qualified men make. Thus, the construction of womanhood has changed in part, yet much remains the same.

SOCIAL CONSTRUCTION OF FEMALE VICTIMIZATION IN SOCIETY

The social construction of womanhood directly affects the social construction of female victims (Garcia & Schweikert, 2010). These social constructs have been institutionalized, as has the concept of *victimhood* (Altheide, 2002; Furedi, 1997; Garcia & Schweikert, 2010; Meyer, Boli, & Thomas, 1994; Rock, 2002; Winter, 2002). According to Berger and Luckmann, "all human activity is subject to habitualization" (1966, p. 53), allowing individuals to avoid having to redefine their interactions anew. During individual face-to-face interaction habitualization retains meaning and is eventually reciprocated. It is this reciprocation that transforms habitualization into patterns, or typification. The more we engage in typification, the more impersonal and generalized these typifications become, allowing us to apply them to individuals or groups without the required interaction. Hence, an institution is born. Since typifications are institutions, the construct of womanhood is an institution. Similarly, because victimization has been typified with constructs of deserving victims and real victims, we can identify the institution of victimhood (Altheide, 2002; Furedi, 1997, p. 95; Rock, 2002, p. 14).

Modern culture has institutionalized victimhood in such a way that when people behave outside of these social constructs, they are not recognized as innocent victims. This is especially true of female victims of violence. Victimhood requires the innocence of any person attempting to claim the status; however, female victimhood goes a step further and requires the victim to not only be innocent but also to be a good woman (Winter, 2002). A good woman, as discussed earlier, is moral, passive, and dependent. Furthermore, stemming from the cult of true womanhood, we still find constructs of good women as mothers, or aspiring mothers. Thus, the good woman is the innocent victim.

However, as pointed out previously, intersections of gender, race, age, income, and sexuality play an important role in society's definitions of the good woman/innocent victim. As a result, the social construction of female victimization denies automatic victimhood to females who are racial/ethnic or economic minorities, young, and lesbian. These females do not fit what society has come to know as the ideal victim (Keitner, 2002).

The ideal victim is innocent of all responsibility for the crime (Garcia & Schweikert, 2010; Karmen, 2010). Innocence, unfortunately, is not always determined by behavior. Examining our social constructs, we find that age is linked to innocence. The very young and the very old among us tend to be defined as innocent (Garcia & Schweikert, 2010; Karmen, 2010). People within these age categories are automatically defined as helpless, unsuspecting, and powerless against the predatory nature of strangers, until their behaviors tell us otherwise. Race, ethnicity, and even immigration are linked to innocence. Our social constructs paint minority groups within these categories as dangerous (Perry, et al., 2009; Smith, 2009). Though research has found that immigrant youth tend to be less criminal than nonimmigrant youth, society tends to see the opposite (Perry, et al., 2009). Finally, considering income, the poor have been globally and historically demonized as vagrant, lazy, and willing to steal and maim for fortune (Chambliss, 1964, 1994; Reiman, 1995).

The combination of these categories and intersections has revealed that females who are young (but not too young), who are racial or ethnic minorities, and who are poor are less likely to be awarded the status of victim (Belknap, 2007; Potter, 2010). Adding to this complexity is the victim/offender relationship. Social constructs reveal that when the victim and offender know each other, members of society tend to ask what she, or he, did to warrant the victimization (Garcia & Schweikert, 2010; Karmen, 2010). In other words, what responsibility does the victim share? When a prior relationship does not exist, we are more likely to give the victim the benefit of the doubt. However, in the case of intimate partner violence, the nature of the crime is that the victim and offender always have some kind of relationship. What is worse, the nature of the relationship is intimate or formerly intimate. As a result, victims of intimate partner violence face the requirement of proving their innocence.

CONCLUSION

Social constructs are powerful in terms of their consequences. As sociologists have claimed for decades, perceptions have real consequences, as these are what our actions are based on (Berger & Luckmann, 1966; Loseke, 1999). These social constructs have real consequences for how society has continued to define intimate partner violence over time. They also have very real consequences for those involved: they blame the victim and excuse the offender. On a structural level, social constructs shape our official definitions of intimate partner violence and guide our understanding of who the victims and offenders truly are. They guide how counselors and advocates address the issue, and they are a factor in determining whether or not and how the community aids victims. These constructs also guide criminal justice decision-making processes and are a factor when lawmakers consider or reject reform, when police make arrests, when prosecutors file official charges, when judges and juries decide the guilt of a defendant, when judges determine the sentence, and when corrections agencies treat the offender. All of these decisions are based in social constructs that were developed on part fact, part myth.

2

UNDERSTANDING THE SCOPE OF INTIMATE PARTNER VIOLENCE

Society's definitions of intimate partner violence have always been dependent on the social constructs of the day. Social constructs tell us which behaviors are acceptable and which are unacceptable. They help us categorize and typify situations that allow us to recognize our surroundings. Without social constructs we are required to relearn the rules and acceptable interactions with each and every social setting. At the same time, social constructs constrain us to limited possibilities. Thus, if the setting does not fit into the institutionalized image of victimhood, we may not see what is right in front of us.

FROM ETERNAL SALVATION TO INTIMATE PARTNER VIOLENCE

Throughout history the social construction of intimate partner violence has changed to align with changing ideologies of gender, family, race, class, age, and sexuality. Prior to the 1970s, most Western industrialized nations defined intimate partner violence as a *private trouble*. Ideologies of gender and family placed women under the protection and control of their fathers and husbands and identified the family as a private institution where the man is the ruler of his

⟋

In 1995 Maria Navarro called 911 because she had just learned that her estranged husband was on his way to kill her. A Los Angeles 911 dispatcher instructed Maria Navarro to call when her husband arrived, stating, "Okay, well, the only thing to do is just call us if he comes over there. . . . I mean, what can we do? We can't have a unit sit there to wait and see if he comes over" (*Navarro v. Block*, 1995). In this case, the threat of violence was considered to be minor, and the L.A. County Sheriff's Department had a policy that did not classify intimate partner violence as an emergency. Maria Navarro and four others were killed and two people were injured by her estranged husband soon after the call to 911 ended.

The Navarro family sued the sheriff's department for deliberate indifference and an equal protection violation but lost their case. Upon appeal, the appellate court affirmed the district court's ruling that the sheriff's department could not be held to deliberate indifference due to the failure of the dispatch operator. However, the court reversed the district court's judgment that equal protection was violated. The appellate court found that "genuine issues of material fact remain as to whether the County had a custom of not classifying domestic violence 911 calls as 'emergencies'" (*Navarro v. Block*, 1995). While the case signifies society's growing willingness to afford women victimhood, it reaffirms practices that minimize and decriminalize intimate partner violence.

Navarro v. Block demonstrates that defining physical abuse is truly difficult. A threat of violence is not considered severe enough to be defined as violent. Add to this the expectation of frequency, and a victim experiencing minor violence or a threat of violence is often ignored. However, the expectation of serious psychological distress is not as serious a consideration as the *Archives of Family Medicine* claimed it to be in 1998 (p. 31). Maria Navarro was distressed enough to call the police for help but was ignored. Furthermore, the Supreme Court did not hold law enforcement responsible for the actions of its dispatch operators or for their proper training. As a result, rejecting deliberate indifference works to reinforce the notion that intimate partner violence may not be a public problem, as it has been claimed to be. On the other hand, the Supreme Court reversal of equal protection was a victory in the fight to eliminate violence against women. The Court's decision that the county sheriff's policy of treating intimate partner violence as a nonemergency call represented an equal protection violation served to acknowledge the oppression that women face in society.

domain. Thus, family violence was a private affair, defined legally as a man's right to chastise his wife and children.

Religious ideologies have also placed women under the control of their husbands. Christian theologians Tertullian (aka Quintus

Septimius Florens Tertullianus, 160–220 A.D.) and Augustine (aka Aurelius Augustinus, or St. Augustine of Hippo, 354–430 A.D.), in applying the Christian doctrine, equated women's differences with vice (Hawkesworth, 1990, p. 31). The Christian doctrine was concerned more with women's weakness of the will, temptations of the flesh, and propensity toward evil. The church's concern was not with a lack of rationality among women but rather with an abundance of the propensity to sin. In the eyes of the Christian church, women were predisposed to evil. This notion was born out of the biblical story of Adam and Eve, in which Eve introduced evil into the world by disobeying God's will and eating the apple. For Tertullian, every woman shouldered the shame of Eve. Women were the reason the Son of God had to die. Accordingly, in order to pay for their sins, women were made to show their guilt in the way they dressed and behaved.

In following the biblical story in which Eve was made from Adam's rib, Augustine identified women as the symbol of material existence. Women symbolized the corporeal side of human nature in a way that Adam did not, and this was what made them more prone to sin. Furthermore, women were viewed as dangerous to men, distracting them from rationality and spirituality (Hawkesworth, 1990). In order to avoid sin, then, men must control women. Early Christian doctrine pronounced that women's eternal salvation depended on their submission to men, who must take the responsibility of salvaging their immortal souls.

The Christine doctrine was the foundation of Eastern European and American culture. In Europe, as well as under common law in the United States, the idea of chaste wives and daughters went from eternal salvation to male responsibility for his property. Women and children had a legal obligation to obey their husbands and fathers, so unless violence against the former by family members was considered to be extreme, such as when it caused permanent damage, the state did not intervene. Though society became more secular over time, the ideologies of family and gender remained patriarchal. The new liberal philosophy became the foundation for the state's approach to intimate partner violence. Philosophers such as John Locke

(1632–1704) "believed that society should restrict its concerns to the maintenance of public order and abjure both trying to regulate private order or eliminate private vice" (Pleck, 1989, as cited in Buzawa & Buzawa, 2003, p. 63). This approach to family and family problems remained in place until the mid-twentieth century.

Well over a thousand years after the formulation of Tertullian and Augustinian Christian doctrine, feminists turned their fight to eliminating violence against women. The 1970s witnessed increased grassroots movement to change social and justice approaches to violence against women. Violence against women was reconstructed as emanating from male domination within a patriarchal society. Departing from the Lockian philosophy, which was the basis of U.S. politics, C. Wright Mills (1959/2008) defined public issues as matters that went beyond the local environments of an individual, past the "range of his inner life" (p. 18). According to Mills (1959/1976), this can be referred to as the "sociological imagination" and allows us to see the relations between history and people and how they affect one another. Thus, violence may occur when a person cannot cope with the lack of control in the social structure. However, this social structure lies behind one's personal troubles.

The sociological imagination became the foundation of second-wave feminism (late 1960s/early 1970s). Feminists argued that "[i]f such violence against women is seen as caused by social relationships of power and domination, it can be redefined as a 'social problem'" (Murray, 1988, p. 2). Beginning in the late 1960s and early 1970s, feminist campaigns that declared that the "personal is political" resulted in the battered women's movement, the shelter movement, and the anti-rape movement.

Naming Violence Against Women

According to social constructionism, *naming* is vital in that it allows society to determine classifications and schemas for dealing with the issue. In the process of creating new constructs of intimate partner violence, advocates and justice officials developed different names (DeKeseredy & MacLeod, 1997). *Family violence* and *family abuse* were commonly used terms as violence against women was socially constructed as a trouble that occurred within the family and home and usually within a marriage relationship. Other commonly used terms included *wife abuse, wife battering* or *beating,* and *spouse abuse* (Belknap, 2007; DeKeseredy & MacLeod, 1997; Karmen, 2010). These constructs of intimate partner violence, however, ignored those victims who were not married to their abusers. These constructs also included child abuse, sibling abuse, and elder abuse and, as a result, did not require society to see the significance of violence against women. The use of the term *wife abuse* was an attempt to recognize the predominant problem of violence against women, but it was short lived.

The term *family violence* was widely used by the criminal justice system, and cases of family violence were processed in family court. Unfortunately, this construction reinforced the idea that the family was a private institution and that family violence should not be treated as a crime. It also placed intimate partner violence within the realm of civil justice in the early 1960s. These cases included only couples who were presently or previously married or cohabitating or who had a child in common. All other cases of intimate partner violence were excluded from the category of family violence and fell under the jurisdiction of the criminal courts, where they were usually dismissed (Belknap, Hartman, & Lippen, 2010). Furthermore, since the police still adhered to norms that rejected intimate partner violence as part of their responsibility, these cases often did not end in an arrest. In fact, until the late 1980s and early 1990s, police academies commonly trained recruits to avoid making arrests in these cases (Martin, 1983).

A newspaper search reveals that the first mention of the term *battered woman* in relation to violence against women was in 1977. Fowler (Feb 17, 1977) describes a New York bill designed to protect victims of intimate partner violence and give them recourse in criminal court. In this article the concept of battered wives was quoted. We can see that government officials had started to construct domestic violence as a crime (also see Schechter, 1982). The National Coalition Against Domestic Violence has been using the term *domestic violence* since 1978, but it was not until the early 1990s that society accepted the feminists' term *domestic violence* as the preferred term over *family violence*. Though this term technically includes only those types of violence within the domestic realm, it has been relatively successful in including violence against women in all intimate relationships. Officially, this term does not recognize a large portion of victims who are dating or who are no longer intimate with their abusers, such as the 21 percent of female intimate partner homicide victims who are killed by their dating partners (Catalano, Smith, Snyder, & Rand, 2009). Since the 1980s, research has uncovered that more serious assaults and injuries occur within marital and ex-spousal relationships, but that dating violence accounts for a higher percentage of total assaults (Erez, 1986).

Vital to the developing construct of domestic violence was the recognition of marital rape, date rape, and stalking. In the mid-1970s marital rape was recognized by the courts as a crime of violence against women. Though many states still continue to impose constraints in codifying marital rape, the construct worked to alter gender and family ideologies by claiming that men do not have unquestionable conjugal rights. In the 1980s date rape was named as a social problem (Belknap, 2007). This construct was a victory for advocates in the anti-rape movement of the 1970s; unfortunately, social constructs tend to separate intimate partner violence and sexual assault, seeing them as two distinct problems. Stalking was also constructed in the late 1980s. Stalking is a usual occurrence within most intimate partner violence cases; however, this crime was brought to the forefront as a result of the widespread media coverage of celebrity stalking and the murder of actress Rebecca Lucile Schaeffer in 1989 (Alpert 2009; Karmen, 2010). Taking advantage of malestream society's claiming of this "new" social problem, feminists of the battered women's movement promoted anti-stalking legislation in the fight against intimate partner violence (Morash, 2006).

In response to the exclusion of so many female victims, the term *intimate partner violence* emerged at the start of the millennium. References to intimate partner and intimate partner violence, and recognition of the status of victims within nonmarital relationships, started to show up in the early 1990s. However, the term itself did not officially take hold until around 2000, and even now most government programs, policies, and laws use the term *domestic violence.* Also important to the social construction of intimate partner violence is that same-sex intimate partner violence is now recognized within the social problem of violence against women. The dialogue about the social construction of violence against women continues; however, the nature and extent of intimate partner violence remain the same: women tend to be the vast majority of victims of stalking and of physical, sexual, psychological, and financial violence within intimate relationships.

NATURE AND EXTENT OF INTIMATE PARTNER VIOLENCE

Intimate partner violence is too complex to allow a simple discussion of the violence within a present or former intimate relationship. Unfortunately, we have only the length of a book to discuss it here. While violence tends to be the main focus for the police, shelters, and crime statistics, intimate partner violence entails so much more. Intimate partner violence also includes sexual violence, stalking, financial abuse, and psychological abuse.

Physical Violence

Physical abuse involves any nonsexual person-on-person or object-on-person violence. Person-on-person violence may include pushing, shaking, pinching, biting, slapping, punching, kicking, stomping, and choking. Object-on-person violence may include the use of any object for the purposes of injuring the victim. Commonly used objects include fire, knives, and guns, or any object that can be thrown with the intent to injure.

In constructing physical abuse within intimate partner violence, social scientists have grappled with the question of what constitutes abuse. In 1998, the *Archives of Family Medicine* recognized that defining intimate partner violence is problematic because society tends to hold to ideal types:

> The stereotyped view of wife abuse depicts frequent, severe, intentional, unidirectional, aggressive behavior in the husband-perpetrator, and serious psychological and physical consequences in the wife-victim (*Archives of Family Medicine*, 1998, p. 31).

Karmen (2010) describes this as normative ambiguity and recognizes that there is a lack of public consensus. Boyd-Jackson (2010) adds that varying definitions also include the destruction of property.

The normative ambiguity makes it very difficult to address the entirety of the problem. It also allows policy and practice to reinforce ideal types. Wife battering as a construct does not force police to address occasional or perceived minor levels of violence. The 1995 murder of Maria Navarro (*Navarro v. Block*, 1995) or the 1982 brutal attack of Tracy Thurman (*Thurman v. City of Torrington*, 1984) demonstrates the criminal justice practice of ignoring threats as serious. In 1994, a woman in suburban western New York called the police in hysterics, demanding that they remove her estranged husband from her front steps. The police sent the husband away and later laughed about it at the police department. They were then informed by another officer that the woman had just been released from the hospital, after an extended stay, owing to the fact that she had been brutalized by her estranged husband (Garcia, 1994).

In 2009, the Centers for Disease Prevention and Control (CDC) released a fact sheet on intimate partner violence. The report revealed that 4.8 million women are victims of physical and sexual intimate partner violence annually, while males are victims of 2.9 million cases of physical intimate partner violence annually (Centers for Disease Control and Prevention, 2009). As we saw in Chapter 1, 4.3 per 1,000 females age 12 and older are victimized, with 99 percent of all cases committed by male offenders (Catalano, et al., 2009). Black females are more likely to be victims of intimate partner violence than white females and are twice as likely to be victims of intimate partner violence homicide. Spouses or ex-spouses were the perpetrators in 24 percent of female homicide victimizations, and boyfriends or girlfriends were the perpetrators in 21 percent of female homicide victimizations. The CDC also reported that medical care, mental health services, and lost productivity attributed to intimate partner violence resulted in a $8.3 billion loss in 2003 (Centers for Disease Control and Prevention, 2009).

Sexual Violence

Sexual violence is a gendered victimization and is a common occurrence in intimate partner violence. Sexual violence includes any unwanted sexual contact or threat of such contact and includes such crimes as touching, fondling, grabbing or injuring breasts or the genital or anal regions, rape, attempted rape, sodomy, and penetration or attempted penetration with an object to the genital or anal regions (National Center for Victims of Crime, 2008). Furthermore, scholars have determined that sexual assault is a crime of power and control and not one of sexual pleasure (Belknap, 2007).

Originally, laws did not recognize anything other than rape as a sexual assault (Fry, 2010). Rape laws criminalized only penile/vaginal penetration in which the male was the perpetrator. This limited definition excluded all other types of sexual violence defined above and rejected the notion of male victims. It was not until the 1970s that rape laws were revised to include sexual assault. The revised sexual assault laws enabled the majority of victims to find recourse in criminal court.

Unfortunately, the social construction of sexual violence has historically and currently reinforced the ideal type, or the *real rape*:

> Real rapes or "classic rapes" . . . are readily identifiable and raise few legal questions or moral doubts. . . . They are perpetrated against unsuspecting females who are ambushed in blitz attacks. The offender is a complete stranger. He is armed with a weapon and pounces out of the darkness to surprise his quarry. The injured party is virtuous and above reproach—she is too young, too old, or too inexperienced to be faulted for attracting his attention and arousing his desires. At the time of the attack, she is engaged in a "wholesome" activity that is above criticism. (Karmen, 2010, p. 262)

The real rape does not encompass the most frequent type of sexual violence, that is, acquaintance rape. Findings from the 2008 National Crime Victimization Survey (NCVS) reveal that 63 percent of all sexual assaults were committed by a nonstranger (Rand, 2009). Forty-two percent of these were committed by a friend or acquaintance, and 18 percent were committed by an intimate partner. Females constitute 94 percent of victims of completed rape, 91 percent of victims of attempted rape, and 89 percent of victims of completed and attempted sexual assaults (Rennison, 2002).

It is vital that such social facts are not ignored or trivialized. Rape and sexual assault laws have used social constructs that are based on the idea of real rapes when they deny the existence of marital rape and date rape, and have required *corroboration* and a *resistance test*. In an examination of New York seduction laws, Donovan (2005) found strong evidence of constructs that held women as untrustworthy. As a result, the laws required that someone other than the victim testify in order to confirm her claims. These corroboration laws were practiced unanimously across the nation until New York repealed its laws in 1974 (Donovan, 2005; Fry, 2010).

The resistance test focused on the "good, wholesome girl" construct of real rapes. This construct is based on the belief that all rapes involve physical force. However, many sexual assaults are committed under psychological coercion. This sexual terror places the victim in fear of serious or fatal injury if she resists. Seventy percent of all completed rapes do not result in additional injury. However, until 1983 the courts required rape victims to demonstrate first "utmost reluctance and utmost resistance," then "earnest resistance" (Donovan, 2005). Unfortunately, while these legal standards no longer exist, we can see continued evidence of corroboration and resistance requirements in many rape cases, especially those involving intimate or former intimate partners.

Marital rape is a recent construct. In 1975 a Michigan court judge spurred discussions of the marital rape exemption in ruling that Judy Hartwell, who murdered her abusive husband, had the right to say no and defend herself against rape. It was not until 1977 that Oregon became the first state to criminalize marital rape. It was not until 1993, however, that "marital rape became a crime in at least one section of the sexual offense codes in all 50 states" (Bennice & Resick, 2003, p. 231). Only seventeen states have no exemptions to marital rape laws. Exemptions to marital rape laws work to allow a husband to force his wife into unwanted sexual contact without recognizing it as a crime. Exemptions have included sexual assault that is not defined as "forcible rape," the victim's mental or physical incapacity, and legal separation. Under these exemptions, the sexual violence of the spouse is not considered a crime. A study conducted by McFarlane and Malecha (2005) revealed that 55 percent of female intimate partner violence victims who were also sexually assaulted were married to the offender; while 15 percent were previously married to the offender.

Date rape is another construct that tends to be disassociated with intimate partner violence. This construct was not named until the 1980s. It was during this time that campus rapes entered the discourse. McFarlane and Malecha (2004) found that 10 percent of female intimate partner violence victims were sexually assaulted by their current boyfriends or girlfriends, while 20 percent were sexually assaulted by former boyfriends or girlfriends. However, while laws have recognized date rape as a social problem, social constructs tend to hinder police investigations and arrest, prosecutorial charging, and judge and jury adjudications of guilty (Belknap, 2007; Karmen, 2010). For example, while rape shield laws (to be discussed in Chapter 3) were created to prohibit victim blaming during cross-examination, exemptions include prior consensual sex with the defendant. In other words, defense attorneys may not badger the witness if she falls under the real rape construct. However, if she is or was married to the defendant or was sexually intimate with the defendant in the past, then her unchaste nature does not afford her victimhood (Donovan, 2005).

Stalking

The National Institute of Justice (NIJ) recognizes Tjaden and Thoennes's definition of stalking as "a course of conduct directed at a specific person that involves repeated (two or more occasions) visual or physical proximity, nonconsensual communication, or verbal, written, or implied threats, or a combination thereof, that would cause a reasonable person fear" (1998, as cited in National Institute of Justice, 2007). Stalking can be accomplished by means of shadowing, mailing, telephoning, or cyberstalking. Cyberstalking is a more recent social construct, recognized as a result of modern technology, and involves "the use of the Internet, e-mail, or other electronic communications devices to stalk another person" (U.S. Attorney General, 1999).

Stalking is by its very nature intimidating, harassing, and threatening. The power and control nature of stalking is intended to make the victim feel fearful and helpless. In a review of state anti-stalking laws, Miller found that most of these laws require that (1) willful multiple acts of stalking occurred, (2) threats were expressed, and (3) the victim experienced fear (2002, p. 14).

Since its construction as a social problem in the late 1980s, stalking, which now has a legal definition, has come to be viewed as rooted in a distorted perception on the part of the stalker. And while stalking is a usual occurrence within most intimate partner violence cases, according to social constructs stalking results from the anger of a discarded lover or an estranged intimate partner. Tjaden and Thoennes found that 59 percent of women and 30 percent of men were stalked by intimate partners, with about half of these cases occurring while the relationship is still intact (Tjaden & Thoennes, 1998). Furthermore, physical assault also occurred in 81 percent of these cases, and sexual assault occurred in 31 percent. Stalking results in mental and physical distress, including "loss of weight, sleep disturbances and nightmares, anxiety attacks, depression, memory loss, and other physical and emotional symptoms" (National Institute of Justice, 2007). Thirty percent of stalking victims seek psychological counseling as a result of the stalking, linking stalking to psychological abuse.

Unfortunately, the NIJ has found that a majority of criminal justice practitioners do not understand their state's anti-stalking laws, which in turn likely results in the vast underestimation of these crimes (2007). The NIJ also found that most states' anti-stalking laws themselves had been developed with some basis in misunderstanding and that many had constitutional problems. Some states make all first-time stalking incidents a misdemeanor, regardless of the offense, while other states do not provide for warrantless arrests for misdemeanor stalking, as do domestic violence laws. This is a problem because, as was the case with domestic violence, this omission does not allow for arrest in most cases (since they are predominantly charged as misdemeanor crimes) and does not protect victims, consequently adding to their psychological distress.

Economic Abuse

Economic abuse is a form of abuse frequently found within intimate partner violence cases, but it is not widely studied. Unless theft or property damage is involved, much of the economic abuse seemingly falls under civil law jurisdiction. As a result, criminal justice does not place much focus on addressing this type of abuse. Vyas (2006) argues that economic abuse must be defined broadly in order to capture the varying forms of abuses involved and to understand the increased dependency and loss of control that result. Accordingly, Vyas defines economic abuse as "the deprivation of the right to employment outside of the home or a situation in which a woman is forced to turn over all of her earnings to her husband/intimate partner or in-laws" (2006, pp. 3–4, italicized words added). Economic abuse involves limiting access to money or stealing money from the victim and/or providing an allowance that makes it very difficult for the victim to meet basic needs.

In an attempt to examine the nature and extent of economic violence, Outlaw (2009) analyzed a subsample of the 1998 NCVS data and found that economic abuse occurs with 2 percent of all study participants but with 8 percent of those who also experience physical violence. It was also found that women were more likely to be victims of economic abuse, reflecting women's peripheral location within the larger economic structure. Most striking was that victims of economic abuse were almost five times more likely to experience physical violence than those who did not experience economic abuse. Unfortunately, as stated by Outlaw, the data have many limitations, including their outdated nature, and so this type of abuse must be examined further.

Though many researchers have examined economic stress as a reason for the violence, this relationship must be investigated further. Feminist advocates and researchers have found that economic abuse is another form of abuse that constitutes an attempt to assert power and control over the victim (Belknap, 2007; Domestic Abuse Intervention Program, 2008; Outlaw, 2009). However, it is difficult to determine if the economic distress is a result of the economic abuse or a result of the physical, sexual, and psychological abuse.

Psychological Abuse

Psychological abuse is perhaps the most complicated form of abuse to examine. Outlaw (2009) separates psychological abuse into the three separate types of abuse: emotional abuse, psychological abuse, and social abuse. According to Outlaw, "emotional abuse involves comments and actions intended to undermine the victim's self-respect and sense of worth. It involves complaints, insults/put-downs, name-calling, public embarrassment, or even accusations" (2009, p. 264). Psychological abuse, on the other hand, entails attempts to make the victim feel mentally unstable. Social abuse involves isolating the victim from social support networks. The isolation from friends and family may involve force, coercion, or persuasion. The widely accepted Duluth Model's Power and Control Wheel (see figure 2.1) provides various examples of these types of abuse (Domestic Abuse Intervention Program, 2008).

The Domestic Abuse Intervention Project created the Power and Control Wheel beginning in 1984 as part of the curricula for male batterers of domestic violence. The wheel demonstrates the complexities of intimate partner violence. Similarly, the Domestic Abuse Intervention Project developed the Equality Wheel (see figure 2.2) to be used in conjunction with the Power and Control Wheel, in order to identify and explore forms of abuse. According to the Duluth

Figure 2.1

Source: Domestic Abuse Intervention Project, Duluth, Minnesota

Model, the Equality Wheel does not demonstrate how to equalize a relationship. Instead, the wheel is used to identify areas that need to be changed in order to eliminate the violence.

Following the Equality Wheel, nonviolence in intimate partner relationships can be achieved through negotiation and fairness, economic partnership, shared responsibility, responsible parenting, honesty and accountability, trust and support, respect, and nonthreatening behavior.

Outlaw's analysis of the 1998 NCVS subsample did not find measures of psychological abuse, so it examines only emotional and social abuse. The analysis found that emotional abuse and social abuse are significantly more common than physical abuse and economic

Figure 2.2

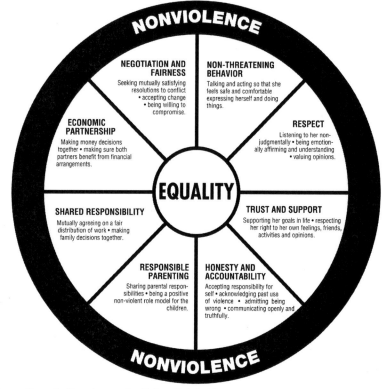

Source: Domestic Abuse Intervention Project, Duluth, Minnesota

abuse. Fifteen percent of intimate partner violence victims experienced emotional abuse, while 12 percent experienced social abuse. Victims who experienced emotional or social abuse were also more than twice as likely to experience physical violence. Outlaw did not find significant gender differences with these types of abuse, guessing that these may be the types of abuse that females are more likely to be able to achieve.

The lack of psychological abuse measures, however, requires that we examine the accuracy of separating these types of nonviolent abuses. Research has found a direct link between nonviolent forms of abuse, such as stalking, and downward mental functioning (National Institute of Justice, 2007). One would be hard-pressed to separate the psychological from the sociological when the result is decaying mental functioning of the victim.

SOCIODEMOGRAPHIC CHARACTERISTICS OF VICTIMS AND OFFENDERS

The scope of intimate partner violence requires that we examine the characteristics of the victims and the offenders, as well as the etiology of intimate partner violence. Demographic characteristics are examined for victims and offenders. Research abounds with female intimate partner violence victim characteristics; however, offender characteristics are difficult to come across. As a result, we extract statistics from the Federal Bureau of Investigation's (FBI) National Incident-Based Reporting System (NIBRS) online via the Easy Access to NIBRS: Victims of Domestic Violence database for 2005 (http://ojjdp.ncjrs.gov/ojstatbb/ezanibrsdv/). Further, victim and offender personalities are covered in the etiology of intimate partner violence.

Who Are the Victims?

Females are significantly more likely than males to be victims of intimate partner violence. The intimate partner violence profile is a black female who is eighteen years of age or older. There are 4.8 million female victims of physical and sexual violence annually (Catalano, et al., 2009). This represented 80 percent of all victims known to the police nationally in 2005 (Adams, Puzzanchera, & Kang, 2008). Females 18 years of age or older are victimized at a rate of 4.5 per 1,000. Black females are twice as likely as white females to be victims of intimate partner violence homicide. The rate of intimate partner violence for Hispanic females is 4.1 per 1,000, while the non-Hispanic rate is 4.3 per 1,000.

Economic status is a difficult factor to examine. Research finds that women of all economic backgrounds experience intimate partner violence; however, those in poverty are more likely to experience severe violence. Women who are poor and homeless and are welfare recipients are more likely to experience intimate partner violence (Josephson, 2005). Women receiving welfare benefits report physical intimate partner violence in 15 percent to 20 percent of the cases, as compared to 0.93 percent of the general population. These women also have a high rate of child abuse victimization. Yet, without further research it is difficult to know if they are poor as a result of the abuse or if the abuse indirectly leads to poverty. It could be that in an effort to escape, these women turn to Aid to Families with Dependent Children (AFDC). Further research found that 60 percent of homeless women in one sample had experienced intimate partner violence in their adulthood, while 32 percent had experienced severe abuse (Browne & Bassuk, 1997).

Who Are the Offenders?

Males tend to represent the majority of intimate partner violence offenders. The profile of the offender is a white male between forty and forty-nine years of age who is dating the female victim. Upon the publication of this book, the Federal Bureau of Investigation's National Incident-Based Reporting System (NIBRS) provided online national data as recent as 2005. Analysis of the statistics reveals that males represent 99 percent of the 250,307 arrests for intimate partner violence against female victims, while females represent 0.81 percent (Adams, et al., 2008). White males are more likely to be arrested for every type of offense recorded (i.e., murder/non-negligent manslaughter, kidnapping, forcible rape, forcible sodomy, sexual assault with an object, forcible fondling, robbery, aggravated assault, simple assault, and intimidation). One must note that these do not include many other forms of intimate partner violence, such as damage to property and most stalking behavior.

Race appears to be a significant factor. White males represent 62 percent of those arrested nationally for intimate partner violence, while black males represent 37 percent. Males between the ages of forty and forty-nine are more likely to be arrested for intimate partner violence (20 percent), while males between twelve and seventeen years of age, the next largest age group to be arrested, represent 8 percent of arrests, and males fifty years and older represent 7 percent of arrestees. Finally, an examination of the relationship between the male offender and the female victim reveals that boyfriends represent 57 percent of arrestees; husbands, 39 percent of arrestees; and ex-husbands, 4 percent of arrestees (Adams, et al., 2008).

A major concern of practitioners has been the involvement of alcohol and drug use and abuse in intimate partner violence. Research has found that binge drinkers are three to five times more likely to engage in intimate partner violence than people who do not drink. During the time of the attack, 32 percent of abusers are under the influence of drugs, while 17 percent are under the influence of alcohol only (Roberts, 1988). However, research has determined for some time that alcohol use and drug use serve as disinhibitors and are not causes of intimate partner violence (Belknap, 2007; Buzawa & Buzawa, 2003).

ETIOLOGY OF INTIMATE PARTNER VIOLENCE

As discussed in Chapter 1, social constructions guide our interpretations of our interactions. These constructs have guided media representations, criminal and civil justice decision making, community activism, and social science inquiry. Because all the actors within the institutions associated with these activities are members of the society that constructs these images, it is difficult to distinguish which came first: the justice response, the community response, or the social/behavioral science response. This section examines the social science response. Three dominant perspectives have driven our scientific understanding of intimate partner violence: psychological/clinical perspectives, sociological perspectives, and feminist perspectives. To be sure, social and behavioral scientists are not the neutral researchers they have historically claimed to be. The social and behavioral scientists' theories and their implications are based upon assumptions that were alive and well within the social constructs of their time (Garcia & Schweikert, 2010).

Psychological/Clinical Perspectives

Early psychological or clinical perspectives historically focused either on the psychopathology of the offender or that of the victim. A large area of psychological research attempted to identify or create *batterer typologies*. Holtzworth-Monroe and Stuart (1994) provide a detailed summary of nineteen batter typologies. They found that typologies tended to be divided into rational-deductive strategies, in which typologies were based on a continuum of rational to irrational choices to engage in the violence, and empirical-inductive strategies, in which a statistical factor analysis determined batterer typologies. With each strategy, researchers identified three dimensions of battering: severity of marital violence, generality of violence (whether toward the victim only or also toward others outside of the relationship), and psychopathology and personality disorders.

From Holtzworth-Monroe and Stuart's meta-analysis, we find typologies falling within the severity of marital violence dimension, and these include the "hitter-batterer" typology and the "infrequent-frequent-mixed batterer" typology. The generality of violence dimension yields the "family only/generally violent" typology. What has been most inhibiting to aiding intimate partner violence victims is the typologies based in the psychopathology/personality disorders dimension. Among these typologies are the "stable/affectionate-dependent/passive-dependent/suspicious-dominating-violent/bullying" typology, which in part incorrectly identified the control the victim has over the offender and the victim's precipitation of the violence. This typology places some intimate partner violence within stable marriages in which the batterer tires of pleasing the victim or where the batterer is dependent on the victim. Other psychology/personality typologies include the "approval seeker–defender–incorporator–controller" typology; the "nonexposed altruist–exposed rescuer–tyrant" typology and the "overcontrolled-undercontrolled" typology. Similar to the rational-deductive strategies, empirical-inductive strategies tended to place the same victim provocation emphasis within their analyses. Unfortunately, these typologies were based within larger constructs that held women partly responsible for the violence perpetrated against them and minimized the offender's responsibility.

Later psychological focus turned to the victim in order to try to understand what made her a victim. Many of the theories characterized battered women as pathological (Campbell, Miller, Cardwell, & Belknap, 1994; Pagelow, 1981). Women who stayed with their batterer were defined as masochistic, weak, or sick, or as women who sought out batterers (Gondolf & Fisher, 1988/2001). Battered women were frequently referred to medical and mental health care providers who told them that they might be to blame for the violence and who feared blaming innocent men. Campbell, Miller, Cardwell, and Belknap (1994) also stress that the more widely accepted theories of learned helplessness, battered woman syndrome, and post-traumatic stress disorder also pathologize intimate partner violence victims.

Lenore Walker (1977, 1978, 1989, 2000, 2001) developed the theories of learned helplessness and battered woman syndrome. Battered woman syndrome (BWS) first emerged as a concept in 1979 (Walker, 2000). According to Walker, BWS is a result of the cycle of violence, learned helplessness, and post-traumatic stress disorder (PTSD). Within the cycle of violence victims experience three phases: the tension building, the acute violence, and then the honeymoon phase. As the violence continuously cycles through these three phases, victims come to learn that they can do nothing to stop the violence, and as a result they learn to become helpless victims. As the learned helplessness progresses, victims experience PTSD, also known as shell shock among soldiers. The DSM-III-R defines PTSD, first identified in 1980, as consisting of three symptoms: (1) feelings of being revictimized or reexperiencing the initial trauma; (2) avoiding any form of related stimuli; and (3) increased arousal and attentional problems (Walker, 2001). The victim then experiences a fight-or-flight response in which she may seek to escape or kill her abuser.

BWS has been used as a self-defense argument for some women who killed their husbands. In some cases, BWS has been successfully used in court. However, many researchers argue that the continued focus on psychological deficiency ignores the facts that, first, most intimate partner violence victims do not experience learned helplessness; second, the cycle of violence is not so much a continuous cycle for many victims but an occasional and sometimes even a spiraling cycle; and third, most victims do not experience PTSD (Belknap, 2007; Campbell, et al., 1994). Further, the BWS theory denies victims agency, ignores the fact that most victims leave their abusers, and denies that intimate partner violence involves nonviolent abuse (Campbell, et al., 1994; Outlaw, 2009; Schram & Koons-Witt, 2004).

Sociological Perspectives

Sociological perspectives have taken four predominant approaches: a family-oriented approach, similar to many psychological theories; a structural approach; a sociocultural approach; and a subculture of violence approach (Buzawa & Buzawa, 2003). Many of the family-oriented approaches focus on explaining violent tendencies within families. Other approaches provide a broader structural focus.

A widely accepted family-oriented approach in the 1980s was Gelles' exchange/social control theory (Gelles, 1983). Exchange/social control theory is based in a structural-functional paradigm in which the function of the family is determined to be reproduction and the socialization of members of society. When the family does not properly fulfill its role, it becomes dysfunctional. In this case, domestic violence may occur. Gelles explains that family units operate on a reward/punishment exchange interaction. Within this exchange interaction, the members of the group understand the roles they are supposed to play and look for reciprocal exchange; that is, if they fulfill their roles, then the other members will reciprocate by fulfilling their roles. The social control focus of the theory claims that if there are no controls to prevent violence, then the violence will continue. Hence, exchange/social control theory has three propositions: violence will occur when (1) the benefits outweigh the costs, (2) social controls against violence are absent, and (3) certain family structures reduce social controls (Gelles, 1983, p. 158).

Problematic to this theory is that, like psychological typologies, it presumes control on the part of the victim. With the lack of criminal justice and community support, many victims try to escape the violence, hence negating the first proposition. Second, even when police arrest the offender, a widely accepted form of social control, the offender will often continue to engage in violence. Research in the early 1990s found that while arrest may work to immediately deter intimate partner violence, its deterrent effects diminish over time (Sherman, 1992).

Some sociologists define the family or intimate relationship as a violent environment and argue that most intimate partner violence involves "mutual combat" (Straus, 1979). This argument is centered on the Conflict Tactic Scale (CTS), which determined that women engage in as much, if not more, violence than men. Within this argument one can see evidence of exchange/social control theory that does not take into account the gendered nature of intimate partner violence. The mutual combat argument has been criticized on several grounds, including the fact that the CTS does not take into account violence used in self-defense or the level of injury inflicted (Belknap, 2007). It has been argued that women cannot be defined as equally violent when their violence is typically minor in relation to men's violence. Nevertheless, the mutual combat theme took hold in the 1980s and 1990s, with increased arrests of women as abusers. Dual arrest worked to fulfill the goal of mandatory arrest policies, demonstrated support for the mutual combat argument, and served as a backlash to the domestic violence movement.

Sociocultural theories examine gender, race, and income as predictors of intimate partner violence (Gelles, 1983). Accordingly, previous research examined whether poverty and minority status were predictors of family violence (Straus, Gelles, & Steinmetz, 1980 as cited in Gelles, 1983, p. 154). Much of the current research further examines poverty and homelessness (Browne & Bassuk, 1997; Josephson, 2005). Research with this focus argues that structural oppression causes sexism, racism, and classism, which in turn make these groups more susceptible to violence.

Sociological theories also place great emphasis on the subculture of violence. One group of subculture of violence theories claims that certain subcultures are more prone to violence, as evidenced by their subcultural norms and values (Wolfgang & Ferracuti, 1982). These theories claim that poor, urban minorities are more likely to be violent. However, as we saw earlier, intimate partner violence occurs within all economic groups (Browne & Bassuk, 1997), and white males are more likely to be arrested for intimate partner violence (Adams, et al., 2008). Further, research has started to focus on intimate partner violence within rural areas, as these victims tend to be more isolated from social support networks, and the abusers are more likely to own firearms for hunting (Johnson & Elliott, 1997; Logan, Walker, & Leukefeld, 2001).

More popular among the subcultural theories is Widom's (1989) *cycle of violence*, also referred as the *intergenerational transmission of violence*. According to this theory, violence within the family predicts future violence. In other words, violence begets violence. Children who witness violence are more likely to become violent as adults. The socialization process reinforces ideological notions of women as property and as submissive individuals. Much of the research testing Widom's cycle of violence has focused on witnessing violence (see Buzawa & Buzawa, 2003); however, a large area of research also examines child abuse as the predominant factor in the cycle of violence (Browne & Bassuk, 1997; Moylan, et al., 2010).

Feminist Perspectives

Feminist theories have worked to deconstruct many of our myths regarding real rapes and ideal types in intimate partner violence. Feminist theorists point to the patriarchal structure of societies and how societies with more gender oppression are more likely to have higher rates of violence against women (Morash, 2006). Within highly oppressive patriarchal societies, families are more likely to be defined as private institutions, allowing for less social control of violence in the home. Further, women are more likely to be forced to stay within the private sphere or on the periphery of the public sphere, minimizing economic resources to escape violence. Morash (2006) also points to the fact that *hypermasculine men* are more likely to define violence as manly and are misogynistic. These men are more likely to use violence to oppress women and increase their sense of masculinity and power.

A widely accepted feminist perspective for understanding intimate partner violence is the idea of *power and control*. According to feminist researchers and advocates, violence against women, including intimate partner violence and sexual assault, results from men's attempts to assert power and control over the women in their lives. Within patriarchal societies, males have more wealth and power. They are considered to be the decision makers and the financial providers. Within traditional families they head the household. The power and control concept declares that within a patriarchal society males are more likely to feel a sense of entitlement to assert their power over women and children. Hence, a hypermasculine male is more likely to assert his power to control the economic and material resources within the intimate relationship.

Another widely accepted feminist theory is intersectionality. *Intersectionality*, as discussed in the previous chapter, concerns the multiple oppressions that women experience within a sexist, racist, classist, and heterosexist society. In the 1970s, black feminists rejected the idea that they had to claim an overarching oppression, such as gender oppression or racial oppression (Della Giustina, 2010). They claimed that "women's social context is created by interconnecting systems of power (e.g., patriarchy, race subordination, capitalism) and oppression (racism, sexism, and classism)" (Della Giustina, 2010, p. 98). In her analysis of femicide, Della Giustina found that cities with greater racial and economic inequality had higher femicide rates; however, cities with greater gender inequality had lower rates of femicide. This finding, though based on an examination of all murders of women and not just intimate partner violence homicide, points to feminist claims that patriarchal societies work to maintain male power, while, as intersectionality claims, multiple structural marginalities are created by interconnecting systems of power.

Intersectionality research on intimate partner violence is growing (Sokoloff & Pratt, 2005). One very notable work on intersectionality and intimate partner violence is Richie's (1996) study of black battered women. Richie found that intimate partner violence was caused by, experienced within, and responded to within intersections of race, class, and ethnicity. Further, victims' ability or inability to respond was limited by the oppressions experienced within their multiple marginalities.

CONCLUSION

Though the Navarro case in box 2.1 represented a significant victory, it also demonstrated the fact that the war raged on. Victims and advocates won one victory, only to lose another. Women were further given recognition of equal status; however, criminal justice was not fully able to provide that equality. Two steps forward, one step back.

The social construction of intimate partner violence over time has demonstrated a definite move in the right direction. As we saw in earlier discussions, women were initially viewed as the cause of sin, then reconstructed as infantile and dependent persons and property. They moved from silent sinners to women with agency. Yet, as we will see, while they change with time and culture, negative social constructs are hard to exterminate. We can find many constructs based in fact; however, society's need to simplify interaction works to create untruths, which we call myths. It is these myths that drive our understanding of and response to intimate partner violence.

3

DECONSTRUCTING CULTURAL IMAGES AND MYTHS OF INTIMATE PARTNER VIOLENCE

Overcoming the Presence of the Past

As previous chapters have discussed, our social constructs of intimate partner violence are based in ideologies of gender, family, race, age, class, and sexuality. Further, these constructs are institutionalized and used to guide victim, justice, and community responses. They are located as essential to society as a whole, as defined by essentialism. Yet researchers have uncovered many untruths that make up these constructions. How, then, do we know that these images of intimate partner violence are socially constructed and not part of the innate nature of social interaction? And how do we know which constructs are truths and which are untruths?

In modern society, theorists and philosophers believed that we could determine and control our surroundings. There are essential facts that may be observed, understood, and changed. In postmodern society, theorists have come to believe that culture is relative. Postmodern social scientists believe that people internalize values and norms that require them to participate effectively with the productive and reproductive labor of their society (Agger, 1991). These norms and values instill compliance and discipline, even norms and values that are oppressive. However, we cannot know what these norms and values are unless we deconstruct our *text*.

The *deconstruction* of thoughts and words became part of the feminist critique during the 1970s. Feminist poststructuralists argued that it is the text that brings these values into society. They utilize a Derridean method of critiquing the text known as deconstruction, which challenges the traditional assumptions about how we read and write. Deconstruction claims that the text is *undecidable*. Deconstructive reading exposes these hidden assumptions and engages with them and invites others to join the dialogue (Abbott & Wallace, 1990; Agger, 1991).

Deconstructive reading and writing are commonly applied to the text of the behavioral and social sciences, revealing the values and interests concealed within these sciences. A major critique is that the behavioral and social sciences deny bringing in assumptions that create, or at least maintain, society's values and norms, for example, the subordination of gender, racial, ethnic, economic, and sexual minorities. Pamela Abbott and Claire Wallace condemn behavioral and social science theories as commonsense theories that are mere prejudices (1990). These theories "blame the victim" and see their environment as natural. In a critique of the widely accepted paradigm of the day, feminists argued that Durkheimian and Parsonian *structural functionalism* places the social as external to people's lives. They did not recognize the fluid and changing interactions that reinforce and change structure and culture at the same time.

Deconstructionism has revealed that members of society internalize norms and values that instill compliance. This compliance requires that we think and behave according to appropriate ideologies of structure, interaction, and status. Considering gender constructs, Acker argued that this compliance demands that we *do gender*, that is, that women behave in a feminine manner, including being passive, nurturing, and dependent (Acker, 1992). Further, we must do gender on a continual basis. Following this same argument, Garcia and Schweikert (2010) argue that social constructs require that we *do culture*. Using the sociological imagination, the feminist campaign of "the personal is political" uncovered what it means to do gender and do culture. This activity of doing became known as *myths*, specifically for the purpose of this book, myths of sexual assault and intimate partner violence. The overarching myth is that the victim bares some or all responsibility for the crimes against her. This was first claimed by victimologists and legal professionals and is referred to as *shared responsibility* (Karmen, 2010). Feminists refer to it as *victim blaming* (Eigenberg, 2003).

VICTIM BLAMING

According to Karmen, *shared responsibility* is "the perspective that the offender does not bear total responsibility for the criminal act" (2010, p. 416). Stating this differently, it is believed that certain victims bear some responsibility for the crimes directed against them. Victimology developed in the 1940s and 1950s in an attempt to distinguish the victim from the nonvictim. Just as the criminology of the day examined what characteristics caused people to turn to crime, victimologists sought to understand what characteristics caused people to become victims. The similar focus on lower-class deviance and a subculture of violence was applied to victims of crime, as discussed in the previous chapter. The inquiry as to why a woman stays in a violent relationship was approached as pathology or deviance on her part instead of as a structural oppression placed upon her.

Victim blaming as an official declaration was able to take root because it fit well with already existing beliefs that we can know and control our surroundings. As already discussed, since the Age of Enlightenment, Western notions of the world declared that we can know, control, and change our surroundings. Victim blaming is based on this ideology. Through scientific observation, we can know who victims are and how to avoid becoming victims. One very popular explanation of why victim blaming occurs is the *just world hypothesis*. In a "just world" people get what they deserve. Similar notions in culture claim that "you are what you eat" or "what goes around comes around." All these beliefs tell us that we have control over ourselves and our environments. This belief in control allows us to feel a sense of comfort in a seemingly chaotic environment. Thus, people who become victims do not have or take control over their lives, as they should.

THE DESERVING AND UNDESERVING VICTIMS

The Deserving Victim

The film *Sleeping With the Enemy* (Ruben, 1991), starring Julia Roberts, provides a portrait of the quintessential ideal intimate partner violence victim. Roberts' character, Laura Burney, is a young, wealthy woman married to a very violent man, Martin Burney, played by Patrick Bergin. Laura is an obedient, hardworking housewife who does everything in her power to keep a clean house and be the wife Martin demands she be. Martin, in turn, is brutally violent and is never satisfied with Laura's efforts. After experiencing a term of learned helplessness, Laura prepares her escape. She stages her own death, creates a new identity, and lives a reclusive life. She is finally hunted down by her husband and attacked. In a departure from battered woman syndrome, though, Laura knows that Martin will ultimately kill her if he is not stopped, so she logically and rationally decides to kill him.

Sleeping With the Enemy brought to the forefront the fact that intimate partner violence occurs in all economic groups and involves not only physical abuse but also stalking and economic and emotional abuse. The film was acclaimed for opening the eyes of society to a hidden social problem. Unfortunately, it also provided reinforcement for the ideal type of victim, that is, the white, middle- to upper-income, married woman whose abuse is extreme in nature. Laura is a good woman who deserves society's sympathy and justice.

The Undeserving Victim

The Oscar-winning film *Thelma & Louise* (Scott, 1991), starring Geena Davis, provides a portrait of the intimate partner violence victim who fits into various myths. In this film Geena Davis plays Thelma, a poor waitress who is married to a beer-guzzling, TV-watching wife beater, Daryl, played by Christopher McDonald. Initially, we see Thelma as a poor woman who does not have sense enough to leave her very unintelligent, abusive husband, even though she has friendship support encouraging her to do so. Thelma is unhappy with her abusive marriage but is committed to being the dedicated wife. Unfortunately, not only does she make poor choices regarding men, but she also makes poor choices when it comes to friends. Thelma is convinced by Louise to take an escape trip away from her husband. Louise, played by Susan Sarandon, is a strong, independent woman and is seemingly a terrible influence on Thelma. Yet it is Thelma who convinces Louise go to a roadhouse, where Thelma proceeds to have too much to drink and to dance too seductively, and is lured outside by a man determined to have sex with her. Thelma resists his sexual advances and is soon fighting off a rapist. Louise intervenes and kills the would-be rapist, and the two women head for Mexico in order to escape persecution. While on the run Thelma convinces Louise to go on a crime spree, and the two, considered dangerous fugitives of the law, are chased across country by federal officers. In the end, Thelma and Louise drive their car off of a cliff, determined to live free or die.

Thelma & Louise was heralded for presenting an image of the complexities of women who may at times be independent and at times timid and helpless. Most importantly, the film presents women with agency, women who can be strong and can choose to fight back. Unfortunately, within the social constructs of the good woman and the deserving victim, Thelma does not foot the bill. She is poor, unintelligent, and makes bad choices when selecting men. She chooses to stay in an abusive relationship although she has the social support to remove herself. Thelma also does not behave like a good woman. Good women do not go away on weekend trips, especially without permission. They do not enter roadhouses without their husbands, have too much to drink, and flirt with strange men. Finally, good women do not initiate robberies, steal cars, or flee from the police. While Thelma seemingly has the support to be defined as a deserving victim, she quickly reveals that she is not a good woman and, therefore, not a deserving victim.

Victim-blaming ideology claims that victims share responsibility through the commission or omission of some activity. As Karmen (2010) discusses, the just world hypothesis includes three propositions: (1) victims are different from nonvictims, (2) something the victim has done or failed to do has resulted in the victimization, and (3) if the victim changes that behavior, then the victimization will not reoccur. The victim has somehow facilitated, precipitated, or provoked the crime against him or her. Similarly, since we can know from others' experiences what behaviors to avoid or what preventative measures to engage in, we can avoid victimization perpetrated against our persons and property. The just world hypothesis maintains an individualized focus on social phenomena, that is, crime and victimization (Ryan, 1976).

Yet an individualized approach to a social problem ignores the gender, racial, class, age, and sexual oppression within any given society. It ignores the fact that victims of robbery living in poor, crime-ridden areas cannot move away, because of structural barriers that maintain their poverty status. The just world hypothesis allows us to envision the victim in many ways, for example, as careless, mentally ill, deviant, even criminal, without direct experience to support our claims. Further, mechanisms we use to reinforce these victim-blaming images include media discourse, legal discourse, and social science discourse.

Victim-Blaming Typologies

Similar to psychological typologies of batterers, early victimologists made attempts to create typologies of victims. Von Hentig was one of the first to lead this practice. Von Hentig's typology included thirteen categories that ranged from no victim responsibility (young/children, females, old/elderly, mentally defective, immigrants, minorities, and dull normals) to low victim responsibility (depressed, wanton, lonesome/brokenhearted, blocked/exempted/fighting) to moderate to high victim responsibility (acquisitive, tormentor, activating sufferer) (1941, as cited in Eigenberg & Garland, 2008; and Hunter & Dantzker, 2005). Addressing no victim responsibility, von Hentig recognized that because of their social status, certain groups of people, such as women, do not have power and are therefore vulnerable to criminal predators. However, von Hentig did posit that others bear some or most of the responsibility because of their actions.

Von Hentig's typology would seemingly disqualify women from being blamed for the violence they experience within oppressive relationships. However, the social constructs of von Hentig's day did not acknowledge marital rape or most forms of intimate partner violence. Furthermore, von Hentig would place some blame on women who were defined as wanton if they were raped by an intimate partner with whom they were previously sexually involved. His typology, following social constructs of the day, would also place intimate partner violence victims as moderately to highly responsible if they were identified as nagging and intrusive (the blocked/exempted/fighting, tormentor, or activating sufferer).

Mendelsohn's (1963) research and typology earned him the label "father of victimology" (as cited in Hunter & Dantzker, 2005). Unlike von Hentig, Mendelsohn was less willing to acknowledge social status and more willing to look for culpability within the social relationship. As a practicing lawyer, Mendelsohn focused on the victim-offender relationship and defined shared responsibility as the primary blame for victimization. Mendelsohn's typology involved six categories: the completely innocent victim, the victim with minor guilt, the victim who is as guilty as the offender, the victim who is more guilty than the offender, the most guilty victim, and the imaginary victim (one who feigns victimhood).

Perhaps the most influential research on the construction of *victim blaming* today is criminologist Wolfgang's investigation of victim-precipitated homicides (1958). Wolfgang tried to understand the complexity of homicide within equivalent groups. Through his examination of murders in Philadelphia from 1948 to 1952, Wolfgang declared to the world that most homicides were "victim precipitative murders." Wolfgang found that precipitative victims were often men who had consumed alcohol, had a history of at least one violent offense, had been the first to use force, or had known the offender prior to the murder. Some victims were described as engaging in a subintentional death by leading a self-destructive lifestyle (Allen, 1980) or as having a death wish in adhering to certain norms of a subculture of violence (Anderson, 1999; Curtis, 1974; Wolfgang & Ferracuti, 1967). Many victims have been attributed the role of instigator of the crime. For example, the murder victim who was the first to draw a knife or the gang member who was killed in a gang war. While similar to von Hentig's typology of victim responsibility, Wolfgang's work was the most widely recognized research on modern-day victim-blaming ideologies within our society.

Thus, the social construction of victim blaming was well developed and well enough ingrained into society to allow the behavioral and social sciences to further its development. While psychology examined offender and victim characteristics that lead to intimate partner violence, victimologists were working to develop a typology of levels of victim responsibility for all crimes. Wolfgang developed the term victim precipitation; however, his typology truly described what society and some victimologists currently refer to as victim provocation. These concepts tend to be applied to most victims of street crimes committed in urban areas. As discussed above, the intersections of social statuses tend to affect members of these groups. So while this book examines victim blaming and the intersections of female victims of intimate partner violence, we can find plenty of examples of victim blaming of males for various types of crimes. Though von Hentig claimed that oppressed groups do not play a role in their victimizations, social constructs fell much more in line with Mendelsohn's typology denying these social facts. Earlier discussions of ideology tell us that young males who are of racial, ethnic, immigrant, or economic minority status are more likely to be blamed for the crimes committed against them.

It was not until Amir's (1971) study of rape in Philadelphia, using the Philadelphia cohort study, that victim blaming was officially applied to female victims of crime within victimology. Amir determined that many rapes can be labeled as *victim-precipitated rapes* because the victim had retracted her permission for sexual intercourse or had not reacted strongly enough to allow the accused to understand that she no longer wished to engage in sex. Amir also identified victim-precipitated rapes as those cases that involve females who were deemed promiscuous or indecent in terms of their language and gestures. In short, Amir used rapists' interpretations to understand offender motivation and blame the victim. The significance Amir's rape study has to victims of intimate partner violence is that these rapes are today classified as acquaintance rape, date rape, or marital rape. Amir brought official recognition to what feminists today call *male entitlement* within the modern-day social sciences.

The degree of victim responsibility has been identified on three levels, according to victim-blaming ideologies: victim facilitation, victim precipitation, and victim provocation. *Victim facilitation* refers to those victims who carelessly and unknowingly make the crime easier to commit. Intimate partner violence victims tend not to be awarded a low level of responsibility, as the level of intimacy in their relationships paints a complex picture of interaction. Von Hentig's typology would seemingly award no responsibility to many of intimate partner violence victims; however, social constructs of the good woman/bad woman would identify the cheating wife who is shot by her husband as von Hentig's wanton and would afford her a little responsibility. The lonesome/heartbroken or depressed woman "looking for love" would be given low victim responsibility as the victim facilitator. Mendelsohn's victim with minor guilt is a facilitator. She was ignorant of her situation and placed herself in jeopardy. As Mendelsohn mainly focused on the victim-offender relationship, his typology would give intimate partner violence victims more responsibility.

Victim precipitation involves victims who ignore the dangers around them and thus are partly responsible for triggering the criminal act perpetrated against them. Von Hentig's blocked, exempted, or fighting victim may be defined as a precipitator or provoker of the intimate partner violence, depending on the situation or the view of the responding officers. However, when responding to intimate partner violence, police often use these terms interchangeably, depending on the degree to which they uphold male entitlement. In unpublished research conducted by one of the authors of this book, the police were often heard describing how the victim provoked her husband to use violence by nagging him or going through his personal possessions (Garcia, 1994). These activities may be viewed as in line with von Hentig's exempted or blocked victim or the tormentor, who would be placed under the label of victim provocation. Mendelsohn's category "victim as guilty as offender" makes the victim the precipitator. Faulk's (1974) dependent/passive batterers, discussed in Chapter 2, are pathological men who are dependent on their wives and become violent in response to their wives' precipitative activities. However, following early Christian doctrine, women are seen as devious or as instigators, so many victim-blaming typologies make women the provoker. This is consistent with Amir's victim-precipitated rapes. Women are sinful and provocative and must be controlled.

Victim provocation concerns victims who are guiltier than their offenders. These women instigate the violence against them with their own violence or tormenting actions. Von Hentig's acquisitive woman seeks her fortune in a husband and precipitates his anger. Faulk's stable/affectionate batterers or Elbow's (1977) approval seekers place most of the blame on the victim. Many of Wolfgang's precipitative homicides are actually provocations to murder. The murder victims provoke the violence through their initial attacks or suicidal ideations.

INTIMATE PARTNER VIOLENCE MYTHS

Victim blaming in intimate partner violence is based in various social constructs of victimhood and womanhood. Victims who are not blamed for the violence perpetrated against them are viewed as innocent, what victimologists refer to as ideal victims. However, those victims who are given shared responsibility are subjected to various myths of intimate partner violence. Applying Kappeler, Blumberg, and Potter's definition of crime myths, we define *victim myths* as "the collective definitions society applies to certain [victim] problems and their solutions" (2000, p. 2, bracketed word inserted). Victim myths are based in overexaggerated descriptions of an event. One can say that victim myths are based in the exception instead of the rule. Below we discuss the ideal intimate partner violence victim. Since sexual assault occurs in at least 18 percent of intimate partner violence cases, in addressing intimate partner violence myths, we also discuss rape myths.

The Ideal Victim

As described in Chapter 2, the ideal type for intimate partner violence is defined as "frequent, severe, intentional, unidirectional, aggressive behavior in the husband-perpetrator, [with] serious psychological and physical consequences in the wife-victim" (Archives of Family Medicine, 1998, p. 31, bracketed word inserted). Mendelsohn's completely innocent victim alludes to an ideal victim, as do von Hentig's categories of the young, old, female, minority, immigrant, mentally defective, and dull normal. However, these categories must be understood within the social construction of womanhood, specifically within the good woman construct. Good women are socially constructed to be heterosexual and married and to be mothers and homemakers who are doing women's work, that is, doing gender (Acker, 1992; Keitner, 2002). When women step out of their socially constructed gender roles, according to the just world hypothesis, they get what they deserve. Feinman (1986) provides a description of this in a discussion of the Madonna/whore dichotomy. In this study Feinman argues that society defines the good woman as the Madonna and the bad woman as the whore. Keitner (2002) refers to this as the victim/vamp dichotomy. However, examining the intersections of gender and race, Young (1986) informs us that women of color are not afforded the good girl category.

Following all that we have learned regarding ideologies of gender, race, class, and sexuality and the social construction of womanhood, the ideal intimate partner violence victim is the white, heterosexual, married woman of middle income with children (or aspiring to have children). We then add our naming of intimate partner violence, discussed in Chapter 2, and we see that the ideal intimate partner violence victim must be a victim of violence to be recognized by most hospitals and by law enforcement, and in many of the federally documented cases. However, after we apply our victim-blaming typologies, we learn that victims who precipitated the abuse or facilitated or provoked the abuser are not included within this ideal type. The problem is that social constructs often define most intimate partner violence as victim precipitated or provoked regardless of the situation. This individualized focus rejects the influence of the social structure on violence against women and requires that women do everything in their power to change conditions they typically have little control of. So who is left? Most victims are blamed for the intimate partner violence committed against them based in various, often correlated myths.

The Manipulative/Nagging Woman

The Western myth of the manipulative woman is based in the Christian doctrine, which describes women as sinful, as was Eve. The manipulative woman is von Hentig's acquisitive victim who attempts to manipulate her abuser to increase her gains and who pushes her abuser to the limit, causing him to have no control. She deserves what she gets. Research has found that culture and the criminal justice system believe that women tend to file for restraining orders in a manipulative attempt to gain child custody (Buzawa, Hotaling, Klein, & Byrne, 1999; Postmus, 2007). According to myths, women use the sympathy that prosecutors currently have for them in order to manipulate the outcomes of their cases, with little evidence in hand (Postmus, 2007). Indeed, during the 1990s date rape backlash led by the mass media, it was claimed that feminists and most victims lie.

This is not as common, however, as the myth that women nag their husbands and boyfriends to the point of uncontrolled anger. In one case of a suburban police department, officers were sympathetic toward the husband-abuser because his wife consistently searched through his drawers and clothes pockets and demanded to know his whereabouts at all times (Garcia, 1994). Officers could understand why the man consistently turned to violence.

The Masochistic Woman

A common myth of intimate partner violence and sexual assault is that women like to be hit or raped (Belknap, 2007; Hockett, Saucier, Hoffman, Smith, & Craig, 2009; Weiss, 2009). Within this myth is the notion that women put themselves in situations in which violence is perpetrated or assumed to be a possibility. Therefore, since they knowingly do not avoid such situations, they must like the violence. The common question, why doesn't she leave? is often answered, "Because she likes to be dominated. She likes to be hit or she likes rough sex."

The claim that she is a victim is often attributed to the notion that "there is nothing like a woman scorned." During the 1980s, when states were undergoing rape law reform, it was common for legislatures to assert that marital rape laws may be abused by women (Barden, 1981). A 1982 New York law stipulated that a man could not be charged with rape if "the force used in the act [did] not produce a fear in the victim of serious physical injury or death" (McFadden, 1982, p. B3, bracketed word added). A Brooklyn district attorney claimed that in their deliberations jurors often took into account the myth that women enjoy being raped (Melvin, 1983). The utmost or earnest resistance and extreme fear requirements for rape cases reveal social constructs of women who like rough sex, otherwise they would have resisted. Further, corroboration laws required that a witness verify a woman's story, as it was often believed that women lie.

Myths of women who like it rough have been linked to the manipulative woman and are not so far in the distant past. The 1991 William Kennedy Smith date rape case resulted in an acquittal based on the belief that the victim was mentally unstable, liked impromptu sex and possibly rough sex, and lied about the date rape in order to blackmail the Kennedy family. The 2003 Kobe Bryant date rape case presented a victim who was promiscuous, having had sex with several partners in one evening, and was interested only in blackmailing Bryant, a wealthy basketball icon.

The Aggressive Woman/Man Out of Control

Intimate partner violence myths often claim that the abuser has no control over his actions and that his anger is often sparked by aggressive women. Psychological typologies of the batterer often portray him as dependent and explain that consistent failures at pleasing his female intimate partner ultimately lead to his loss of control and violence against her (Holtzworth-Munroe & Stuart, 1994). Similarly, batterer counseling frequently still emphasizes anger management and psychopathology more than addressing an abuser's choice to engage in violence. For example, White and Gondolf (2000) suggest that batterer treatment programs should largely focus on cognitive-behavioral treatment components that address the self-image of mostly narcissistic and avoidant personalities.

The question, why doesn't she just leave? suggests that the woman is really the one in control. She forces her abuser to lose his temper, so she deserves the violence. Research shows continual acceptance of this myth. People are more likely to blame the victim if she is verbally aggressive, using antagonizing or obscene language

(West & Wandrei, 2002). Similarly, the mutual combat myth, which claims that women are just as violent as men, if not more so, and which took hold of the nation in the 1980s (Straus, 1979), continues to influence police arrest of intimate partner violence victims (Belknap, 2007; Klein, 2004).

The most extreme case of the aggressive woman that has been used to fuel this myth is the woman who kills her abuser. Most cases of this nature do not end in a successful battered woman syndrome defense. In many cases, jurors do not understand the simple concept of imminent danger (Wallace, 1999) and hold the woman to the ideal victim standard. Since battered woman syndrome places a lot of stress on psychological abuse and since the ideal victim experiences consistent severe physical abuse, juries are often unable to put aside the ideal victim myth and apply the legally acceptable standard of battered woman syndrome (Belknap, 2007; Wallace, 1999).

The Mentally Unstable/Crazy Woman

The myth of the victim as mentally unstable can be linked to early psychological and clinical typologies of intimate partner violence offenders. Just as we saw the male abuser being labeled as pathological, we also witnessed the female victim constructed as pathological (Campbell, Miller, Cardwell, & Belknap, 1994; Pagelow, 1981). As described in Chapter 2, women who stay in violent relationships are often defined as masochistic, weak, and sick, or as women who sought out batterers (Gondolf & Fisher, 1988/2001). Even today abused women are frequently referred to medical and mental health care providers. In fact, as will be discussed in Chapter 8, many shelters mandate counseling for their residents.

Although social constructs have also incorporated less extreme labels of "the crazy woman" myth, Walker's learned helplessness, battered woman syndrome, and post-traumatic stress disorder have also worked to pathologize intimate partner violence victims. These theories have been used with some success by women who have killed their abusers. Unfortunately, the double-edged sword has revealed a return to the pathology of the victim (Belknap, 2007).

Male Entitlement and Sexism

Male entitlement is a concept developed by feminists to describe the male position of power that is taken for granted within a patriarchal society (Belknap, 2007). According to this concept, males within a patriarchal society believe that they are entitled to control the intimate relationship and the family. Furthermore, hypermasculine males are more likely to believe that they have the right to assert their control through violence and psychological manipulation (Morash, 2006). This sexist ideology has been termed ambivalent sexism. We find that people, especially males, with high levels of ambivalent sexism are more likely to minimize the seriousness of intimate partner violence (Yamawaki, Ostenson, & Brown, 2009). Benevolent sexism is the belief that men should protect women; however, women must behave within their socially prescribed gender roles in order to deserve that protection. We find that both males and females with high levels of benevolent sexism tend to have higher levels of victim-blaming ideologies when intimate partner violence victims step out of their gender roles (Yamawaki, et al., 2009).

Religion has also been found to further male entitlement ideologies. Under the teachings of the Christian doctrine, religious leaders tend to approach intimate partner violence within marriages as a test of strength and liken the victim's suffering to Jesus's suffering. "Wives be subject to your husbands as you are to the Lord" (Fortune, 2000, p. 375 as cited in Pyles, 2007, p. 284) is a central message of this religious teaching. Directly supporting male dominance, other religious leaders have counseled battered wives that "God's design for family life is characterized by strong male leadership and submissive female nurturance" (Nason-Clark 2000, p. 355, as cited in Pyles, 2007, p. 284).

Media Images as Cultural Images

Perhaps the most common mechanism for reproducing intimate partner violence myths is the mass media. The media are a reflection of cultural images and premise decisions of newsworthiness on issues that fit comfortably into ideology (Chermack, 1995; Garcia &

Schweikert, 2010; Graber, 2002; Marsh & Melville, 2009; Surette, 1998). The media can reinforce our images of the lying and manipulating woman, as in the William Kennedy Smith and Kobe Bryant date rape cases (Connor, 2004; CourtTV, 2004), or the 1990s backlash of date rape as a social myth (Jhally, 1994). The media can also reinforce legislative claims of victim blaming, as was seen in the 1970s and 1980s, during the time of rape reform, or they can bring these antiquated ideologies under public scrutiny (Barden, 1981; McFadden, 1982).

In a recent study it was found that media victim blaming was not as prevalent as had been assumed but that victims of sexual assault were more likely to be blamed for the violence committed against them (Garcia & Schweikert, 2010). Media images of victims are more likely to present victims as careless. Further, ideal rape myths are engaged in, denying victimhood in date rape or marital rape cases. Ideas of deserving and undeserving victims are presented within media presentations. Accordingly, *deserving victims* should be recognized as victims and provided all the help available by the justice system and the community. Deserving victims represent ideal victims. *Undeserving victims* are those who are blamed for the crimes committed against them and are fit into victim-blaming myths.

MYTHOLOGY IN CRIMINAL JUSTICE PRACTICE

The above description of intimate partner violence myths included several examples of the practice of mythology in criminal justice. This brief section provides further and more organized examples of intimate partner violence mythology within policing, the courts, and corrections.

Policing

The early police approach to intimate partner violence was essentially a *do nothing response*, as will be discussed in Chapter 5. This response was based on the earliest myths that intimate partner violence was a private affair. Since the advent of the battered women's movement, however, the police have adopted mandatory arrest, pro-arrest, and presumptive arrest policies. These policies were the result of successful advocacy and research that reconstructed intimate partner violence as a public issue. However, arrest practices do not reflect policy to the letter. First, NCVS data tell us that 49 percent of female intimate partner violence victims reported the crime to police (Catalano, Smith, Snyder, & Rand, 2009). Second, UCR data reveal that 37 percent of all intimate partner violence intimidation, simple assault, and aggravated assault incidents resulted in arrest (Hirschel, 2008). What official statistics do not tell us is why 63 percent of the incidents do not result in arrest.

We know that facts of evidence and probable cause must be in place in order for police to make a legal arrest. Research also tells us that the police are more likely to forestall a response and an arrest when the victims are African American (Potter, 2010). These women are more likely to be viewed as suspect and even as primary aggressors in their claims of violence and abuse. We also know that the aggressive woman myth has taken hold: official statistics tell us that over 1 percent of all intimate partner violence cases result in dual arrest (Hirschel, 2008). However, Chesney-Lind points out that national data are severely lacking and cites research that shows that over 15 percent of intimate partner violence cases result in dual arrest (Chesney-Lind, 2002). In fact, in the 1990s dual arrests tripled in some states.

Prosecution and the Courts

Even with the lack of an official police response, this segment of criminal justice is found to be more progressive than prosecutors and judges (Belknap, Hartman, & Lippen, 2010). With the reconstruction of intimate partner violence as a social problem, prosecutors nationwide have implemented *no-drop policies*. According to these policies, victims are not permitted to drop criminal charges against their offenders and are compelled to serve as witnesses. However, these policies are based in part on the myth that women manipulate the system: using the police to scare their abusers but not wanting further punishment, they lie about the facts or are uncooperative and resistant (Belknap, et al., 2010; Buzawa & Buzawa, 2003). Further, research has revealed that prosecutors do not prosecute in 66 to 79 percent of intimate partner violence cases (Belknap, et al., 2010).

The courts and judicial decision making in cases of intimate partner violence have not been widely studied. Areas of inquiry have predominantly focused on orders of protection, domestic violence courts, and battered woman syndrome. Seeking orders of protection has been a common recourse for battered women; however, myths prevail that often minimize their accomplishments. Myths utilized in awarding protection orders include the assertions that women are manipulative and wasteful of court resources, and that restraining orders are not effective and may cause more problems for victims (Postmus, 2007). The deterrent effects of restraining orders were found to vary by study. Further, judges who deal with awarding protection orders tend to be magistrates or commissioners who are untrained in the law and tend to define intimate partner violence as a private affair (Klein, 2004).

Battered woman syndrome will be discussed in depth in Chapter 6. In brief, battered women syndrome tends to involve the jury's use of ideal victim myths as well as an ignorance of the law. Further issues of the battered woman syndrome defense involve the promulgation of women as mentally unstable and increasingly violent. Furthermore, intersectionality reveals that African-American women are significantly less successful in using this defense (Belknap, 2007).

Corrections

Probably the least studied area of the criminal justice response to intimate partner violence has been corrections. This will be discussed in detail in Chapter 7. The primary focus for corrections has been batterer treatment, since most offenders are not sentenced to jail or prison. Furthermore, treatment tends to revolve around myths of batterer pathology, dependence, and exchange theory (Gelles, 1983; Holtzworth-Munroe & Stuart, 1994; White & Gondolf, 2000). Regardless, judges still hold to constructs of intimate partner violence as private problems, or to ideal type myths, and are more likely to utilize pretrial diversion followed by probation (Klein, 2004).

CONCLUSION

Victim blaming is not an arbitrary task. It is premised within ideologies of patriarchy, womanhood, race, class, and sexuality. Social psychology attempts to explain the need to blame the victim. Accordingly, it is natural to deny the suffering of the victim in our attempts to rationalize injustice and to avoid feelings of vulnerability (van Wormer & Bartollas, 2007). However, in so doing, we tend to blame the victims when their situations do not fit neatly into our ideals. The denial of the victim has the negative result of denying structural influences on such victimization. It also works to reproduce social constructs based in myth. This reproduction of myth is apparent in the criminal justice and community response to the victim. They work to keep women trapped in abuse situations. And they work to perpetuate self-blame.

LEGAL JURISPRUDENCE AND THE HISTORY OF INTIMATE PARTNER VIOLENCE

To state that intimate partner violence is as old as man seems like an exaggeration. However, this is not far from the truth. Certainly there is documentation of intimate partner violence in every country throughout recorded history. More troubling is that intimate partner violence has been socially and legally acceptable, until very recently. This chapter tracks the legal and social history of intimate partner violence and explains why we stand at a crossroads today as our legal and criminal justice systems attempt to keep pace with social constructs of the victims and perpetrators.

EARLY LEGAL AND SOCIAL HISTORY

The earliest legal system to address violence against women is the Code of Hammurabi. As all legal history has revealed, legal codes have their foundations within the social ideologies. These ideologies dictated that husbands ruled the family—with violence, if necessary—as well as the public arena. Legal codes were also dictated by religious ideologies, which prescribed family life, as well as the role of men and women within society. While the legal system of the United States is not as closely linked with religious ideology as it once was, we can still see strong religious influences. Tracing ancient legal traditions through to English common law and then to the American colonial legal system and the current U.S. legal system reveals the links of the past to the present.

The Ancient Legal Tradition

The earliest codification of law was the Code of Hammurabi (circa 1780 B.C.). The code included extensive details concerning specific arrangements between husbands and wives (Hale, *History of Pleas of the Crown*, p. 629, as cited in Horne, 1915). Marriage was entered into as a contract, usually arranged by the father of the bride. Women were seen as possessions and were protected by male relatives. The law permitted husbands to divorce their wives, but they were required to return the dowry. However, if there were children from the marriage, the husband was required to provide his wife with a means to support the children. If the wife wanted to leave the marriage, the husband had to grant permission. If he did not grant permission, the wife would be converted into a house servant and the man could take another wife.

There is a strong historical foundation within the Code of Hammurabi for men's domination over women and children. Patriarchy, according to many experts, is the basis for the inequality between the sexes in this legal and social arena. It is the foundation that provides our current normative assumptions of male superiority and intimate partner violence. Consequently, husbands were afforded the right to punish their recalcitrant wives in most societies. This was the underlying rationale for brutality against women. Others argue that this was life's order for social survival.

Laws of the Roman Empire

During the reign of Romulus (circa 461/463–476 A.D.), the civil law of Rome placed the male as the sole head of the family, with full legal powers over his wife, children, and their descendants. The physical discipline of one's wife and children was legal under the Laws of Chastisement. These laws held that husbands had absolute power over wives and children and had the right to discipline them. Under the laws, a husband was legally and socially liable for the crimes of his wife and children. As a result, the laws protected husbands from harm caused by the actions of their immediate family by allowing them to beat their wives with a rod or switch, the circumference of which could not be larger than the base of a man's thumb, thus the *rule of thumb*. It was the Romans that gave us the rule of thumb and not English common law, which is often credited with the idea. Under Roman law, wives could not divorce their husbands. However, husbands were granted divorce rights when their wives had used drugs or magic or had committed adultery. In these instances there were no penalties. Husbands were granted divorce rights under other conditions, but they had to forfeit part of their estates (Lefkowski & Fant, 2005). At the end of the Punic Wars (circa 140 B.C.) the changing family structure was reflected in the increased freedoms women gained, including the right to own property and the right to sue their husbands for unjustified beatings.

The Early Christian Doctrine

Christianity reproduced patriarchal authority within the family. Scripture commanded the subordination of wives to their husbands, requiring women to be silent, obedient, and accepting of their husband's authority (Ephesians 5, pp. 22–23). Subordination's unconditional doctrine was supported by the church's actions. In fact, the first Christian Roman emperor, Constantine the Great, was the first emperor to execute his wife. He had her scalded to death in a cauldron of slow-boiling water because of suspected adultery in 298 A.D. He was later canonized a saint by the Roman Catholic Church. At this time, the church began to waiver in its philosophy and edict, allowing wife beating yet teaching compassion in the degree of allowable punishment. Friar Cherbubino of Sienna wrote the *Rules of Marriage* in the late 1500s (as cited in Lemon, 1996). He admonished husbands not to resort immediately to physical beatings. Instead he encouraged scolding. But if this did not resolve the issue(s), then corporal punishment was an acceptable form of punishment, not out of anger, but for the good of her soul.

Russian Laws

Historian Natalia Pushkareva contends that women held positions of power and status in Russia before Christianity (1997, as cited in Gosselin, 2000). Women had property rights as a means of support in the case of the death of their husband. This was unique for the time. However, the Russian Orthodox Church through scriptures clearly established that men were permitted to control their wives. In fact they were expected to, and men who permitted their wives to rule them were scorned. During the reign of Ivan the Terrible (1530–1584), the state church of Russia issued the Household Ordinance, describing when and how a man was to effectively beat his wife (Martin, 1983). A husband was to soundly thrash his wife, but the beating should not include the face or head, because that would damage the husband. The value of the wife would diminish if she were to become blind or deaf. However, the husband could kill his wife for disciplinary purposes. In the late 1500s to 1600s Russian women revolted over the brutal treatment they received from their husbands. When victims killed their husbands for the violence they suffered at their hands, the punishment was being buried up to the neck and left to die, a visual reminder of the superiority of men.

English Common Law

Western civilization embraced patriarchy as the basis for the social arrangement of the family. Under English Common Law, women and children were seemingly no longer considered property. However, when a man and woman married, the husband and wife became one in a legal and social manner. Therefore, a woman's rights became subordinate to the rights of her husband. In essence, the woman and man became one person in law, suspending the legal existence of the woman during the marriage or consolidating it with her husband's. It was under his protection, cover, and wing that she did everything (Gosselin, 2000). As discussed earlier, the phrase rule of thumb is often credited to Sir Francis Buller. The law dictating this practice was perhaps a show of compassion, as it replaced the law that permitted a husband to beat his wife with anything.

In the 1500s, Lord Hale, a British judge, established the tradition of the nonrecognition of marital rape. According to Lord Hale, "the husband cannot be guilty of a rape committed by himself upon his lawful wife, for by their mutual matrimonial consent and contract the wife hath given up herself in this kind unto her husband, which she cannot retract" (Hale, *History of Pleas of the Crown*, p. 629, as cited in *People v. Liberta*, 1984). This contractual consent theory was utilized to condone marital rape and wife beating into the 1970s and 1980s. To some extent, marital rape exceptions still hold to the contractual consent edict.

French Law

The French legal system did not address the rights of women in its Declaration of the Rights of Man and the Citizen. Instead, Napoleon Bonaparte's formal legal code defined women as legal minors. Under the Napoleonic Code, wives could be beaten and even disfigured for minor transgressions. However, divorce for a woman who was battered was rare, but it was permissible if the beatings reached the level of attempted murder. France's code of chivalry would accept nothing less. However, some French historians raised the issue that notwithstanding a husband's authority, allowing the murder of the wife did not make sense (Martin, 1983).

American Legal History

The early settlers to America were originally Puritans, whose ministers spoke against wife beating in England. The Puritans were the first group to legally prohibit intimate partner violence. Puritan law established penalties for battering, including corporal punishment and fines. An interesting enforcement technique used by Puritans was the process of holy watching (Gosselin, 2000). This was one of the first forms of social control in America. The Puritans considered wife beating to be a social problem that affected the entire community. Enforcement included watching your neighbor (holy watching) so that transgressions were detected and corrected. According to the 1642 American Puritan legal criminal code, "[e]verie marryed woman shall be free from bodilie correction or stripes by her husband, unless it be in his own defense upon her assault" (Gosselin, 2000, p. 36). The settlers based many of their original laws on British common law, which explicitly permitted wife beating. Early American laws tolerated the practice. In fact, in places where wife beating was prohibited by law (exceeding the level of permissiveness), it was rare for courts to hear cases of such violence that were brought before them. Between 1633 and 1802 only twelve cases of intimate partner violence were prosecuted in the Plymouth colony.

In a Mississippi Supreme Court decision the court upheld a husband's right to administer only "moderate chastisement in cases of emergencies" (*Bradley v. State*, 1824). In 1857, in the case of *Commonwealth v. Fogerty* a Massachusetts court recognized the spousal rape exception for the first time in the United States (*Commonwealth v. Fogerty*, 1857). Relying almost solely on Lord Hale's decision, the court found that marriage to the victim was a defense of rape.

Unlike the dominant U.S. culture, some early Native American cultures were based in matriarchy. Among the Navajo, mothers were the heads of households, and heritage was traced through the mother's side of the family (Martin, 1983). Family last names, bloodlines, and inheritances came from the mother. However, while formulating the Treaty of 1868, negotiated between General Sherman and the Navajo Nation, Sherman insisted that the Navajo select male leaders, thereby taking the decision-making power away from women. Furthermore, Navajo children were sent to boarding schools where they learned Anglo values. These combined to concentrate power in the hands of Navajo men, who were introduced to paternalism and patriarchy and learned the tradition of abusing their women by robbing them of their economic and political power ̇ ̣, 1983).

The first state to reject a husband's legal right to beat his wife was Alabama *(Fulgham v. State,* 1871). Shortly thereafter the state of Massachusetts followed the lead of Alabama. Several years later the United States Supreme Court heard a case regarding the constitutionality of an Illinois law requiring that the offices and positions within the courts be held by men only. The Supreme Court ruled in favor of the state of Illinois, claiming the law did not abridge any of the privileges or immunities of United States citizens (*Bradwell v. Illinois,* 1872).

The courts slowly came to reflect the growing sentiment in the country that wife beating was socially repugnant. However, women had little success in prosecuting their husbands for wife beating, and instead of the practice being stopped, it moved behind closed doors. Many states enacted laws to get around the "prohibition" of wife beating. Some states enacted the stitch rule, which made wife beating permissible unless the injuries required stitches. North Carolina's curtain rule (*State v. Oliver,* 1879) allowed police interference in a husband's actions against his wife only when permanent injury was inflicted, life and limb were endangered, or the violence was malicious beyond all reasonable bounds (as cited in Belknap, 1992).

Maryland was the first state to criminalize wife beating. The abusive husband faced a possible punishment of forty lashes or one year in jail. In 1890 the North Carolina Supreme Court removed the last of the restrictions on the legal liability of a husband in assaulting his wife and prohibited a husband from engaging in such conduct. In 1894, a Mississippi court abolished the right to administer chastisement (*Harris v. State,* 1894). To close out the nineteenth century, North Carolina condemned a husband's participation as a third party in the rape of his wife (*State v. Dowell,* 1890).

The beginning of the twentieth century found the country split in addressing the problem of intimate partner violence. A Texas court convicted a husband of assault with the intent to commit rape, but an appeals court overturned the ruling of the lower court, essentially restating Lord Hale's rule of immunity (*Frazier v. State,* 1905). Oregon enacted legislation in 1906 similar to that passed in Maryland. This reform period was too brief, ending around the beginning of

World War I, when the concern faded and courts rarely intervened in domestic affairs (Gosselin, 2000). No significant changes occurred again until the 1960s.

In the early stages of the twentieth century intimate partner violence in the form of wife beating was no longer a sanctioned crime. One must keep in mind the historical context in which these legal actions took place. Women were not viewed as equal partners in marital relationships or as citizens equal to men as a matter of constitutional law. Not until 1919, with the passage of the Nineteenth Amendment to the Constitution, did women gain the right to vote. And the matter was not truly settled until 1922, when the United State Supreme Court ruled that the amendment was properly adopted (*Leser v. Garnett*, 1922).

LAW AND POLICY

The ideology of family adds to the social construction of a woman's place in society. Prior to 1960 women were trapped by the *family ideal*. This included a two-parent household and minor children. Consequently, there were three barriers to the reform of laws pertaining to intimate partner violence: (1) domestic privacy, that is, family life was separate from public concerns and the government was expected to practice a noninterference policy; (2) the belief that the husband was the head of the household and had dominion over his wife, children, and servants; and (3) the preservation of the family, which stipulated that a woman sacrifice her individuality for the sake of the family unit. As the head of the household, the husband could compel his wife to engage in sexual intercourse at his pleasure, and he was permitted—in fact, he was expected—to correct family members' transgressions, including by the use of force. Unfortunately, women's desire for autonomy and personal liberty posed a threat to family stability. Women engaging in political activism were viewed as threatening the very fabric of American life—the family. This behavior was thought to be outside the role of the *ideal woman*. Ignoring the fact that women had held the family together, and the country, to a large degree during World War I, only made this stereotyping more insidious. It is possible that the lack of emphasis on reforming laws pertaining to intimate partner violence after World War I was an attempt to regain males' dominant role within the family. A quick solution was to allow men to perform their traditional head of household responsibilities, including their correction practices, free of government intervention as a way to stabilize the primary social unit, the family.

World War II ushered in an era when women were recognized as being able to maintain their family roles as well as being productive members of the workforce. As discussed in Chapter 1, women contributed to the war effort by working at jobs they were precluded from prior to this time. In fact, women were praised for their efforts in support of the war. When the war ended and men returned home, women were once again relegated to traditional roles within the family and to the lower-paying jobs traditionally held by women.

During the 1960s, violence against intimates, marital and family, remained private affairs. Intimate partner violence continued despite not being legally sanctioned. The criminal justice system's response to the growing clamor that family abuse required intervention was to train police officers as counselors and mediators. The response was to separate the parties for a cooling-down period. Couples could be referred to the appropriate social and psychological services to work on their problems. In extreme cases, victims were referred to the court in order to file a private complaint. The rationale for the lack of legal/criminal pursuit was that in most cases arrest was not possible, because statutes prohibiting intimate partner violence treated the assaults as misdemeanor offenses. Legally, police officers needed to witness a misdemeanor assault in order to make an arrest at the time of the complaint filing.

In New York wife battering was recognized as cruel and inhumane treatment and was grounds for divorce. However, the plaintiff was required to prove that a "sufficient number of beatings" had occurred in order to establish grounds for divorce. At about this time, the first national study concerning domestic violence was completed, and it showed that spouses were struck by their partners in one out of every six households in America (Gosselin, 2000). Coincidentally, a Chicago study in 1966 revealed that 46 percent of major crimes against women were perpetrated in the home and that police spent more time on intimate partner violence calls than on murder, rape, aggravated assault, and other service calls. Subsequent studies found similar results (Martin, 1983).

Along with the dissatisfaction over women's oppression, these studies helped to usher in the battered women's movement in a new wave of domestic violence awareness. In the last half of the 1970s several key events and court decisions changed the landscape of intimate partner violence forever. Police department policies that instructed police officers not to intercede in most intimate partner violence situations were called into question. A lawsuit filed against the Oakland Police Department in 1976 and settled in 1979 required that the department no longer instruct and train its officers to avoid domestic violence calls (Schetcher, 1982). In 1977, Oregon became the first state to legislate mandatory arrest for domestic violence, and in 1979 President Carter established the Office of Domestic Violence. During this same period Nebraska made marital rape a crime, and California followed suit. Despite all these reforms being introduced into policing, it was not until 1984 that significant and irreversible change took place.

FROM THE LAW, TO THE POLICE, TO THE COURTS

The landmark legal case that took control of intimate partner violence practices was *Thurman v. City of Torrington* (1984). *Thurman* recognized the legal responsibility of the police to respond to and protect victims of intimate partner violence, as will be discussed in detail in Chapter 5. The plaintiff in the case, Tracey Thurman, was awarded $2.3 million. At the time, all states had legal remedies in place as a response to the demands of the battered women's movement, but police practices dictated nonintervention in family matters. *Thurman* changed those practices forever.

The first controlled randomized experiment to test police responses to intimate partner violence was the Minneapolis Domestic Violence Experiment, conducted in 1984 (Sherman & Berk, 1984). The results of the experiment showed that arrest was a more effective deterrent to intimate partner violence than the previous practices of separation or mediation. As a result of these findings and the *Thurman* decision, most states implemented mandatory arrest laws. Although replica studies found that deterrent effects of arrest were valid only for the first six months immediately following the incident, large city police departments adopted pro-arrest policies based on probable cause (Sherman, 1992).

Although police were making changes to their procedures by adopting pro-arrest policies and legislatures were passing mandatory arrest laws, courts around the country took longer to catch up. In 1984, New York struck down the marital exemption in rape laws when Mario Liberta appealed his conviction of nonmarital rape of his former wife, Denise Liberta (*People v. Liberta*, 1984). Mario Liberta argued that the restraining order was the determining factor of the nonmarital rape conviction. Without the restraining order there would have been no separation and the rape would have fallen under the marital exception to rape, which was not a crime. Mario Liberta also claimed a violation of equal protection. "The defendant then argued that New York law violated equal protection by punishing rape by 'unmarried' men but not by married men with respect to their wives" (*People v. Liberta*, 1984).

The appellate court's decision provided proof of the changing social constructions of husbands' rights to beat their wives. In its decision, the court cited Lord Hales's edict that wives cannot be raped by their husbands, but stressed that Lord Hale had no legal citation to his claim and therefore could not be considered.

We find that there is no rational basis for distinguishing between marital rape and nonmarital rape. The various rationales which have been asserted in defense of the exemption are either based upon archaic notions about the consent and property rights incident to marriage or are simply unable to withstand even the slightest scrutiny. We

therefore declare the marital exemption for rape in the New York statute to be unconstitutional. (Judge Wachtler in *People v. Liberta*, 1984)

The appellate court agreed with Mario Liberta that the exemption laws were a violation of equal protection and thus struck down
the marital rape exemption in the statutes. However slow the courts
were in making this decision, there was a recognition that judges
needed to be sensitized to the complexity of intimate partner
violence, as well as to the "archaic notions about the consent and
property rights incident to marriage" (*People v. Liberta*, 1984). Striking down marital rape exemptions often resulted in the need for
training judges. In fact, Nevada actually closed the courts for a day
in order for judges to attend training.

Further altering our social constructs, Lenore Walker developed
the theories of learned helplessness and battered woman syndrome
(BWS) in 1979. As described in Chapter 2, Walker claimed that BWS
was a result of cyclical violence that consisted of three phases: (1)
the tension building phase, (2) the acute violence phase, and (3) the
honeymoon phase. As the violence continued to cycle through these
phases, victims learned they could do nothing to stop it and became
helpless. The case of Francine Hughes (whose story is told in the book
and film *The Burning Bed*) illustrated the reluctance of the courts to
accept the BWS defense. Hughes was found not guilty of murder
by reason of temporary insanity. Her case was not won through the
BWS self-defense argument. It was not until Walker made her final
leap in the logic of the battered woman syndrome, claiming that the
cycle of violence resulted in post-traumatic stress disorder (PTSD),
that this defense received proper attention by the courts.

Another act of reform, specialized domestic violence courts were
established in many jurisdictions. The purpose of the domestic violence court was to combine the criminal and civil elements of the
complex intimate partner violence cases under one court to more
efficiently deal with the problem. The punishment of the offender
and the protection of the victims were the goals of these courts.

Courts also frequently issued orders of protection, prohibiting
contact between the victim and the perpetrator. These orders ranged

from emergency orders, generally issued by police with judicial approval, to temporary orders of protection, issued by judges *ex parte* (Fagan, 1996). Final or permanent orders of protection were issued only after a court hearing with both parties present, affording the accused the opportunity to present evidence that the order should not be issued. The success of the orders was at best spurious and mostly relied on the values of the perpetrator and not the legal restrictions.

Prosecutors, like the police, began to adopt policies that were more aggressive and that were aimed at victim protection. In 1986 the Los Angeles District Attorney's office created the country's first domestic violence prosecution unit. Burt Pines, then city attorney, believed that vigorous prosecution would stop the revolving-door cycle of violence that characterized intimate partner violence. The policy also involved frequent contact with victims to advise them about what to expect every step of the way and to familiarize them with prosecutorial procedures. Many other prosecutors adopted similar programs. In the late 1970s and the early 1980s, victim assistance programs showed promise in encouraging prosecutors to cooperate with intimate partner violence victims.

Another promising innovation within prosecutors' offices was the idea of evidence-based prosecution. Prosecutors worked with the police and investigators to build cases on evidence other than the victim's testimony. Rules of evidence prohibited hearsay information, so prosecutors trained police and investigators to develop evidence from medical personnel and social workers, as well as from information received by the responding officers. The equivalent of a legal end-run, these tactics proved to be successful in prosecuting intimate partner violence abusers.

LEGAL REFORMS

The Violence Against Women Act

The Crime Bill, enacted by the United States Congress in 1994, expanded federal jurisdiction over certain intimate partner violence crimes. As part of the Crime Bill, Congress passed the Violence

Against Women Act (VAWA), which identified certain intimate partner crimes as federal crimes and provided training and funding in order to address this problem. The VAWA also required that states and local jurisdictions adopt mandatory or pro-arrest policies and policies for order of protection violations in order to receive federal funding. An additional piece of the Crime Bill provided for the criminalization of gun-related intimate partner violence crimes under the Gun Control Act. Although most intimate partner violence crimes fall under state jurisdiction, the VAWA and the Gun Control Act served as groundbreaking changes by providing federal tools to prosecute intimate partner violence offenders in certain situations involving firearms or interstate travel or activity.

Several key provisions of the VAWA illustrate the acknowledgment on the part of the United States Congress that there was an epidemic of violence against women from those who were closest to them, partners and spouses. The sections of the law titled Interstate Travel to Commit Domestic Violence, 18 U.S.C. & sect; 2261 and 18 U.S.C. & sect; 2261(a)(1) state:

> It is a federal crime for a person to travel interstate (or to leave or enter Indian country) with the intent to injure, harass, or intimidate that person's intimate partner when in the course of or as a result of such travel the defendant intentionally commits a violent crime and thereby causes bodily injury. The law requires specific intent to commit domestic violence at the time of interstate travel. The term "intimate partner" includes a spouse, a former spouse, a past or present cohabitant (as long as the parties cohabitated as spouses), and parents of a child in common. The intimate partner definition does not include a girlfriend or boyfriend with whom the defendant has not resided unless protected by state law. There must be bodily injury for prosecution under this statute.

Congress believed that women attempting to flee abusive relationships should be protected when the abuser crossed state lines in pursuit with the intent to commit further violence. Recall that intimate partner violence was a misdemeanor in many states and the punishment was often a "slap on the wrist" or probation, both of which had little deterrent effect. With the passage of the interstate sections of the VAWA, the federal government recognized correctly that if an abuser pursued his victim across state lines, there was reason to believe the violence would be serious, as the intent was clearly present to exert power over the victim and often equated to more severe forms of violence. Subsequent sections of the legislation also prohibit interstate travel to violate valid orders of protection. Penalties for these violations were based on the extent of the bodily injury to the victim, with prison terms ranging from five years to life.

Federal firearms statutes were also amended to prohibit the possession of a firearm while subject to an order of protection or the transfer of firearms to a person subject to an order of protection. In the case of law enforcement or military personnel, there was an "on duty" exemption. However, persons convicted of a misdemeanor intimate partner offense in a state or local jurisdiction were prohibited from possessing a firearm, even if the offense occurred prior to the passage of the legislation. The restriction applied to those who, in the course of the conduct that led to the conviction, attempted to use or threatened to use physical or deadly force with a weapon. There was no law enforcement or military exemption from this portion of the legislation. The maximum term of imprisonment for a violation was ten years.

The original VAWA provided for victim recourse through civil lawsuits. Unfortunately, the U.S. Supreme Court struck down the civil suit provision of the VAWA in 2000 (*United States v. Morrison*, 2000). In *United States v. Morrison* the Court held that Congress did not have the constitutional authority to enact the statute under the Commerce Clause or the Fourteenth Amendment, since interstate commerce was not affected. Chief Justice Rehnquist wrote that "no civilized system of justice could fail to provide [Brzonkala] a remedy for the conduct of . . . Morrison," which must be provided by the state under our federal system (*United States v. Morrison*, 2000). The dissenting opinion pointed to the fact that the Commerce Clause needed to be altered to provide civil justice for victims. It was also stressed "that [the] VAWA contained a mountain of data assembled by Congress . . . showing the effects of violence against women on interstate commerce" (*United States v. Morrison*, 2000).

The original law was amended in 1996 and in 2000. Principally, these reauthorizations continued the tradition of the federal government's role in combating intimate partner violence through partnerships with state and local governments. The 2000 reauthorization added additional crimes classified under the laws (e.g., crossing state lines for the purpose of stalking), and additional funds were allocated to increase the training of personnel in the police and the courts. The Office on Violence Against Women (OWA) was created to administer financial and technical assistance nationwide in order to update programs, policies, and practices that addressed intimate partner violence, sexual assault, and stalking (Office on Violence Against Women, 2000).

The passage of the Violence Against Women Act marks a true attempt to institute legal reform and right the country's history of neglect by not only recognizing the national problem of intimate partner violence but also by allocating federal funds to combat it. The VAWA leads states to strengthen their laws prohibiting intimate partner violence and to provide training for criminal justice personnel most involved in the processing of and assistance to victims.

Rape Shield Laws

As discussed in Chapter 2, social constructs came to include sexual assault as a form of intimate partner violence. Rape laws are steeped in the tradition that women who are viewed as outside the socially constructed ideal are more likely to be malevolent and therefore are unworthy of legal protection. Historically, rape laws held that the sexual history of a woman alleging rape was relevant to the truth of her allegations. Chaste women were more likely to be truthful in their allegations, whereas unchaste women were more likely to have consented and later lied about their rapes (Donovan, 2005). Embedded in rape laws was the underlying presumption that women must remain chaste in order to obtain legal protection. The social

In 2003, basketball icon Kobe Bryant was arrested by the Eagle, Colorado, sheriff for the sexual assault of a nineteen-year-old hotel employee, Katelyn Faber. Faber accused Bryant of raping her in his hotel room on July 1 at the Lodge and Spa at Cordillera in Cordillera, Colorado. Though Bryant admitted to having sexual relations with Faber, he claimed that it was consensual.

The alleged victim claimed that after she gave Bryant a tour of the hotel, they went to his room. There she became uncomfortable as he was flirting with her. As she got up to leave, he asked her for a hug and kissed her. The kiss lasted about five minutes, and she admitted that both the hug and the kiss were consensual. However, as she moved to leave, Bryant grabbed her about the neck and bent her over a chair, raping her from behind. Though there were details of the incident that were inconsistent, on July18, 2003, Kobe Bryant was formally charged with sexual assault.

During pretrial hearings the defense charged that Katelyn Faber appeared for her rape exam wearing underwear stained by another person's sperm and that there was evidence of intimate contact with a white male. The defense accused Faber of having sexual relations with another man almost immediately after her alleged encounter with Bryant. The judge ruled that the sexual behavior of the victim within seventy-two hours of the alleged incident was relevant and therefore was admissible. On September 1, 2004, the charges against Bryant were dismissed when Faber informed prosecutors that she was no longer willing to testify. Prosecutors and the media speculated that she was motivated by concern that her sexual history would become part of a very public record, as well as by several other personal matters. However, Faber filed civil action against Bryant. Without admitting any wrongdoing, Bryant settled the case, the terms of which were undisclosed and sealed.

This case exemplifies the way judges circumvent rape shield laws by using their discretionary powers. Bryant and Faber are the only ones who really know for certain what took place on the night in question. However, the rape shield law in this case was not adhered to and not worth the paper it was written on.

construction of the ideal victim of rape is both a powerful and normative statement (Anderson, 2002).

Beginning in the mid-1970s, *rape shield laws* emerged, prohibiting the cross-examination of complainants on their sexual history. By the early 1980s most states had some form of shield laws. Legislators concluded that it was unfair and humiliating to enter a victim's sexual history as evidence of consent for a specific case. Legislators, with the passage of rape shield laws, acknowledged that we cannot assume that sexually active women are bad women and liars. However, rape shield laws were not the panacea hoped for. Many laws allow the defendant to admit as evidence the sexual history between the victim and third parties. They also provide for exceptions by allowing as evidence (1) any previous intimacy between the victim and the defendant, and (2) any evidence of prostitution and other forms of promiscuity (Anderson, 2002).

Though the laws were intended to eliminate archaic notions of the chastity and goodness of women, the exceptions to the rape shield laws permit the continued use of these constructs. The exceptions fail since, according to the Department of Justice, more than half of known rapes are committed by spouses, ex-spouses, boyfriends, or ex-boyfriends (Rand, 2009). The second exception is broadly misinterpreted by judges, and when the victim is deemed promiscuous, it is often more broadly interpreted. Other exceptions of judicial ruling are judicial discretionary powers of third-party conduct where a pattern of promiscuity can be established, prior prostitution, prior sexual conduct with the defendant, and prior sexual conduct in public with others. All of these exceptions fail to address the real issue: non-consent in the particular incident. Victims of intimate partner violence by definition have had an intimate relationship with the abuser; therefore the exceptions are a crass attempt to minimize the intimate partner violence victim's right to refuse the sexual advances of her abuser.

We are brought full circle to the original construct of male entitlement and chaste women. Anderson (2002) recommends new rape shield laws that strike a balance between the victim's right to real protection at trial and the preservation of the truth-seeking function of a trial. Anderson proposes the following rape shield law:

> Evidence of the complainant's sexual conduct and sexual communication with the defendant on the instance in question is admissible. Direct or opinion evidence of the complainant's sexual conduct and sexual communication prior or subsequent to the instance in question is inadmissible, subject to the following three exceptions: (1)

Evidence of an alternate source for the semen, pregnancy, disease, or injury that the complainant suffered. (2) Evidence of negotiations between the complainant and the defendant to convey consent in a specific way or to engage in a specific sexual act at issue. (3) Evidence of the complainant's bias or motive to fabricate the charge of rape. (Anderson, 2002, p. 10)

Under this proposal the complainant's sexual conduct is admissible only relative to the instance of conduct in question, with few, very specific exceptions. Until recently rape shield laws have not provided victims of intimate partner violence the necessary protection. Changes in marital rape laws were the first significant steps to protecting wives from their husbands. Amending rape shield laws to conform to Anderson's recommendations will provide protection for all intimate partner violence victims, including gay and lesbian couples and non-cohabiting couples.

Intimate Partner Violence as a Hate Crime

Perhaps American society has reached a point where the protection of all intimate partner violence victims is better served by expanding hate crime laws to include intimate partner violence. The discussion is paradoxical. Equating hate with intimacy seems almost absurd. Yet we know that intimate partner violence is most often not an isolated incident, but a crime repeated over and over with increasing ferocity. Cognitive dissonance permitted social ignorance of intimate partner violence for most of the twentieth century.

Intimate partner violence includes same-sex partners as well as opposite-sex partners. Only twenty-seven states include gender in their hate crime laws. Gender is not included in federal hate crime laws; however, federal law does include the Violence Against Women Act, which, many argue, provides similar protections. One area that hate crime laws address is the harm to society by criminal actions based on hate. Certainly one could argue that the inclusion of intimate partner violence in this category would bring increased attention to these crimes.

Opponents of including intimate partner violence in hate crime laws argue that they will consume these laws by their sheer volume, while feminists fear that much of the progress made will be subsumed by the hate crimes and much of the attention to violence against women in intimate partnerships will be lost (Gerstenfeld, 2010). Some argue that the inclusion of intimate partner violence crimes in hate crime laws is unwarranted as most offenders do not hate women.

There is little academic or policy literature concerning the inclusion of intimate partner violence in hate crime legislation. It is hard to argue that the physical, emotional, and psychological harm inflicted on women over the years as a result of intimate partner violence has not affected society in ways similar to violence against other groups protected by hate crime legislation. The academic literature demonstrates a reasonable assumption that the harm caused to women as a class is considerable. One could argue that the debilitating effects of abuse and the accompanying criminal justice responses through most of the twentieth century left women vulnerable to the abuse and in need of greater protection. Not until recently has women's fight against intimate partner violence resulted in substantial social change. For some victims, fighting back has led to increased violence.

Most state laws consider intimate partner violence a misdemeanor. Inclusion in hate crime laws would certainly allow intimate partner violence to be classified as a felony, and the accompanying punishment may have a deterrent effect on abusers. Certainly the incapacitation effects would increase if offenders were facing prison sentences and not just jail time. With the emphasis on punishment as the prevailing ideology for criminal justice policy in the last twenty-five years, it is odd that intimate partner violence has been exempt from the increased penalties most other groups of crimes have faced. One could argue that the inclusion would serve as a penalty enhancement for offenses that shock the conscience of society and cause harm not only to the individual but to the group as a whole, thus increasing the overall harm to society. Perhaps it is time to begin an earnest debate about the designation of intimate partner violence crimes as hate crimes and the establishment of gender as a class worthy of protection under these laws.

CONCLUSION

The jurisprudential side of intimate partner violence spans a good deal of history. From early times through at least half of the twentieth century, cultures either openly or secretly permitted intimate partner violence. In fact, in most cultures the practice was expected and condoned. The long and arduous fight against violence toward women remains unsettled. It appears that we take two steps forward and one step backward. Progress has been slow. Although state and federal governments have enacted laws and established policies to combat intimate partner violence, it remains a serious problem. Throughout history the problem seems to have been addressed, only to slip out of respectability again. This chapter documented the history of jurisprudential and criminal justice action with regard to intimate partner violence. The question remains, is it enough? Perhaps it is time to consider those who repeatedly engage in intimate partner violence as domestic terrorists, as women haters. The application of hate crime statutes may be the next effort to combat intimate partner violence.

5

POLICING INTIMATE PARTNER VIOLENCE

L aw enforcement officers, primarily the police, are the face of the criminal justice system. Police are the gatekeepers of the criminal justice system and are among the first responders in a crisis. Police are charged with enforcing the law and maintaining order within our communities. They provide services in medical emergencies, fires, and when our children are missing. Many citizens residing outside of major cities believe that the police should serve their personal needs. Children are instructed to find a police officer when they are scared, uncertain, or lost. Most schools invite police to assemblies in order to foster a better understanding among children about the role police play in society. For most people in distress, the police are a welcome sight and are trusted to provide some order to chaos.

Female intimate partner violence victims are among the groups within society who for centuries did not receive police protection. Since their victimizations were socially constructed as private troubles within the private domain, the police, as the first responders and gatekeepers to the criminal justice system, did not provide the protection and assistance these women desperately needed in violent situations that had the potential to turn lethal. When female intimate partner violence victims turned to the police for help, they received an ambivalent response.

The case that has had the most impact on the police response to intimate partner violence is the historic case of Tracey Thurman (*Thurman v. City of Torrington*, 1984). Tracey Thurman took her infant son and fled to her hometown of Torrington, Connecticut, to escape her abusive husband, Charles Thurman. She moved in with friends, and a short time later her husband found her and attacked her. Tracey's hosts, the property owners, called the Torrington Police Department and requested that Charles Thurman be kept off their property. Several weeks later Charles Thurman returned and physically took his son from the premises. Tracey and one of the property owners complained, but the police refused to accept either the kidnapping complaint or the trespassing complaint. Several days later Charles attacked Tracey as she sat in her car. He screamed threats at her as a police officer witnessed the incident. He eventually broke her windshield while Tracey remained in the car. At that point Charles was arrested. He was convicted of breaching the peace and was sentenced to six months. As part of the sentence he was told to stay away from Tracey and her residence and to avoid further criminal conduct.

Charles was given a two-year probation term with the understanding that if he abided by the aforementioned conditions, the case would be dismissed. Charles left the state for several weeks but returned. He did not leave Tracey alone. Repeated calls to the Torrington police by Tracey and others, reporting that Charles continued to call and threaten her with violence, were ignored, and Charles' violation of the conditions of his probation was left unchecked. A day later the police were notified that Charles was now threatening to shoot Tracey and her hosts. Police took a report from Tracey and filed the complaint but refused to take a report from her hosts. The police told Tracey to report to the police station in three weeks, when an arrest warrant would be available. Tracey filed for an order of protection the next day, and the superior court issued a temporary restraining order, requiring Charles to refrain from assaulting, threatening, or harassing her. The Torrington police were notified of the order.

Three weeks later Tracey requested police protection so that she could get to the police station safely. Upon her arrival she was told that the warrant was not ready and to return in several days. She did and was then told that the only officer who could help her swear out the warrant was on vacation and that she would have to wait until he returned. That day Tracey's brother-in-law called the Torrington police to complain about Charles' behavior, and he was told that Charles would be arrested in twelve days. No such arrest took place.

After Charles' subsequent arrest and release, Charles went to Tracey and her hosts' home and demanded to speak to Tracey. Tracey called the police and requested that they arrest Charles for violating the order of protection. About fifteen minutes later she went outside to plead with him not to hurt or take the baby. Not long after Charles began stabbing Tracey repeatedly about the neck, throat, and chest. Approximately twenty-five minutes after Tracey's initial call to the police, a single officer arrived at the scene. In plain view of the officer, Charles dropped the bloody knife and kicked Tracey in the head. He ran into the house and returned with their baby, dropped the child on a bleeding Tracey and again kicked her in the head. Three more officers arrived and allowed Charles to continue to threaten Tracey. A crowd had gathered by now, and as Charles approached Tracey again, this time as she lay on a stretcher, the police finally arrested him.

Tracey survived the attack and sued the City of Torrington and the police for violating her civil rights by not performing and poorly performing their duty. The city responded that the police had discretion in deciding how best to respond to an alleged crime and were immune from suits challenging their discretionary actions. The United States District Court ruled that although the police had broad discretion, that discretion did not extend to permit discrimination against certain groups of citizens. The court permitted the case to move forward. In this case, the court found that the city had a policy of nonintervention in domestic violence. The court further stated that if such was found at trial, it would be tantamount to "an administrative classification used to implement the law in a discriminatory fashion, violating the Fourteenth Amendment to the United States' Constitution" (Klein, 2004, p. 94). The court also admonished the city by stating that the notion that a husband could physically discipline (assault) his wife was both outdated and unconstitutional. Therefore police officers had an obligation to intervene in such situations.

The city also tried to justify its noninterference policy by claiming that it permitted couples to promote domestic harmony. The court rejected that claim, as well. It found no evidence that Tracey Thurman had wanted to reconcile with her husband. In addition, the court emphasized that although the city could not be sued because of the actions of its employees, it could be sued if the actions were the result of an official policy or if there was a pattern of behavior that supported the assertion that the city had such a policy. In this case, the court found that because the abuses of Tracey Thurman occurred over a period of eight months and the police were not disciplined for their actions, a pattern was clearly established and the city was liable.

The court noted that there might have been other police departments that had similar policies. However common the practice, the court ruled that police have an affirmative responsibility to act to protect the personal safety of citizens. Failure to perform this duty constituted a denial of equal protection under the law and was a violation of the Fourteenth Amendment to the United States Constitution. The city settled the suit for $2.3 million. Charles Thurman was convicted of felony assault and was sent to prison. Immediately after the case was settled, the Connecticut legislature passed a mandatory arrest law for intimate partner violence. Similar suits followed *Thurman* and have continued to the present.

In this chapter we provide evidence of the implementation within law enforcement of social constructs of intimate partner violence. These constructs can be seen in the "classic police response," and the substantive, legal, and procedural reforms that removed the barriers to responsible police response to intimate partner violence. The consequences of hastily implemented arrest policies dealing with mutual combat and the mandatory arrest reveal a backlash to the demand for police to recognize the rights of women to live free of violence. However, one fact remains: the police have made greater reforms to policies related to their response to intimate partner violence than any other segment of the criminal justice system.

THE CLASSIC POLICE RESPONSE

Throughout most of the twentieth century the *classic police response* to intimate partner violence was to avoid a dangerous and unpleasant situation by spending as little time as possible with these calls in order engage in *"real police work"* (Buzawa & Buzawa, 2003). The classic police response to intimate partner violence for most of the twentieth century can be termed the *do-nothing response*. As all family matters were defined as private troubles, officers typically distanced themselves from a task they felt was outside their jurisdiction (Melton, 1999). The lack of police involvement resulted in a lack of documentation of the abuse, hindering action by the criminal justice system. Police behavior was further reinforced by the "covert tolerance" of judges, prosecutors, and police administrators, who tacitly supported this response (Berk, Loseke, Fenstermaker Berk, & Rauma, 1980). Until recently, intimate partner violence was a misdemeanor. Police in these incidents were unable to make an arrest without a warrant unless they actually witnessed the assault personally. Since most intimate partner violence incidents took place in the privacy of homes, police were limited in their ability to make an arrest, reinforcing the typical response of doing nothing, or at most having the abuser walk it off.

Police attitudes allowed officers to rationalize their do-nothing response. Police officers did not see intimate partner violence as more than a private, personal dispute that should be resolved by the involved parties. Officers wanted little to do with undermining the "rights" of men to assert authority over women. Relying on normative assumptions of men's right to dominate women, the police did not enforce the law in these cases (Berk, et al., 1980). This allowed police to justify their actions and attitudes. Added to this, intimate partner violence calls were considered to be among the most dangerous calls the police responded to.

The police commonly stressed that the Federal Bureau of Investigation (FBI) presented proof of how dangerous these private troubles were (Buzawa & Buzawa, 2003; Garcia, 1995). Until the 1980s the FBI released statistics revealing that most officer deaths and injuries occurred while responding to domestic disturbance calls. Statistics revealed that one-third of police deaths resulted from these calls between 1960 and 1984 (Garner & Clemmer, 1986). When the FBI released its statistics to the police departments, it created a panic among officers, and police precincts started screening domestic violence calls. In 1976, the International Association of Chiefs of Police (IACP) training instructions on "Investigation of Wife Beating" declared that:

> [i]ntervening in wife assault cases is a formidable task. The police officer is exposed to the threat of personal injury every time he responds to a family disturbance call. . . . Police officers must be aware of the danger involved in disturbance calls. Since 1966, 157 officers have lost their lives responding to disturbance calls. (As cited in Garner & Clemmer, 1986, p. 2)

Garner and Clemmer revealed that the FBI's definition of *domestic disturbance* included "bar fights, gang calls, general disturbances (short of riots and civil disorders), and incidents where a citizen is brandishing a firearm—in addition to disputes or assaults among family members" (Garner & Clemmer, 1986, p. 2). In 1982, the FBI separated "family quarrels" from other crimes within the domestic disturbance category and found that between 1973 and 1982, only

62 out of 1,085 officer deaths, just under 6 percent, occurred as a result of domestic violence incidents. This is a very small number considering that the police spend much more time on intimate partner violence calls than on any other call.

Buzawa and Buzawa (2003) found that many precincts employed untrained personnel to screen these calls. These individuals did not understand the seriousness of such calls and many times were not able to detect severe danger. Additionally, police academies trained the police to employ certain tactics. When in a victim's house, one officer separated the couple into two different rooms but kept himself or herself within view of his or her partner. All weapons were removed from the house, and all people were kept out of the kitchen. These are all logical tactics for any officer; however, these tactics are based on the assumption that the victim is hostile, along with the offender, further victimizing her. In an unpublished study, one officer claimed that what makes these calls more dangerous is that "you don't know what you are getting into. At least in a shootout, you know that there are guns involved" (Garcia, 1995, p. 17). Officers also claimed that when a woman saw her husband getting arrested, she realized that she was losing him and might attack the officer.

The do-nothing response was also consistent with police promotional policy. Promotions were generally based on arrests and convictions. Most intimate partner violence incidents were not witnessed by police, making an arrest impossible in most cases. These calls were also time-consuming and were perceived to be more time-consuming than they were in reality. As a result, officers saw little payoff in involving themselves in intimate partner violence incidents. The police believed that if they were responding to an intimate partner violence call, then they could not respond to calls that would be more productive in terms of promotions. Therefore, intimate partner violence calls were considered counterproductive.

Fagan (1996) argues that although efforts to deter intimate partner violence fell to the police, that burden might have been unfairly placed. The police were limited in their options. Arrest might reduce further violence, but sanctions were the responsibility of the judicial branch, i.e., judges. The failure of these actors to punish intimate partner violence offenders might have lent credence to officer perceptions that intimate partner violence offenses were better left a private matter, best settled by the participants.

An area that has failed to get much attention and scrutiny from researchers and the media alike is the police response to same-sex intimate partner violence. Contextually, the laws have been expanded from tradition heterosexual violence between husband and wife to other forms of intimate partner violence, including those involving same-sex couples. Of course, much of the research and political discussion have addressed the effects of legal changes toward the control of traditional intimate partner violence, including the sweeping changes in police training and enforcement. Little attention has been paid to same-sex offenders. Today, however, the social construction of the ideal/deserving victim has expanded the application of the law and, consequently, its enforcement. Recognizing that intimate partner violence victimization in same-sex relationships is equally as serious as heterosexual victimization has expanded police responsibilities over the last several decades.

The limited research in this area is based on small samples or inferred from heterosexual couples (Renzetti, 1992). While some research indicates that gay and lesbian couples experience intimate partner violence at similar rates to their heterosexual counterparts, prevalence rates for these victimizations have not been examined (Lilith, 2001). Regardless of the methodological problems with much of the research, the consensus is that intimate partner violence is a serious problem within the gay and lesbian community and perhaps is much more dangerous than one suspects.

In some ways the police response to intimate partner violence in gay and lesbian communities mirrors the classic police response. Absent mandatory arrest laws, there is little difference in the arrest patterns of male offenders in same-sex couples versus different-sex couples. Police seem to have a more hands-off response to lesbian couples in intimate partner violence incidents absent mandatory arrest laws. Pattivana et al. (2007) posit that this is the result of police attitudes that women are the victims, not the abusers, or that women abusers are not capable of inflicting serious injury. The current police response seems to be driven by the specificity of mandatory arrest laws in cases of same-sex intimate partner violence. Research indicates that the police response to same-sex intimate partner violence would follow traditional lines if not for the broadening of legal definitions of intimate partner violence to include same-sex relationships.

The reforms in the police response to traditional intimate partner violence incidents and the expanding legal definitions are important for examining the general category of policing intimate partner violence. Police have instituted more reforms in their response to intimate partner violence than the other segments of the criminal justice system. The reforms were mostly due to changes in the political and legal climates in the 1960s and 1970s, largely as a result of the efforts of the women's movement. The centuries of neglect toward the oppression of women could no longer continue. The consciousness of society was awakened, and people became aware of the issue of inequality suffered by women and grew in empathy. The issue of violence in the home began to take center stage, and the criminal justice system's abysmal response was called into question by reformers, who pressured legislatures around the country.

A shift in attitudes toward crime and the formal response to crime demanded that law enforcement be enhanced to prevent crime, not just react to it. The federal government established the Law Enforcement Assistance Administration (LEAA) to afford states a revenue source to address the growing crime problem through innovative tactics. States began to change their sentencing structures, becoming harsher on crime. More acts were criminalized, permitting the public to see intimate partner violence as criminal and to focus on the need for legislation to address it. Given the legal liability of police departments for failing to provide women equal protection under the law, as guaranteed by the Fourteenth Amendment to the United States Constitution, police departments and individual officers were subject to civil rights claims and large damage awards (Melton, 1999).

The LEAA also provided for the development of criminal justice as an academic and social science discipline. As a result, more studies of crime and delinquency and the systematic response to them were conducted. Studies of violence between intimate partners, in the form of domestic violence studies, proliferated. In 1973, a landmark study of the LEAA intervention in family violence revealed that the police could have a profound effect in the fight against intimate partner violence (Bard, 1973, as cited in Melton, 1999).

Probably the most influential of all criminal justice research on policy change relative to intimate partner violence was the Minneapolis Domestic Violence Experiment (Sherman & Berk, 1984). Its purpose was to examine the deterrent effect of arrest on misdemeanor violence. The study protocol required each participating officer to carry color-coded forms representing one of three possible treatments for misdemeanor domestic violence assault: arrest, separation, and counseling. When officers arrived at the scene of an eligible offense, they would follow the procedure required by the color-coded form that was on top of their packet. The Minneapolis study found that arrest had the lowest rate of recidivism (10 percent), leading to the conclusion that arrest was more likely to prevent repeat incidents of intimate partner violence when compared to either separation or counseling. Over the caution of Sherman and Berk, the findings hailed arrest as the best practice of response. In a wave of reform, police departments started changing their policies to mandate arrest or to mandate presumptive action by officers handling misdemeanor assaults between intimates.

MANDATORY ARREST/PRO-ARREST POLICIES AND LAWS

The Minneapolis study was fraught with internal and external validity issues (Sherman, 1992). As a result, six replica studies funded by the NIJ were conducted in Atlanta, Georgia; Charlotte, North Carolina; Colorado Springs, Colorado; Dade County (Miami), Florida; Milwaukee, Wisconsin; and Omaha, Nebraska (Pate & Hamilton, 1992). Although the studies varied in their outcome, there was consistency in the finding that in general arrest does not significantly reduce the long-term frequency or intensity of violence between intimates (Pate & Hamilton, 1992). However, police departments began to expect their officers to make arrests whenever possible, especially in misdemeanor assault cases. Legislatures enacted laws removing previously existing barriers to arrest. By 2000, all states, and the District of Columbia, had adopted laws permitting warrant-less arrests of intimate partner violence misdemeanor offenders (Klein, 2004).

The majority of states went further, mandating that arrests be made in intimate partner violence cases. Thirty states mandated arrest for violations of orders of protection, eight states made arrest the preferred or *presumptive response* of police to intimate violence, and thirty states enacted primary physical aggressor laws, meant to distinguish the abuser from the abused (Klein, 2004). Research indicates that success has not been universally achieved under man-datory arrest policies. If reducing recidivism is the goal, arrest is not significantly or consistently contributing to this outcome. In later research Sherman (1992) summed up the investigation of manda-tory arrests by pointing out that:

(1) arrest reduces repeat offending only in some cities,
(2) mandatory arrest reduces intimate partner violence among employed offenders but increases it among the unemployed,
(3) arrest has short-term deterrent effects, but intimate partner violence increases over time, and
(4) police are capable of predicting which couples are most likely to engage in future violence, but our constitutional protec-tions are too highly valued to allow preventative action on the part of law enforcement.

Victims do not always want the offender arrested. Instead, they may only want the violence to stop at the time. Many victims fear, often correctly, that arrest will escalate future violence. Victims are concerned with empowerment, and they see arrest as removing their power yet again (Melton, 1999). There is the real potential for negative long-term consequences. Victims may experience more severe abuse in the future and may believe they have no place to turn, because the police are required to arrest the abuser despite the wishes of the victim. Therefore, victims of repeat abuse may be reluctant to report repeat incidents of violence to the police.

Feminist social constructions of intimate partner violence have also strongly emphasized empowerment. Many feminists argue that to empower victims, they should be given the option to determine if arrest is warranted. On the other hand, feminists have also argued that intimate partner violence must be acknowledged as a public or social problem. The paradox we face is that to leave arrest decisions up to the victim is to return violence against women to the private sphere once again. Additionally, since we already know that many victims fear retaliation, would it not be logical to assume that fearful victims may be too afraid to ask the police to make an arrest? Yet, when we examine victim preferences, we find that the police ignore the victim's preference to arrest in 75 percent of intimate partner violence cases, whereas this is reduced to 40 percent for stranger violent crimes (Potter, 2010).

As is often the case in effectuating criminal justice policy, laws often disproportionately target economic and racial/ethnic minorities. Intended or not, the result is insidious. It allows the state to shape the private lives of citizens and increases the social control functions of the so-called dangerous classes. Following a conflict perspective, many social scientists have claimed that many African-American women do not call the police for intimate partner violence incidents for fear that they are all too willing to arrest already persecuted African-American men. However, Potter (2010) reviews past research and her own findings in revealing that African-American women are more likely to call for police assistance and are more likely to desire arrest than are white women. Still, there is the consistent feeling among African-American women that the police respond in a racist manner and are more likely to question the validity of their victimization claims.

In contrast, there is much literature asserting the pro-arrest side of the debate. A major argument is that, at its core, battering is a violation of women's civil rights (Stark, 1993). It is a method of using control, through power and violence, to exploit the sexual inequality of women. As a result, the pro-arrest policies help women over-come these violations and allow them to gain more power in their struggles for equality.

A second dominant argument in support of arrest policies is that mandatory arrest is a control measure for police conduct. The laws and policies assert accountability for police behavior and hold officers responsible for their actions or, as was the case with pre-mandatory arrest, their inaction. Despite the objections of the police to the mandatory arrest policies and laws, arrests for intimate partner violence increased significantly after the passage and imple-mentation of these laws within police departments.

A third argument is that mandatory arrests bring immediate relief and protection to the victims, at least in the current violent incident. Mandatory arrest provides the victim with time to consider her options. For those victims who are ready to leave their partners, it allows them time to find suitable arrangements. It also provides victims with a degree of understanding that the criminal justice sys-tem will, in fact, protect them.

A fourth argument declares that mandatory arrest elevates inti-mate partner violence to a special category of offense. It acknowl-edges society's outrage and interest in controlling this behavior while at the same time recognizing the dehumanization of women at the hands of their male intimates. These policies also send a strong message that society considers battering outside the boundaries and the batterer as a deviant and criminal.

Although most studies conclude that the efficacy of arrest in reducing intimate partner violence is at best inconclusive and most likely spurious, Maxwell, Garner, and Fagan (2001) reanalyzed the data from previous studies and found when using self-reports from victims of intimate partner violence for outcome measures that pro-arrest policies did reduce re-assault (also see Dugan, 2003). Analysis of data from the National Crime Victimization Survey showed that mandatory arrest and pro-arrest states experienced less household violence and less repeat violence.

Chesney-Lind (2002) points out that when analyzing official statistics, it appears that men of color are more likely to recidivate, whereas victim surveys suggest that white men are more likely to repeat their violence. This may be because African-American women are more likely to call the police (Potter, 2010). Additionally, police willingness to arrest men of color has been adequately demonstrated in much of the criminal justice research. An alternative explanation is that white women are more likely to have the financial means to seek private medical and social care, keeping them from law enforcement detection and skewing the official report data (Potter, 2010).

THE LATENT AFFECT OF MANDATORY ARREST POLICIES

The initial goals of arrest were to protect women from the abuse of their partners, to provide some immediate relief from victimization, and perhaps to provide them some time to sort out their next move. These are all laudable goals, but as is often the case, laws are fraught with latent or unintended consequences not foreseeable at the time of implementation. Mandatory arrest and pro-arrest laws are no exception. Equal protection under the law requires that law enforcement officers not discriminate on the basis of gender (among other things). Research has found that when women gained a modicum of equality in the 1970s, the criminal justice system responded with a backlash and increased arrests of females without a respective increase in their offending (Belknap, 2007; Chesney-Lind, 2002). Similarly, arrests of women perpetrators of intimate partner violence are increasing. Chesney-Lind (2002) argues that the increase in female arrests for intimate partner violence offenses is due to the arrest decisions of police officers and the misapplication of the laws. As an example, Comach, et al. (2002) found that the zero-tolerance policy adopted by Canadian police showed a more dramatic effect on the arrest of women than their male counterparts (as cited in Chesney-Lind, 2002). While both male and female arrests increased, female rates doubled. However, a closer examination of the data reveals that in 35 percent of the cases involving a female arrest, it was the female who called the police for help. This was true in only 5 percent of the male cases.

Extra legal factors contribute to police officers' decisions to arrest. Included in this list are intoxication, the severity of the injury, race, class, marital status, and prior police contact with the household for intimate partner violence incidents. We find that women are more likely to be arrested, either mutually or alone, when police have been called to the home previously and when females violate stereotypical norms or act outside prescribed gender roles, or are young, black, or hostile toward police. Mutual arrest is more likely when the woman is unmarried, cohabitating, and young (Frye, Haviland, & Rajah, 2007). An examination of female *dual arrest* defendants reveals that they are less likely to have been victims of previous intimate partner violence incidents, have higher incomes, and are involved with drugs or alcohol more frequently than males in dual arrests or females in single arrests (Frye, et al., 2007). As a result, we find that victim characteristics and behaviors are important factors in police decisions to arrest women.

Chesney-Lind (2002) indicates that as many as 25 percent of all intimate partner violence arrests are women. This figure may indicate a shift away from the traditional definition of intimate partner violence as a male perpetrator abusing a female victim. There is a growing debate regarding how seriously scholars should take female violence. Male advocacy groups have wasted no time in carrying this debate into the political and legal arenas, contending that existing intimate partner violence laws, court proceedings, and federal funding are discriminatory toward males. They argue that these laws and policies characterize victims of intimate partner violence exclusively as females. An unintended consequence of mandatory arrest and pro-arrest laws and policies is that police departments and officers may be bolstered in their feelings of justification in making more female arrests for intimate partner violence.

As described earlier, some states have enacted primary aggressor laws. These laws remove police liability for not making an arrest in intimate partner violence cases and instead define which party to arrest. The National Council of Juvenile and Family Court Judges' Model State Code for Family Violence offers four criteria for defining the aggressor:

(1) prior complaints of domestic violence,
(2) the relative severity of the injuries,
(3) the likelihood of future injuries to each person, and
(4) whether one person acted in self-defense (Klein, 2004, p. 100).

There are other definitions posited for the primary aggressor, but the issue here is to account for the rising proportion of female arrests for intimate partner violence. Without proper police training, police frequently label women acting in self-defense as the primary aggressor since the women often use weapons in self-defense, such as knives and guns, as well as other objects, to ward off their attackers and to equalize the combat. Thus, police officers arriving on the scene of a domestic dispute may be confronted by a woman brandishing a weapon and appearing to be the aggressor. In the case where only the male has visible injuries, it is possible that the woman's injuries may not have developed yet, as in the case of strangulation. Prior to mandatory arrest and pro-arrest policies, police may have been reluctant to make an arrest, but under current laws and policies, officers are under pressure to make an arrest (Henning, Renauer, & Holdford, 2006).

Recall that initially, the intimate partner violence laws were aimed at domestic violence in the traditional meaning of the phenomenon, that is, a husband battering/beating his wife. As the social construction of domestication expanded to include cohabitants and with the eventual recognition of gay and lesbian partnerships, domestic violence morphed into intimate partner violence. Research into same-sex intimate partner violence has examined the phenomenon from a heterosexual perspective. Most states do not address same-sex intimate partner violence directly. As a result, the role of the police in confronting same-sex intimate partner violence shows a disturbing trend. Furthermore, the police often ignore the potential seriousness of same-sex incidents and fail to make any arrests or to intervene (Comstock, 1991). They ignore the standard police procedures for handling intimate partner violence incidents, even to the point of disregarding the primary aggressor identification and arrest policies. What is clear from recent research is that the police hold more negative feelings toward gay men than they do toward lesbians.

Pattavina, et al. (2007) found little difference in arrests of intimate partner violence perpetrators for heterosexual and same-sex partners when sex was not controlled for within same-sex incidents. However, when male and female same-sex couples are considered separately, differences in police response become more evident. Mandatory arrest laws seem to influence police to make arrests in lesbian intimate partner violence cases when the injuries are minor. In contrast, gay couples require a more serious injury for an arrest to be made. Within states where mandatory arrests laws include specific language concerning same-sex crimes, males are arrested more often under those provisions than in states lacking those provisions. Again, women do not seem to be affected by the lack of such specific language. It appears that the police are more willing to arrest females when laws simply indicate they can. However, male same-sex arrests seem to be dependent on more specific language. The bias may simply be an extension of the intimate partner violence controversy that began in the 1960s, that is, that women victims need to be protected by the police. The police may be more reluctant to see males as victims of intimate partner violence until a serious (felony) assault is evident.

Despite the original rationale for the mandatory arrest and pro-arrest policies of the 1960s and 1970s, the police response to intimate partner violence has emerged as the primary line of defense against intimate partner violence. The unintended consequences of the mandatory arrest policy have adversely affected both heterosexual and lesbian women. Consequently, the increase in arrests of female perpetrators of intimate partner violence demands attention from the public, scholars, and practitioners.

THE POLICE-VICTIM ENCOUNTER

There are numerous situational and personal factors that have been examined relative to police-victim interactions. Among those factors is the gender of the responding officer. Female officers improve how the police handle intimate partner violence cases, and the encounter between the victim and female police officers is viewed more positively than encounters between male officers and victims (Johnson, 2007). One reason given for this satisfaction difference is that female officers tend to give victims additional information about the legal and social services that are available, while at the same time providing an intervention and protection. Male police officers are more likely to handle intimate partner violence cases in a formal, legal manner. Their role is to protect victims and prevent the perpetrator from harming the victims or the officers. White women seem to express more satisfaction with police during their encounter than do African-American women. One could posit that the latter has less satisfaction with the police because they are less likely to receive additional protection information from the police. Potter (2010) found that the police hold images of African-American women as strong and self-reliant, as less likely to be victims than aggressors, but also as more likely to handle to their own problems.

Police–victim encounters have changed over the years. There remains some distrust in the racial minority communities concerning involving the police in matters that increase the social control of the state over the community. There seems to be equal concern in the gay and lesbian communities, as well. Lesbians state that police homophobia and stereotyping have affected the police–victim encounter. Gay males also complain that the police are unlikely to accept the fact that a male can be the victim of intimate partner violence (Wolf, Ly, Hobart, & Kernic, 2003). The police and victims often have differing ideas that can cause encounters to erupt into serious debates. One issue that seems consistent within the literature is that victims want the police to listen to them. Victims are more satisfied when the police take their wishes into consideration. Although there is generally the belief that mandatory arrest policies have improved the victim–police encounter, as discussed earlier, victims do not always want the police to make an arrest (Hirschel & Hutchison, 2003). Victim satisfaction seems to increase when the police's decision to arrest or not arrest is consistent with the victim's wishes. Failure on the part of the police to consider the wishes of the victim exacerbates an already unpleasant situation (Johnson, 2007).

Police–victim encounters are not always one-sided, that is, offender-focused. The police react to certain stimuli created by the victim. The police are more likely to ignore victims who are under the influence of alcohol or drugs, or who are loud and disruptive and are creating a public spectacle. When victims want police officers to stop the immediate abuse but not to arrest the abuser, the police see this as contrary to the mandatory arrest laws and are often nonresponsive to the wishes of the victims. On their part, victims frequently characterize the police as minimizing the situation, not believing the victims, not showing care and concern, and exhibiting arrogance in their attitudes toward the victims.

Race plays a special role in the victim–offender encounter. White women are likely to claim gender discrimination, asserting that police attitudes are sexist, while African-American victims are more likely to claim racial bias on the part of police (Potter, 2010). These attitudes of the victims and the police are not isolated, and they have often prevented women from reporting a crime or have increased their anxiety in reporting future incidents of intimate partner violence. As is the case with many of the underlying issues concerning police conduct in intimate partner violence cases, these issues are complex and intersecting. Race, class, and gender are significant factors that should be taken into consideration when evaluating the satisfaction of victims and the police-victim encounter.

POLICE ORGANIZATIONAL EFFORTS

Much of the discussion thus far has centered on the implementation of the mandatory arrest and pro-arrest policies in the handling of intimate partner violence cases. However, new laws are not enforced by the simple passage of legislation mandating some action on the part of the criminal justice system. One often overlooked factor in how police respond to intimate partner violence is training. Police training in the area of intimate partner violence has undergone a series of changes over the last four decades. Most states have laws or regulations that require police academies to provide both new officer training and in-service training in intimate partner violence. This training tends to be very broad in nature and utilizes other responders to intimate partner violence, such as shelter staff and experts, in order to provide information to officers about the array of services available to victims. Furthermore, it is necessary to train not only police officers but also police dispatchers and crime scene investigators (Klein, 2004). As described in Chapter 2, *Navarro v. Block* (1995) demonstrated the lack of dispatcher knowledge of, training about, and care for victims of intimate partner violence. As a result, most jurisdictions train dispatchers to understand the seriousness of threats of intimate partner violence and to send police to the scene.

Crime scene investigation training is an important component of intimate partner violence cases. Most intimate partner violence crimes are misdemeanors and therefore depend on the officer's ability to gather corroborating evidence at the scene. Prosecutors rely on the victim's cooperation in most instances. Unless there is other evidence supporting the facts in the case, the case often boils down to "he said/she said." As misdemeanor offenses rarely warrant the follow-up support of detectives, it is up to the investigating officers to obtain additional information to corroborate the criminal claims. Many departments have training for officers in evidence gathering for intimate partner violence cases. This is a major difference between intimate partner violence and other misdemeanor crimes (Klein, 2004).

CONCLUSION

In many ways, the police are the criminal justice system in the minds of ordinary citizens. They are the responders that initiate all other actions within the system. How the police are viewed is often based on the personal interactions we have with them. The same is true for victims of intimate partner violence. The determinants of victim satisfaction with police handling of intimate partner vio-lence are not dissimilar from other police–victim encounters. The initial interaction, coupled with police empathy and assistance, are important factors in the satisfaction of the victim. Mandatory arrest and pro-arrest policies limit police discretion. These policies were meant to protect the victim and, to some degree, as evidenced in the *Thurman* case, to insulate the police and the local government from liability. These policies have had an impact on the satisfaction of the victim. However, victims do report that the police are often arrogant, sullen, and disingenuous when it comes to arresting an abuser or intervening in intimate partner violence incidents.

The historical analysis presented here accounts for why changes to the laws occurred and how police responses have adapted to the changing social construction of intimate partner violence. One must keep in mind that originally the laws were formulated to address the traditional domestic violence situation, that is, a husband abusing his wife. As the laws evolved and the social construction of intimate partner violence expanded, the police were confronted with chang-ing legal and social norms. The traditional domestic violence cases were complicated by the fact that women were asserting themselves and defending themselves. The police were faced with the require-ment to enforce the laws without regard to gender, and women began to be arrested in greater numbers as mutual combatants or as primary aggressors. Mandatory arrest policies were enforced regard-less of gender.

The definition of intimate partner was expanded to include same-sex couples. The police had already formed biases regarding this group. And while the police found it more convenient to defend female victims regardless of the fact that the assailant was of the same sex, we must question police attitudes toward male victims of same-sex intimate partner violence. Gay and lesbian communi-ties are suspicious of the police in general. Their experiences with the police in intimate partner violence incidents have done little to lessen these suspicions.

The definition of intimate partner violence has continued to expand, and it now covers violence between non-cohabitants who are presently involved or have been involved in a personal relation-ship. The behaviors deemed criminal have also expanded to include stalking and terroristic threats. The police response to intimate part-ner violence continues to evolve as the legal definition changes to become more inclusive. How the police respond is as important to victims as the final outcome of the process. For the police, victims' satisfaction is effected by race, gender, sexual orientation, class, and the relationship between the victim and the abuser. Intimate partner violence now extends to violence between middle- and high-school children who are dating. How police adjust to this change will need to be examined by the research.

6

INTIMATE PARTNER VIOLENCE IN THE COURTS

We are taught that courts are places where justice is blind and the law reigns supreme. Justice is depicted as a woman with a blindfold holding a set of balanced scales. However, nothing could be further from the truth. As Matthew Robinson (2009) depicts in his book *Justice Blind? Ideals and Realities of American Criminal Justice*, Lady Justice is peeking through her blindfold and the scales are tipped. As so many legal and social science theorists have found, the law and justice are premised in a hegemonic ideology that favors white, wealthy Americans. Feminists have also added the fact that the law and justice are created and determined by males using male experiences. Justice is anything but blind.

For female victims of intimate partner violence, the journey through the courts is often daunting. Victims are concerned with safety and being heard, while prosecutors are primarily concerned with their record of convictions. As a result, women who are not ideal victims are often neglected. Their cases are defined as weak and are dropped because the evidence does not point to the ideal victim. Females as a rule have been defined as too emotional, hysterical, and uncooperative. Additionally, female victims of intimate partner violence are often defined as hostile.

Similar to the organizational and cultural changes within policing, prosecutors did not give victims of intimate partner violence equal attention until the battered women's movement took hold. Ironically, it commonly took class action suits and consent decrees (court orders) to move prosecutors toward the fair treatment of these victims, such as in Cleveland, Ohio, in 1975, Los Angeles in 1979, and Tarrant County, Texas, in 1979 (Klein, 2004). In this chapter we will examine the progress made by prosecutors and judges when handling intimate partner violence crimes.

The majority of victims approach the courts in order to obtain orders of protection. These are the staple for victims in their fight to stop their abusers and protect themselves and their children. Although protection orders are a seemingly strong tool in the fight against intimate partner violence, victims have found that the enforcement of protection orders is not as it should be. The courts have little power to enforce protection orders, and so they rely on the police to assure that abusers who are not in compliance are arrested and remanded back to the court for further disposition. However, the police are not always aware of the orders and are not always enthusiastic about their enforcement. In addition to police reluctance to enforce protection orders, victims frequently face judges who are resistant to helping them. Judges often use outdated concepts of intimate partner violence or lack appropriate training, as is frequently the case with town judges, commissioners, and magistrates. As a result, victims often find that their safety remains uncertain.

At the other end of court case processing is the issue of the court's response to female victims who fight back. In the occasional instance, victims take matters into their own hands and fight back to such an extreme that the criminal justice system identifies them as serious offenders. These cases involve extensive injury to or the death of the abuser, as in the cases of Lorena Bobbitt or Francine Hughes. The battle for victims and other advocates of the battered women's movement has been in pressuring the courts to recognize their victim status above their offender status (Walker, 2000).

Courts have rigid rules of evidence and a set of legal defenses that have evolved slowly. Courts were even slower to examine claims that female victims of chronic abuse suffer psychological harm far greater than their physical injuries. Following a malestream definition of self-defense, courts often failed to recognize that the female victim turned perpetrator might be suffering from psychological trauma, which might account for her actions (Belknap, 2007; Walker, 2000). Legal and academic scholars proffered the defense of battered woman syndrome as an explanation for women taking the unusual action of murdering their abusers when there was no imminent threat of death or bodily harm, which is the requirement for self-defense claims. There was little acceptance in the courts of this defense strategy. However, when psychology experts classified this syndrome in male terms, as post-traumatic stress disorder, the courts became more accepting of the defense. The complexity of this defense and its nationwide acceptance, however, has often hinged on social constructs of ideal types.

In other areas of court reform, some jurisdictions have developed specialized domestic violence courts in order to address the more common intimate partner violence cases. Domestic violence courts bring together criminal and civil law in order to address intimate partner violence holistically. There is no consensus, however, on how these courts should be structured. As a result, we find varying models utilizing various means to handle these cases. We examine their effectiveness in this chapter.

Courts should have a better track record than they do in handling intimate partner violence cases. Victim worthiness is a determining factor in how justice is decided in intimate partner violence cases. The definition of the deserving victim has changed over the years (DeKeseredy & Schwartz, 1998). The social construction of the ideal intimate partner violence victim now includes heterosexual male and female couples, gay and lesbian couples, and persons in non-cohabitating relationships. Intimate partner violence constructs have also been extended to include teen dating couples, as well as former intimates. Regardless of the expanded definition of the intimate partner violence victim, we find that there are differences in how these victims are processed by the judicial branch.

THE PROSECUTION OF INTIMATE PARTNER VIOLENCE OFFENDERS

Intimate partner violence prosecution is seemingly conditioned by the seriousness of the offense. However, the presence of injury does not determine the severity of the charge (Buzawa & Buzawa, 2003). Premeditation and the use of a weapon are stronger determinants to charging decisions. Unfortunately, as Buzawa and Buzawa point out, intimate partner violence incidents are treated as isolated events, and thus persistent patterns of violence are denied as evidence of premeditation. As a result, prosecutors maintain the police practice of treating most intimate partner violence cases as less serious misdemeanors. In fact, research has uncovered that prosecutors are reluctant to file criminal charges in these cases.

While the research has placed a lot of focus on police refusal to arrest the perpetrators, we find that prosecutors have been just as reluctant to prosecute. In 1984, only 2 percent of all police arrests in the Minneapolis experiment resulted in prosecution. Research in the 1990s revealed that intimate partner violence cases charged as misdemeanors were treated more leniently than simple assault cases (Martin, 1994). A more recent study found that slightly over half of intimate partner violence cases are dismissed by the prosecutor, with only 5 percent of cases adjudicated ending in a guilty verdict (Belknap, Hartman, & Lippen, 2010). In a 2001 evaluation of its victims' rights amendment, Rhode Island found that appealed misdemeanor dismissals were twice as prevalent as dismissed appealed felony cases (Botec Analysis Corporation, 2001). The diminished treatment of this type of victimization reinforces social constructs of violence against women as a private trouble and deprives women of legal protection, thus adding to the social problem.

Felony prosecutions fall under the jurisdiction of county prosecutors. These officials are most often elected, although in some instances they are appointed by the governor of the state. Felony cases are heard in courts of general jurisdiction or in trial courts, located in county seats and less visible to the public. Each state has an attorney general who exercises a varying degree of authority over local and county prosecutors. Often the attorney general serves in a quasi-supervisory capacity. Attorneys general issue legal interpretations, opinions, and instructions to local and county prosecutors concerning the uniform implementation of the laws within the state. Since most cases are charged as misdemeanors, they often do not come under close scrutiny of the attorney general. In any governmental structure, however, prosecutors are political actors and represent law enforcement. As such they tend to embrace the same constructs of intimate partner violence and its victims as do police.

The history of the prosecution of intimate partner violence cases is relatively short. Strong lobbying efforts by a variety of feminists and women's groups resulted in significant changes to how the criminal justice system in general and prosecutors in particular address intimate partner violence. Traditionally, prosecutors were reluctant to prosecute intimate partner violence cases. Legal action in Ohio, California, and Texas led prosecutors to adopt a more demanding prosecution policy. In Texas, a class action suit was filed after two women were murdered by their husbands (*Miller v. Curry*, 1979, as cited in Klein, 2004). Prosecutors began to adopt a set of policies that mirrored the public sentiment about and the growing outrage over intimate partner violence. Among these were absolute and soft no-drop policies and mandatory prosecution policies.

As the police adopted their pro-arrest policies, prosecutors were to some degree forced to make reforms in their prosecution of intimate partner violence cases. There was a conundrum evident in police policy and prosecution reluctance. Although the burden of proof for arrest (probable cause) is considerably lower than the prosecution standard of beyond a reasonable doubt, the failure to prosecute intimate partner violence cases routinely negatively reinforced police action. It sent a message to the police that their efforts to arrest intimate partner violence perpetrators were unnecessary and pointless. It reinforced the police's reluctance to make arrests in the first place (Buzawa & Buzawa, 2003; Klein, 2004).

There are several reasons, both legitimate and illegitimate, for not prosecuting intimate partner violence cases. First is the lack of evidence. Since intimate partner violence often occurs behind closed doors, with only the victim, the offender, and perhaps the children as witnesses, the case becomes one of he said/she said. If the police are not properly trained to identify the primary aggressor, they may not adequately record evidence of injury. And while we now understand the traumatic effect that witnessing this violence has on children, we also know that they may be too afraid or traumatized to serve as witnesses in the case. Furthermore, neighbors who call the police for help often do not witness the violence, but rather hear the chaos of a violent interaction. Often this limited information is not enough to be defined as strong evidence. Bauman, Messner, and Felson (2000) found that prosecutors often drop cases because they believe the victim not to be credible. The problematic part is that race, income, and demeanor are often tools used to determine credibility (Karmen, 2010; Neubauer, 2005; Potter, 2010).

A second, related reason for not prosecuting intimate partner violence cases is the lack of victim cooperation. Until recently prosecutors relied on victim cooperation as their primary or sole form of evidence when pursuing intimate partner violence cases. In many instances, victims are reluctant to testify, resulting in case dismissals. However, the idea of the uncooperative or reluctant victim is more dynamic than one would think. Research as early as the 1970s shows that police and prosecutor attitudes often encourage victims to drop the cases or to refuse to testify (see Buzawa & Buzawa, 2003). In 2000, as many as 50 percent of victims recanted their story or refused to cooperate with Rhode Island prosecutors (Klein, 2004). Belknap, Hartman, and Lippen (2010) found that prosecutors reported that victims were uncooperative in only 20 percent of the cases. When examining the reasons for case dismissals, however, it was found that 75 percent of victims did not show up to the court proceeding (70 percent) or did not cooperate with the prosecutor.

It has long been known that the prosecutor's perception of the uncooperative victim/witness often derives from experiences with victims who cannot be contacted or victims who want dispositions or charges the prosecutor does not agree with (Karmen, 2010; Neubauer, 2005). Victim-witness assistance programs, which operate nationally out of the prosecutor's office, report understaffing, which results in failing to contact the victim, illegible police reports, and a lack of awareness of a change in the victim's address. Prosecutors commonly come across a victim who cannot be located, because she has fled the jurisdiction for a safer place. However, these failed efforts aside, prosecutors have been found to be negligent in their efforts to work with victims. For example, one study found that in 88 percent of all cases prosecutors had no phone contact with victims, and in 52 percent of all cases prosecutors had no face-to-face contact with victims (Belknap, et al., 2010).

A third factor in determining not to prosecute intimate partner violence cases is the belief that it is in the interest of justice to drop criminal charges or to attempt to handle cases in a diversionary manner. In either instance, it is evident that mandatory arrest policies and feminist groups pressure prosecutors to increase their efforts. One solution to this problem was the *no-drop policy* adopted by many prosecutors. No-drop intimate partner violence policies were the response to uncooperative or reluctant victims. A major problem with victim-witnesses is a fear of retaliatory violence, which is often more severe and, in many cases, more frequent (Belknap, 2007). When the victim is physically injured, she becomes acutely aware of the potential harm that can be caused to her. Belknap (2007) argues that the threat of further and more severe abuse is more real once the victim has been physically assaulted. She knows firsthand the capabilities of the abuser and fears retaliation. As the courts were not very successful in protecting the victims against repeated violence in many instances, victims' reluctance is understandable. Bennett, Goodman, and Dutton (1999) found four obstacles to victims' participation in intimate partner violence court cases:

(1) the process was confusing,
(2) the process was frustrating,
(3) fear of the abuser and/or concern that the court was unwilling or unable to protect her, and
(4) the victim's interpersonal conflict over the prospects of their partner's incarceration.

NO-DROP POLICIES AND EVIDENCE-BASED PROSECUTION

Under no-drop policies prosecutors do not rely on the victim's testimony to move cases to trial. Instead prosecutors rely on other evidence to reach their burden of proof. Prosecutors adopted *evidence-based prosecution policies* that required the police take detailed statements from victims during the course of the initial and subsequent investigations. Prosecutors use 911 tapes, photographs, medical records, and statements made to medical personnel concerning the injuries, as well as information gathered by social workers, as evidence to build cases against abusers. The victims' statements are authenticated by investigators and the police, medical personnel, and social workers.

To follow prosecutorial dictates, the police and 911 operators are often trained in how to question victims and callers in order to gain testimonial evidence (Jaros, 2005). Of course, defense attorneys claim that these statements violate the hearsay rules and are inadmissible in court. In 1995, the court held that an *excited utterance* serves as an exception to the hearsay rule because the victim or witness provides the statement under the stress of excitement (*State v. Sims*, 1995); however, when the victim or witness has time to reflect on the statement, the stress of excitement is called into question and the statement can no longer be deemed an excited utterance (*State v. Barnes*, 1996). The courts have ruled that excited utterances are not likely given to incriminate the defendant but are reasonably related to the victim's treatment. Further, corroboration, which tends to be higher for intimate partner violence cases, is often provided via statements by police, doctors, and counselors. The totality of the circumstances provide for the hearsay exception.

The courts continue to hear cases relevant to the excited utterance exception. Almost a decade following *State v. Sims* and *State v. Barnes*, the United States Supreme Court further clarified this exception in *Crawford v. Washington* (2004). In this case, the Court examined the confrontation clause and ruled that any statement made by a victim or witness that served as a testimonial statement in lieu of the absent victim or witness is a violation of the defendant's Sixth Amendment right to cross-examine the evidence.

The Court determined that statements made with the intention of prosecuting the defendant must be supported with court testimony. As mentioned earlier, many police and 911 dispatchers have been trained to question the caller in a way that the information gathered can be used as evidence in court. As the U.S. Supreme Court did not define what constituted testimonial statements, lower courts are left to make this determination. As a result, 911 calls have been redefined from excited utterances to testimonial statements that require victim cooperation (*People v. Moscat*, 2004). As pointed out by public defender Jaros (2005), this interpretation can serve as a severe blow to evidence-based prosecution.

The success of evidence-based prosecution relies on the collaboration between the prosecutor and the police. Specialized intimate partner violence caseloads or units were successfully developed throughout the United States to address the revolving-door syndrome of family abuse and victimization. Specialized units do not follow one model. However, the important element of each model is to determine the role of personnel from intake through adjudication to ensure that victims are kept informed about and are familiar with the case processing. These specialized units have increased prosecution rates around the country. They were developed as a result of legislatures adopting pro-prosecution policies for intimate partner violence even over the objection of victims. The criminal prosecution of intimate partner violence by these specialized units means that intimate partner violence is no longer treated as a private matter.

Specialized prosecution units have anywhere from one to thirty-seven prosecutors (Klein, 2004) and additional trained personnel to assist in the care of victims and to ensure that the necessary evidence is compiled for criminal convictions. Specialized prosecution units have investigators trained in intimate partner violence law to work with arresting police officers. Evidentiary issues are resolved by the police and investigators, who have expanded the definition of witness by relying on third-party witnesses, specifically children. Children have proven to be reliable and relevant witnesses, often having a remarkable sense of the situation. They have proven to be knowledgeable of the events leading up to the incident and are able to identify the aggressor. Children who call 911 are especially viewed as reliable witnesses.

Evidence-based prosecution has proven to be successful, though cases such as *Crawford v. Washington* (2004) and *People v. Moscat* (2004) have been setbacks. The success of evidence based prosecution is a result, in part, of the current training given law enforcers in gathering evidence in a manner that lends itself to conviction. The police no longer make their cases based exclusively on witness testimony. Instead they immediately gather evidence and information at the scene, as well as at hospitals. They also follow up with possible witnesses, including children. This process allows for stronger evidence, a second reason for the success of evidence-based prosecution, as perpetrators frequently express a willingness to plea-bargain once they see that the victim-witness's testimony is not the entire case against them. Offenders often realize that intimidating the witness into dropping the charges is not a viable option and resign themselves to the fact that a guilty plea will result in a more favorable sentencing outcome than a trial.

Critics of evidence-based prosecution cite cost as the primary objection. However, research demonstrates that the cost of conviction does not depend on the lavishness of the programs' budget. There appears to be little difference between well-funded programs and those of a more modest nature (Belknap, Graham, Lippen, & Sutherland, 1999; Klein, 2004). Prosecutors that commit the necessary time to intimate partner violence cases have a highly successful conviction rate regardless of budgetary affluence. However, prosecutors' success is also determined by the ideology of the court and the judges they are working with. Just as police efforts can be all for naught with uncooperative prosecutors, prosecutors find they may hit a wall when dealing with judges and juries.

JUDICIAL RESPONSES

Misdemeanor offenses, which comprise the majority of intimate partner violence offenses, are the purview of courts of limited jurisdiction (National Center for State Courts, 2006). In many instances, municipal judges are appointed to their positions. In some instances they may be elected. Since most intimate partner violence cases are still charged as misdemeanor crimes, most cases fall under the jurisdiction of municipal or town courts (courts of limited jurisdiction).

One problematic area for victims and prosecutors is judges' lack of expertise within town courts (Neubauer, 2005). While larger suburban and urban jurisdictions have highly structured courts of limited jurisdiction, most of the country is divided into smaller jurisdictions and has town courts. Judges in town courts are often elected or appointed residents and are not required to hold a law degree. These officials are commonly referred to as town court judges, magistrates, or commissioners. Magistrates or commissioners used in larger jurisdictions and within limited and general jurisdiction courts tend to handle bail, process fines, and oversee order of protection hearings. In most jurisdictions these officials may oversee trials of minor criminal and civil issues. In many instances, intimate partner violence cases are placed within the minor category. While these judges are required to undergo legal training once elected or appointed to office, this training does not equate to a law school background.

National trends reveal that town judges and magistrates often do not define intimate partner violence cases as real crimes. For many of these officials, community popularity has placed them in office. These officials are unprepared and have had no training about the dangers of intimate partner violence (Garcia, 1994). Even when police and prosecutors make every effort to help victims of intimate partner violence, town court judges often dismiss these cases. This becomes particularly problematic when these are the judges who issue orders of protections to victims. Judges often fail to provide this protection to intimate partner violence victims who do not fit the ideal type of victim, who is married, has children, is a "good" woman, and has been subjected to extreme violence. Without the needed legal training, these judges cannot appreciate the rule of law and do not know how to truly keep current with changing case law and legislation.

Orders of Protection

Orders of protection are civil remedies available to victims of intimate partner violence. They were developed in the mid-1970s to protect victims of intimate partner violence. Orders of protection, also referred to as restraining orders or no-contact orders, have not yet been found to be the best response to end the violence; however, they have often served as the only recourse for victims. In the 1970s, the criminal justice system refused to inject itself into the "domestic arena." However, since 1976 all states and the District of Columbia have enacted laws allowing intimate partner violence victims to seek orders of protection. The orders specify that there shall be no more contact between the abuser and the abused. They may also include mandates to vacate the premises, attend batterer treatment, and pay child support during the separation, and they may contain visitation provisions. Since the 1994 Crime Bill, orders often mandate that offenders surrender firearms to police.

As intimate partner violence research has expanded our understanding of this phenomenon, orders of protection have taken various forms based on the circumstances of the violence and the needs of the victim. Jurisdictions may provide emergency orders when courts are not open. The police issue the orders on judicial authority and they remain in effect until the court opens the next business day. The more formal process begins with a temporary order of protection. The defendant is not present during this court hearing. The victim tells her story to the judge. If there is credible evidence to believe that the victim is in danger, the judge will issue the temporary order of protection against the defendant. This order will remain in effect until a formal hearing can be conducted, at which time the defendant will have the opportunity to present evidence to refute the claims of the victim. As this is a civil matter, the level of evidence needed by the victim remains a preponderance of the evidence. If the victim prevails at this hearing, a permanent order of protection is issued. The order generally remains in effect for six months to three years depending on the jurisdiction. The victim may petition the court to have the order vacated. If a victim fails to appear to have the temporary order made permanent, the temporary order will be vacated by the judge in most scenarios.

Orders of protection are issued to protect victims, their property, and their families and associates from their abusers. Many states now issue injunctions against harassment. These injunctions can include orders levied on the abuser to have no physical contact with the victim away from the household (e.g., at work, at church, while shopping, etc.), and prohibit telephone calls to the victim or engaging in property damage or theft (Belknap, 2007; Johnson, Luna, & Stein, 2003). In these circumstances, the abuser is ordered to remain a specified distance from the victim. However, this does not prohibit offenders from intimidating victims by waiting outside of their place of employment or other frequently patronized locations while maintaining the required distance. Their mere presence can be as intimidating as other forms of harassment.

Though orders of protections are potentially a lifesaving recourse, victims have frequently been faced with judicial resistance to issue these orders. Tracey Thurman, for instance, fought for months to obtain her order of protection. Only 20 percent of petitioning victims are granted an order of protection (Durfee, 2010; Holt, Kernic, Lumley, Wolf, & Rivara, 2002). In Rhode Island only 44 percent of intimate partner victims are able to secure orders of protection (Botec Analysis Corporation, 2001). Unfortunately, many victims claim that the court process is too difficult. Furthermore, victims who are financially dependent on their abusers and those who experience more severe abuse do not complete the process (Belknap, 2007). Apparently, the system fails to provide enough protection to ensure that victims feel safe enough to file for an order of protection. However, even those who obtain orders of protection are not always safe. Tjadan and Thoennes (2000) found that 60 percent of temporary orders are violated within twelve months.

One problem with the orders of protection is serving the defendant. Courts issue the order but rely upon the sheriff's deputies to serve the abuser with the order of protection. If the offender cannot be located promptly, the order may go unserved for a long period of time. Some critics have noted that the orders may actually be served but are not properly recorded, so that their existence for execution by law enforcement may not be immediately known. This hinders local law enforcement's ability to enforce the court order should a violation occur or be reported.

The research examining the efficacy of orders of protection is inconclusive (Holt, et al., 2002; Johnson, Luna, & Stein, 2003). Grau, Fagan, and Wexler (1985) studied the efficacy of protection orders in Pennsylvania, finding that these orders were generally ineffective. However, they did find that protection orders were more effective in cases where offenders had engaged in less violence and where offenders had a less serious history of intimate partner violence. The effectiveness of orders of protection also varies when considering the abuse and the type of order. Victims who obtain temporary orders of protection are more likely to experience subsequent psychological abuse than victims with no order, while victim who obtain permanent orders of protection are less likely to experience violence than victims with no order (Holt, et al., 2002). Other research has found that the effectiveness of these orders is dependent on how comprehensive they are (Keilitz, Davis, Efkeman, Flango, & Hannaford, 1998).

Belknap (2007) and Erez and Belknap (1998) found that although the police encourage women to seek orders of protection, there is strong evidence that the police are reluctant to enforce the orders once they are issued. Regardless, victims tend to feel more confident and empowered once they start the process of filing for an order of protection (Keilitz, Davis, Efkeman, Flango, & Hannaford, 1998), revealing the fact that orders of protection serve as a step toward stopping the violence. The decision to apply for a protection order, and not the issuance of the order, has a significant influence on lowering recidivism (McFarlane, et al., 2004). That is, public contact (of any kind) works to decrease subsequent violence over the short and long term.

Orders of protection are not the panacea that advocates and feminists would like them to be. The evidence is less than convincing that women who obtain orders of protection are safer for their troubles. We do know that social constructs work against victims who attempt to secure their safety through these orders. Postmus uncovered four myths surrounding orders of protection that are linked to social constructs:

1. Women who seek restraining orders are not really abused but want a quick way to get custody of their children.
2. Battered women rarely follow through with the hearing; hence, they waste the court's time.
3. Compared to men, battered women are awarded unfair stipulations and benefits in restraining orders because of judicial bias and the presence of an attorney.
4. Restraining orders are not effective and may cause more problems for victims (Postmus, 2007, p. 348).

The first myth is easily accepted as it falls in line with cultural schemas that portray women as manipulative and scorned (Belknap, 2007; Garcia & Schweikert, 2010). Uncovering this myth, we find that victims request child custody or restricted visitations in less than half of orders of protection (Gondolf, McWilliams, Hart, & Stuehling, 1994; Harrell & Smith, 1996; Hart, 1992). Holding to the myth of the manipulative woman denies a woman the right to demand freedom from violence and from hiding, and to live in a safe and permanent home.

The second myth claims that victims rarely follow through with the case. As we discussed above, the myth of the uncooperative victim can frequently be linked to prosecutors' false assumptions about victim credibility, lack of testimony, or use of ideal types. As a result, the myth becomes a self-fulfilling prophecy when prosecutors do not even attempt to contact victims (Belknap, et al., 2010). Furthermore, victims will often drop their request for an order of protection as a result of offender retaliation (Harrell & Smith, 1996; Keilitz, Davis, Efkeman, Flango, & Hannaford, 1998).

The third myth, that women receive unfair benefits, has also been debunked by the research. As stated before, less than half of the victims are able to secure the requested child custody provisions. Half of all women are able to obtain orders of protection (Holt, et al.,

2002), and half are able to secure a no-contact provision (Gondolf, et al., 1994; Harrell & Smith, 1996). When female victims file for orders of protection, they often do not use attorneys, since they cannot afford them. Female victims who utilize attorneys are more likely to obtain orders of protection (Durfee, 2010), and an attorney's presence increases the chances of obtaining the desired provisions (Finn & Colson, 1990). Hence, it appears that income would be the greater determinant. Finally, as detailed above, the effectiveness of orders of protection is often dependent on the type of order, the comprehensiveness of the order, the use of an attorney, or the very act of filing for an order of protection. Hence, though over 50 percent of orders of protection are violated (Johnson, et al., 2003; Tjaden & Thoennes, 2000), when victim empowerment is the construct and purpose for the order of protection, the order is positively viewed by recipients in the majority of cases. This may result from the fact that women may see the order of protection as the first in a series of steps they need to take to advance beyond the abusive relationship. An order of protection is often seen as a necessary document to compel legal and social service agencies to assist victims in extricating themselves from their abusive relationships (Johnson, et al., 2003). Those somewhat knowledgeable of the legal process understand that orders of protection will increase the likelihood that felony charges can eventually be brought against the abuser. Empowerment seems to be as important an indicator of success as the traditional reduction in the frequency and/or intensity of the violence.

However, there is growing evidence that abusers are becoming increasingly aware that they can avoid the service of the orders of protection. The orders are civil documents and do not allow officers to enter the premises or force the person to accept these documents absent a subsequent court order. As a result, orders of protection may go unserved for long periods of time. Little research has been conducted on the effect of this phenomenon. On one side, clearly the abuser knows the victim has initiated legal action against him. Some research shows that if the abuser is more educated, is white, and is middle-class, he will likely be deterred from openly violating the order. Others may in fact become enraged, and the violence could ensue prior to the actual service of the order simply because the abuser avoided the service of the order. This is a critical issue that requires further attention.

BATTERED WOMAN SYNDROME

As pointed out earlier, courts have been slow in recognizing the trauma of abuse that can transform female victims of chronic abuse into female offenders who maimed or killed their abusers. Understanding the complexities of increasingly severe abuse, psychologists introduced the concept of battered woman syndrome in the 1970s to explain this phenomenon (Walker, 2000). The use of battered woman syndrome as an explanation or legal justification for the acts of battered victims who kill their partners in response to their partner's threats and aggression remains controversial. It is a justification defense that has self-defense as its legal foundation. Traditional "self defense rests on the belief that a person may take reasonable steps to defend themselves from physical harm" (Russell & Melillo, 2006, p. 220); however, the harm must be imminent.

Battered woman syndrome typically includes a recent battering incident that the victim believes will continue and most likely will cause her death. This fear is not unwarranted. Typically, the murder of the abuser takes place after the victim has endured indignities, previous death threats, and frequent and severe physical attacks, and it is often driven by alcohol or drug abuse (Huss, Tomkins, Garbin, Schopp, & Kilian, 2006). The abuse is often relentless and escalating in nature. The victim has little hope that it will ever subside. Victims fear for their lives or the lives of their children. The danger to children is often considered a flash point, the point when the victim feels there is no alternative but to kill the abuser to prevent the death of her children or herself.

Battered woman syndrome was first identified by Lenore Walker in 1977. She identified three stages of the syndrome: (1) tension progressing to an explosion, (2) an acute battering incident, and (3) a calm, even loving, respite (Walker, 2000). Walker's later research revealed that victims do not stay in abusive relationships because they have a psychological need to be victimized; instead, they stay out of sheer terror that leaving would lead to further and more severe battering or death.

It is easy to see the scars, bruises, and cuts from physical abuse. The manifestations of physical violence also allow trained medical personnel to demonstrate a pattern of abuse, quantifying and documenting it. Furthermore, the horror of the injuries often allows a jury to render a verdict of self-defense. Battered woman syndrome is predicated as much on psychological abuse as it is on physical abuse, maybe even more. The social construct of psychological abuse was not well established in the psychiatric, psychological, or legal communities before Lenore Walker's introduction of battered woman syndrome. One of the major difficulties with establishing a definition of psychological abuse for battered woman syndrome was the variety of factors upon which the definition depends. These factors include abuse intensity, frequency, intent, and the level of fear of the battered women (Tolman & Bennett, 1992). Additionally, psychological abuse also includes the creation of fear, economic abuse, and threats to children, among others. The social and behavioral science discourse on these topics appears clear; however, they become much more complicated in a courtroom. One major factor that enters into the legal debate is how to qualify and quantify when the abuse has reached critical mass.

The amount and intensity of abuse to reach a threshold level varies from victim to victim and makes the legal limits difficult to establish. Some argue that convicting a woman of murder under these circumstances is unfair, especially considering the relentless abuse. The debate has centered on culpability (Huss, et al., 2006). Some argue that at the very least, battered women should be held less culpable for their actions, while some argue that they should not be held culpable at all in light of their long-term suffering. Others argue that such a stance—that is, diminishing culpability in these instances—puts a strain on normative legal values.

As is often the case, law and research often experience a dissonance. The law often lags behind science, and social science in particular. Advances in social science are often statistically driven and difficult for the law to encompass. Additionally, social science lacks the degree of certainty required by the law (McManimon, 2010). Others argue that the antiquity of self-defense laws puts battered women at an extreme disadvantage. Finkel (1995) posits that current self-defense laws expect women to react dispassionately when they are anything but dispassionate. Finkel recommends amending the laws to make it possible for battered woman syndrome to meet the legal requirements of self-defense. Others, of course, argue against such action. Regardless of the feasibility or advisability of modifications to the self-defense laws, the killing of batterers poses difficulties for the legal system, as the facts in these cases do not lend themselves to the straightforwardness of the self-defense laws.

Often left out of the debate concerning the use of battered woman syndrome in the courtroom is the reaction of jurors to this line of defense. Ewing and Aubrey (1987) found that both men and women hold strongly to certain social constructs that blame the victim. In a public opinion survey, Ewing and Aubrey found that more than half of the men surveyed believed that battering occurred because the couple experienced "serious marital problems," that women could simply leave abusive spouses, and that if women sought counseling, they could prevent the abuse. Similarly, 50 percent or more of the women surveyed believed that the couple experienced "serious marital problems," that women could simply leave abusive spouses, that women who stayed in abusive relationships were masochistic and/or emotionally disturbed, and that if women sought counseling, they could prevent the abuse.

Jurors may also be influenced by the typicality of the defendant. Jurors have less trouble with a stereotypical or ideal case than with those that deviate. Because of the apparent difficulty in coming to a consensus about the typical battered woman, it may be more edifying to examine some issues jurors do find convincing in the battered woman syndrome defense. Expert testimony has been cited as one factor influencing juror decisions. Schuller (1992) found that when jurors were provided with expert testimony specific to BWS, sentences were lighter. Huss et al. discovered that the "(1) level of premeditation, (2) general culpability, and (3) severity of abuse" (2006, p. 1073) significantly influence jury decisions. Jurors clearly identified women who exhibited fewer signs of premeditation as less culpable; however, the length and severity of the abuse suffered by the victim/defendant were less convincing to male jurors.

Russell and Melillo (2006) identify several characteristics that laypersons believe the prototypical battered woman exhibits that can impact verdicts. They refer to this as *defendant typicality* and include demographic characteristics (age, motherhood, financial dependence on abuser), biosocial characteristics (frayed and fragile), social characteristics (lack of social interaction, hiding signs of abuse, excusing abuser, trying to please abuser) and psychological characteristics (depressed, guilt-ridden, confused, fearful). All these traits represent the ideal victim, as discussed throughout this book, and were determined through a detailed review of social science research. Russell and Melillo found that victims/defendants who were not ideal victims and who had "an active response history" (i.e., fighting back) were viewed as less credible and were more likely to receive a guilty verdict. Similarly, victims/defendants who were ideal victims and who had a "passive response history" (i.e., manipulated by their abusers) were viewed as more credible and were more likely to receive not guilty verdict. Unlike Ewing and Aubrey's research, males held more firmly to older social constructs of the ideal victim and were more likely to render guilty verdicts in all situations.

These findings support the major argument of critics of battered woman syndrome as a defense. That is, battered woman syndrome reinforces the construct that victims are mentally unstable (Russell & Melillo, 2006). Furthermore, unless victims/defendants demonstrate a passive response history, reflected on the learned helplessness component, jurors reject their defense, characterizing it as an excuse instead of a justification. The use of battered woman syndrome as a defense thus denies victims' agency and their right to defend themselves when the justice system fails to protect them. Yet there remains a real concern for the psychological plight of the victim/defendant.

Juror reliance on traditional legal lines of premeditation and culpability (Huss, et al., 2006) reveals the difficulty that the legal system has with the self-defense claims emanating from battered woman syndrome. Many of the problems seem to be associated with the social construct of psychological abuse. The manifestations of psychological abuse are concrete, and depression, often severe, is reported among groups of abused women with lower self-esteem as significantly correlated with abuse. The ineffectiveness of the battered woman syndrome defense to elicit not guilty verdicts consistently has caused it to be replaced over the last decade with the post-traumatic stress disorder defense.

POST-TRAUMATIC STRESS DISORDER (PTSD)

Post-traumatic stress disorder was originally known as shell shock and was diagnosed in veterans returning from World War I who were experiencing the psychological effects of war. Post-traumatic stress disorder is now used to explain the mental deterioration of persons who have experienced psychological trauma from a variety of sources, including physical and psychological abuse at the hands of an intimate partner (American Psychiatric Association, 1980). Studies examining lethality in women conclude that there is little difference between women who kill their abusive partners and those who do not. Victims of severe and frequent abuse may develop a series of escape strategies when they distrust the criminal justice system to adequately respond to the intimate partner violence and fear abuser retaliation if they attempt to leave. The progression includes substance abuse or an increase in alcohol consumption, suicide attempts, and possible murder of the abuser. Houskamp and Foy (1991) found that there is a high correlation between the symptoms of post-traumatic stress disorder and Walker's battered woman syndrome. Because the psychology and psychiatry communities recognize post-traumatic stress disorder as a disease or disorder, the intensity and severity of it can be quantified relative to abuse, as outline in the DSM-III/DSM-IV (1980, 1994). The criminal

In 1977, in the tiny town of Dansville, Michigan, the most famous intimate partner violence case was heard. It began the public debate over battered woman syndrome. As evidenced by this book and many others, and the ongoing research into this phenomenon, the debate about battered woman syndrome rages on today. Many do not remember the names of the parties involved, but they remember the "case of the burning bed," detailed in a book (McNulty, 1980) and then in a movie (Greenwald, 1985).

Francine Hughes was a twenty-nine-year-old housewife. One spring evening she poured gasoline over her sleeping husband, stepped back, lit a match, and dropped it onto the bed. James "Mickey" Hughes was burned to death in his sleep, and the house surrounding him was burned to the ground. The subsequent murder trial uncovered thirteen years of unthinkable violence that took place within that house. Equally as troubling were the inadequacy of the criminal justice system and the civil justice system and the total lack of understanding about the depths of intimate partner violence. During the murder trial, Francine Hughes' attorney laid out a set of facts that were unthinkable in a civilized society. Francine Hughes had endured repeated vicious beatings at the hands of her husband. She had been subjected to repeated threats of physical abuse and death and to intimidation. Her years of humiliation had not been endured in silence. Francine Hughes had attempted to escape from her husband by actively seeking help from lawyers, judges, social services, and the police, to no avail. She had been trapped in a repeated cycle of violence that offered her only despair and a future she feared was certain death at the hands of her husband. So Francine Hughes had done the only thing she could do. She had taken her safety into her own hands and killed her husband.

At trial, the defense was confronted with a legal conundrum. Francine Hughes had not been in imminent danger or fear for her life, so self-defense was going to be a difficult defense to mount. It was also clear that she knew right from wrong, the legal requirement for an insanity plea. But her attorney proceeded with the claim that she should be found not guilty because of self-defense. The jury returned a verdict of not guilty by reason of temporary insanity, indicating the difficulty with the self-defense claim, but recognizing that the level of violence suffered by the victim might have caused her to lose her ability to determine right from wrong.

In the decades since the verdict, advocates for victims of intimate partner violence and feminists have been troubled by this verdict, not the acquittal so much as the idea that a women who kills her abusive husband must be insane. Lenore Walker posits that in cases of repeated violence and abuse, the victim in fact does believe she (and, in many cases, her children) is in imminent danger of losing her life. It is the assurance that the abuse will happen again. The repeated threats and the escalation of violence appear to warrant self-defense for the victim. Lenore Walker was the first person to propose the cycle of violence theory and battered woman syndrome. Much of what we know about intimate partner violence is the result of the introduction of this syndrome. Although battered woman syndrome was anathema to prosecutors, who claimed it would be open season on husbands, it nonetheless has gradually made its way into the legal lexicon and is now recognized as a viable defense in the form of post-traumatic stress disorder. As mentioned earlier, the reframing of the diagnosis from battered woman syndrome to post-traumatic stress disorder has eased the way for the syndrome's acceptance within the criminal justice community. Many feminist scholars, practitioners, and researchers credit the Francine Hughes case as the catalyst for awakening America to the scourge of intimate partner violence. Prior to the incident many rightfully claimed that intimate partner violence was a secret locked behind the closed doors of the family home.

justice system and the law have caught up to the science, making post-traumatic stress disorder a viable defense.

One reason for the increase in the judicial acceptance of the post-traumatic stress disorder defense is the repetitive nature of the abuse suffered by victims/defendants. Furthermore, "traditional defenses of duress, necessity, justification, self defense, defense of others, and impairment have evolved in contemporary legal circles, as has posttraumatic stress disorder" (McManimon, 2010, p. 299). Studies have found that women who killed their husbands or intimate partners were more likely to be severely victimized over significantly longer periods of time when compared to their nonlethal counterparts. Mann (1988) found that 59 percent of the women in her study who killed their partners and claimed self-defense were severely beaten over long periods of time. On the other hand, she also found that 58 percent of the women in her study indicated premeditation, a condition that invalidates the generally accepted self-defense argument. Her conclusion was that self-defense may be relevant only when premeditation is not involved.

A battering husband or partner is not an excuse for murder. Although there is acceptance of the post-traumatic stress disorder (self-defense) claim, traditional and stereotypical women do not resort to violence. When they do, their response is to enter a guilty plea. However, judicial acceptance of the post-traumatic stress disorder defense has faced stiff resistance primarily from male judges, who see the actions of women who use lethal force as counter to traditional American roles of women. Additionally, post-traumatic stress disorder is characterized by discernible symptoms, identifiable to most in the mental health community. The breakthrough came when psychologists were able to diagnose high levels of post-traumatic stress disorder symptoms in offender populations that killed their abusers. This finding gave credence to the defense and made it more acceptable to the criminal justice community. As judges became more willing to admit expert witness testimony related to the post-traumatic stress disorder defense, the psychiatry and psychology communities became more efficient in detailing for the court the verifiable symptoms of the disorder and connecting them empirically to victims of intimate partner violence and in explaining the disorder's role in the criminal behavior of battered women (Sigler & Shook, 1997).

One factor often overlooked in the discussion of the battered woman syndrome defense is the fact that post-traumatic stress disorder is classified as an affirmative defense, or in layperson terms, a defense that needs to be proved. In these instances, if the prosecutor meets the burden of proof that the elements of a crime were present, it is now the burden of the defense counsel to prove this affirmative defense, that is, that the victim was suffering from post-traumatic stress disorder. Unlike a normal defense, where the presumption of innocence is with the defendant, affirmative defenses most be proven. This is a task not easily accomplished. Advocates argue that this is an unfair burden, one that victimizes women who believed they had no other alternatives available to them. Perhaps as intimate partner violence continues to play out in the media, and women have more services and resources available to them, they will see the other alternatives, presumed by so many to exist. Perhaps society will also understand the depths of the abuse and the inefficiency of the criminal justice community in addressing this most serious problem.

DOMESTIC VIOLENCE COURTS

Domestic violence courts were developed in the United States in the late 1990s as a form of therapeutic jurisprudence. The philosophy of therapeutic jurisprudence is that it allows the law to increase the mental health, psychological, social, and physical functioning of the victim while also addressing the multi-legal complexities that victims and offenders are entangled in. As a result, while the domestic violence courts must adhere to rules of evidence and due process procedures, a major focus is to ensure victim and child safety, obtain needed services for victims and their children, and mandate batterer treatment for the offender (Sack, 2002).

Following the therapeutic jurisprudence philosophy, courts nationwide developed varying models of domestic violence courts. Nationally, there are six overarching models for domestic violence courts, including: (1) integrated courts, (2) civil protection order dockets, (3) the criminal model, (4) domestic violence courts with related caseloads, (5) the unified family court, and (6) the coordinated court (Sack, 2002). Other research has found that as early as 2000 there were two hundred established domestic violence courts (Karan, Keilitz, & Denard, 1999; Winick, 2000).

One must consider, however, that domestic violence courts are innovative or specialized courts existing within traditional criminal or family courts. As a result, we must examine if the philosophy of domestic violence courts has been successfully implemented within such well-established institutions. According to Meyer and Rowan (1977), the rationalized elements of networks are societally ingrained and reflect societal understanding of social reality. Furthermore, these elements are reinforced, supported, and even demanded by public opinion, the power elite and other influential groups, legitimated knowledge, and the law and law enforcement agents (i.e., the government). These elements reflect highly institutionalized rules that bind formal structures. The stressed factor here is that networks must adopt these institutionalized rules in order to survive. In their adoption of these rules, interorganizational networks must take on the acceptable institutional form that engages in acceptable institutionalized technologies; otherwise, they chance illegitimacy. In the case of intimate partner violence, the transference of social constructs and business as usual tend to threaten to override the good intentions of domestic violence courts (Karan, et al., 1999; Keilitz, et al., 2001/2003).

Specialized drug courts provided the model for intimate partner violence courts. The foci of domestic violence courts are therapy, intervention, treatment, and restoration. Domestic violence courts have veered away from the punitive orientation of criminal courts in general. Drug courts are viewed positively for their reduction in recidivism, as well as their cost-effectiveness. Domestic violence courts seem to build on restorative justice models in their commitment to providing comprehensive services to victims and batterers alike (Coulter, Alexander, & Harrison, 2005).

Domestic violence courts recognize the weaknesses, noted by many critics, in the judicial handling of intimate partner violence cases in traditional courts. Intimate partner violence cases are often a low priority in traditional courts. Criminal justice resources are allocated more on the basis of the perceived detriment to community safety, as violence involving strangers is perceived to be more serious than violence between intimates (Coulter, et al., 2005; Fagan, 1996). Thus, stranger cases receive a higher priority in traditional courts. Furthermore, the attitudes of court personnel relative to the seriousness of intimate partner violence and victim blaming have an adverse effect on the outcome of intimate partner violence cases in the victims' eyes.

Erez and Belknap (1998) posit that court personnel's underestimation of the seriousness of their biases can have a catastrophic effect on victim safety. These same biases can also have an effect on the willingness of victims to engage in the process. Victims see the biases and negative attitudes of court personnel as barriers to their satisfaction and to a sense of fairness in the judicial system. One important consideration is the potential for victim actions in subsequent incidents. Victims who feel their concerns are not heard or who do not experience a sense of fairness in the judicial system are less likely to feel empowered and to return to the formal process.

They are likely to seek resolution outside the system in the future. Specialized courts for intimate partner violence that are geared to victims' preferences and demonstrate concern and a sense of priority are viewed positively by victims (Coulter, et al., 2005). To this end, these specialized courts emphasize the training and education of court personnel in the issues of intimate partner violence, engage in community outreach and education, and increase responsiveness to victims' needs.

An evaluation of these specialized courts is difficult because "establishing comparison conditions internally or across communities is difficult" (Fagan, 1996, p. 20). As is the case with all evaluation research, cross comparisons are often impossible, because the outcomes evaluated are different. Evaluations of specialized courts are often restricted to cost and recidivism. These, of course, are the easiest measures to evaluate, and that may be the reason they are so often the focus. However, intimate partner violence victims are concerned with the continuation and severity of the abuse.

Intimate partner violence is a complex social problem defined by a set of values, beliefs, and attitudes, inclusive of the victim and abuser, the criminal and civil justice systems, and the personnel that work within these systems. The perceptions of court personnel concerning the services provided to victims as adequate or better are not shared by the victims (Coulter, et al., 2005). When victim satisfaction in the process is evaluated alongside the perceptions of court personnel, the differences are stark. Victims feel that safety in the courts is inadequate, and that the policies and procedures of the legal system are too confusing and complicated. Although assistance is available to victims, victims still need to do the "legwork" to find those services. One important reality is that victims need to be involved in court processes for countless hours. Coulter, Alexander, and Harrison (2005) interviewed one victim who estimated that her court involvement exceeded three hundred hours. Coulter, Alexander, and Harrison conclude from their research on Florida's court system (both specialized and traditional courts handling intimate partner violence cases) that "while some court personnel feel that court processes may be improved through the establishment of specialized courts, improvements are not evident. Most notably, change in the areas of training of court personnel and provisions of increased support and safety for victims are imperative" (2005, p. 105).

CONCLUSION

Just as changing social constructs altered police practice, so, too, did they alter prosecutorial and judicial practice. Unfortunately, the judicial branch of government is deeply steeped in tradition and legal precedent, which makes needed change slow and interminable. What appears to the layperson as endless is to the judicial branch speedy. It is not surprising that discussions about intimate partner violence continue and are truly in their infancy stage, especially in legal terms. Yet prosecutors, as law enforcers, adapted a bit more quickly to the demands to treat intimate partner violence cases as crimes. The prosecution of intimate partner violence has undoubtedly improved. Prosecutors now recognize that the very reporting of violence can increase the danger to the victim considerably. However, myths about uncooperative victims still tend to override many prosecutorial decisions, as many victims are reluctant to follow through with complaints, fearing for their safety and that of their children. Regardless of the persistence of victim-blaming constructs, no-drop policies, evidence-based prosecution strategies, specialized prosecutorial units, and victim-witness assistance programs operated out of the prosecutor's office have drastically improved the justice response to victims. Additionally, while there is improvement still to be made, victims today are more satisfied with how their cases are handled.

The judicial processing of intimate partner violence cases has also changed for the best. Orders of protection (emergency, temporary, and permanent) provide victims with both civil and criminal recourse. Social constructs run amuck here as well, as most victims are not successful in obtaining permanent orders of protection or in obtaining the desired provisions due to victim-blaming ideologies held by judges. Additionally, police are often reluctant to enforce orders of protection, and offenders frequently violate them. Nonetheless, victims often use orders of protection to provide a record of violence that cannot be denied by the justice system. Furthermore, the orders often serve to empower victims.

Nothing has strained the senses of the judicial branch as much as the debate over women who kill their abusers. Women who kill their abusers have not fit neatly into traditional legal definitions of self-defense. However, changing social constructs of imminent danger were accepted with Lenore Walker's battered woman syndrome and post-traumatic stress disorder. The paradox that has presented itself is that while feminists have worked to empower victims, strengthening their agency, battered woman syndrome and post-traumatic stress disorder cast victims as mentally unstable, once again stripping their agency. Furthermore, victims who do not fit the learned helplessness or extremely depressed categories are denied the right to fight back.

Specialized domestic violence courts are evidence that the judicial system recognizes the complexities of intimate partner violence. Modeled after drug courts, specialized domestic violence courts emphasize restorative justice and therapeutic treatment, using punishment as a mechanism to ensure compliance. However, recognizing the complexities of intimate partner violence and delivering services are not the same thing. Research demonstrates that the attitudes and biases of court personnel in these specialized courts do differ substantially from those of traditional courts. As a result, there is conflicting evidence about the protection afforded victims and their safety. Despite the many positive accomplishments of specialized domestic violence courts, victims still raise concerns about the lack of services and information, and the time they spend attending case hearings. That in these courts civil law and criminal law are brought together under one roof is a very positive development. Giving intimate partner violence cases the priority they deserve through the creation of these courts is a positive in the eyes of the victims. The continued evaluation of specialized domestic violence courts on a variety of outcome measures is important to strengthening the judicial commitment to address intimate partner violence for the long term.

7

CORRECTING INTIMATE PARTNER VIOLENCE

Deterrence, rehabilitation, retribution, and incapacitation are the central ideologies concerning punishment in the United States. Departments of corrections are not victim-centered. They are offender-focused, and as a general rule, victims receive little thought or service from correctional agencies. We have discussed throughout this text the need to understand contextually the victim-abuser dynamics in the criminal justice response to intimate partner violence. In fact, many of the changes in criminal justice responses resulted from these realizations. However, unlike police and court personnel, corrections has never played a direct role in providing services to victims. One may argue that victim needs are served when corrections takes custody of, incapacitates, or rehabilitates offenders. However, these needs are not served when offenders are not actually punished. The punishment for intimate partner violence offenses must follow similar progressive ideologies used to apprehend, try, and convict offenders and should also resemble ideologies of non-intimate criminality. So, how is intimate partner violence punished in relation to the severity of the crimes?

Social constructs of intimate partner violence have been deconstructed and reconstructed to warrant a criminal justice response. Supreme courts and legislatures have altered their approach from laissez-faire government of the family to stronger social control of the family. Intimate partner violence is now a crime punishable by imprisonment. In today's punitive environment one would think that the severity of the offense and the criminal history of the offender would provide the guiding principles for sentencing intimate partner violence offenders. In reality, though, most male intimate partner violence offenders are not sentenced to jail or prison (Canales-Portalatin, 2000). And while probation is the most common custodial punishment, many are not sentenced to terms of probation. Diversion is the most frequent punishment received. Even when probation is the sentence, probation officers are reluctant to revoke probation for repeated incidents of intimate partner violence. Being offender-centered, corrections ignores victim protection to concentrate on providing offenders with another opportunity to change. To that end, there has not been a movement to revoke probation for intimate partner violence offenders, unless the subsequent incidents are at a felony level.

Rehabilitation has reemerged in the correction of intimate partner violence offenders in the form of batterer treatment programs. Like with many treatment programs, there is the one-size-fits-all mentality. Programs are based on either a feminist ideology or an offender ideology, and the results are not very encouraging. Yet we continue to require offenders to participate, with little success and high dropout rates. What is more troubling is that offenders who drop out of these mandated treatment programs do not face serious repercussions for violating their sentences, thus rendering impotent the programs' and the justice system's efforts to protect victims from future battering.

More insidious is the *criminalization* of victims of intimate partner violence. Girls are often criminalized when they run away from abusive homes. They are adjudicated status offenders or criminals, and little regard is given to their victimization. The patriarchal structure of the family seems to overrule all logic. When girls and women act outside the socially expected boundaries, the punishment is frequently disproportionate to the severity of the action (Belknap, 2007). The failure of the system to recognize that criminalization in the face of the long-term brutalization of women diminishes women's right to protect themselves. Furthermore, race seems to play an important role in who is deemed worthy of victim or offender status.

SENTENCING BATTERERS

Traditionally sentencing involves the formal assignment by a judge of a convicted offender to a fine or a term of treatment, community service, probation, or incarceration, in accordance with the laws of the jurisdiction where the offense occurred. The terms of the sentence are prescribed by law, with judges having some discretion in the selection of the sentence, as well as the length and the conditions of the sentence. Probation is the most often-used sanction in American jurisprudence. Sixty-five percent of all criminal offenders are sentenced to a term of probation (Clear, Cole, & Reisig, 2010). Intimate partner violence offenders, on the other hand, are more likely to receive pretrial diversion, treatment, or sentence deferment pending the completion of an informal period of probation (Canales-Portalatin, 2000; Gondolf, 1997; Klein, 2004).

Batterer Treatment

The most frequent sentence given offenders since the acceptance of formal judicial processing of intimate partner violence has been court-mandated treatment (Ventura & Davis, 2005). Judicial sentencing was frequently premised in early offender typologies, which identified various categories of offenders as pathologic and as having various personality disorders, a loss of self-control, or codependency (Holtzworth-Munroe & Stuart, 1994). Though this clinical approach to intimate partner violence was based within the larger constructs that held women as partially responsible for the violence and minimized offender responsibility, this approach was nonetheless widely accepted, as it was based on normative assumptions of the day.

The evolution of intimate partner violence treatment takes a social-political path, traveling through a maze of individual incident-based treatments to culture-focus treatments. In addition to psychiatric/psychological counseling, changing approaches to intimate partner violence treatment have included group anger management programs, as well as feminist-based education programs that couple cognitive techniques and behavior management techniques centered on the belief that intimate partner violence is learned behavior and can be unlearned (Hansen & Harway, 1997; Klein, 2004). Originally, males were referred to treatment only when they killed their spouses. This was an artifact of the patriarchal attitudes that prevailed into the 1980s, as nonlethal battering was largely ignored.

Initially, lethal batterers were referred to psychiatrists for individual counseling, and in many cases the deaths were partially blamed on the victim's precipitation of the violence or masochistic behavior (Elbow, 1977; Faulk, 1974). Victim blaming is an old, reliable excuse for the aberrant behavior of batterers, and is part of society's normative assumptions. Further, murderers were often diagnosed as suffering from depression and low self-esteem, which, when coupled with the victim's own behavior, resulted in the lethal attack. Absent any possibility of the victim contradicting the batterer's version of the incident, early batterer treatment relied on counseling for these clinical maladies and was supervised by the mental health community. As a growing number of nonlethal cases of intimate partner violence began to reach the courts, the criminal justice response remained one of individual therapy, primarily overseen by the mental health community.

The reliance on psychiatric and psychological treatment of an individual nature for batterers began to lose favor in the early 1980s, when the rehabilitation model generally fell out of vogue. The criminal justice system's affection for treatment was replaced with a growing appetite for retribution and public safety. For the first time, the primary concern of the criminal justice system was for the safety of victims of intimate partner violence (Schechter, 1982). Many batterer treatment programs evolved into feminist-oriented models that define violence more broadly to include issues of power and control, which had to be addressed as part of the programs (Hansen & Harway, 1997; Klein, 2004). These models require that batterers divest themselves of their sexist beliefs and attitudes. Anger management and improved modes of communication are also important components within the modern treatment modalities. Many programs replicate the Duluth Model, whose curriculum centers on identifying behaviors of batterers as compared to non-batterers: "physical violence/non-violence; intimidation/non-threatening behavior; emotional abuse/respect; isolation/support and trust; minimization, blame and denial/accountability; sexual violence/sexual respect; male privilege, children and economic abuse/partnership; and coercion and threats/negotiation and fairness" (as cited in Klein, 2004, p. 222). As noted in Chapter 2, the batterer is described with the Duluth Model's Power and Control Wheel, while the non-abusive partner is described by Duluth's Equality Wheel (Domestic Abuse Intervention Program, 2008).

Although many programs address the problems of power and control outlined by the Duluth Model, there are no standards for the length of programs. Some programs may last for two days, while others last for one year. Many programs exclude heterosexual women or gay and lesbian batterers, and many smaller communities do not have the resources to serve a diverse ethnic population. As many of the programs are privately conducted, there is pressure from criminal justice agencies to keep programs short and therefore affordable in order to handle a larger number of offenders. Although these programs were originally designed to rehabilitate individual offenders, the explosion of intimate partner violence in both the civil and criminal justice arenas has led to a one-size-fits-all approach. This approach has diminished the ability of many of these programs to effect change in batterers.

Regardless of the programs' effectiveness, social constructs have maintained the need not just to punish offenders for their crimes but also to change them via treatment. Most states have passed batterer treatment, counseling, and intervention laws. The legislation ranges from mandating treatment as a condition of probation to terminating probation once treatment is completed. However, states do not need legislation to refer batterers to treatment. New York courts refer on average 76 percent of batterers to treatment, and the vast majority follow the progress of their referrals as a matter of policy, not law (Klein, 2004).

Debate exists concerning the treatment modality and the efficacy of programs in general. Treatment programs tend to be psycho-educational and focus on having batterers confront their behaviors and take responsibility for their actions and problems, and on raising the conscience of offenders concerning power and control (Lee, Uken, & Sebold, 2007). Anger management and effective and equal communication between batterers and their partners are also key treatment components. These programs are referred to as feminist-cognitive behavioral treatment programs and have contributed significantly to the treatment of intimate partner violence offenders. However, these programs are not based on offender motivation. Rather they are usually required as a condition of court/correctional mandate. Practitioners working with batterers report that offenders are resistant to treatment, defensive, and unmotivated. Non-completion rates range from 75 percent to 92 percent of batterers recommended for traditional treatment (Cadsky, Hanson, Crawford, & Lalonde, 1996; Murphy & Baxter, 1997).

Lee et al. (2007) examined the effectiveness of a self-determined goal program and found initial evidence that self-determined goals had a positive impact on reducing recidivism among batterers. Batterers who are specific about their goals are more likely to continue to work on their goals, even after the treatment period ended. While the research was limited in size and did not include a control group for comparison, there was evidence that offenders could be motivated to reduce or refrain from future battering if the treatment was centered on their goals and motivations. The use of language and symbols of self-determination are important constructs for the control of intimate partner violence.

The effectiveness of traditional batterer intervention programs has been called into question. Evaluations indicate that traditional batterer intervention programs have only a small effect or no effect on batterer recidivism (Davis & Taylor, 1999; Davis, Taylor, & Maxwell, 1998; Feder & Forde, 2000). Unfortunately, much of the research fails to examine the effects of different types of intervention on batterers of different racial/ethnic backgrounds (Buttell & Carney, 2005). The findings indicate there may be a need to specialize treatment programs according to racial/cultural differences. For example, according to the National Crime Victims Survey, African-American women have a higher incidence of intimate partner violence (Buttell & Carney, 2005). Furthermore, African-American men drop out of treatment at a significantly higher rate than their white counterparts in the same programs (Buttell & Carney, 2005; Gondolf, 1997). While there is some evidence that court-ordered batterer treatment may be equally effective on psychological variables for both African-American and white male batterers, evidence also reveals that the effectiveness of programs for both racial groups is very poor.

Therapeutic jurisprudence continues within court sentencing today. We can see strong evidence in the continued development of domestic violence courts throughout the United States (Sack, 2002). While these courts are organized in order to address intimate partner violence within the criminal justice system, they are also concerned with the treatment of the victim and the offender. Some research has found that batterers who are mandated to treatment have less recidivism than offenders who voluntarily enter treatment (Gondolf, 1997). Gondolf (2009) points to the fact that research has placed increased focus on trying to differentiate the most violent offenders: those who are depressive/compulsive and have narcissistic/antisocial tendencies. However, clinicians have learned that batterers tend to have differing and dynamic problems, ranging from severe mental health issues to substance abuse to childhood victimization. This adds to the programs' difficulty in effecting treatment.

In his more recent examination of batterer treatment success, Gondolf (2009) found that batterers undergoing batterer treatment and supplemental mental health treatment as mandatory referrals by a court referral system (which he refers to as "intent-to-treat") did not show improvement in their re-offending. Furthermore, while their female intimates felt slightly safer during the referral period, this feeling did not last, as the violence continued once the treatment period ended. On the other hand, rearrest for subsequent events of violence was less likely to occur for abusers with mandatory referrals for mental health treatment than for abusers with no referrals. However, Gondolf speculates that the referral process may influence the victim's likelihood of reporting subsequent crimes and not the actual crime themselves.

The current approach to treatment as a criminal sanction serves dual purposes from the court's standpoint. First, there is the fact that offenders are being tried and convicted, with a definite sentence imposed, without adding to the prison and jail overcrowding problem. This demonstrates that the court is treating intimate partner violence with seriousness and holding offenders accountable. Second, it provides a means by which offenders can be aided in decreasing their violence. Unfortunately, the lack of court supervision of these sanctions can prove problematic when offenders do not fulfill their sentences (Gondolf, 2009).

Offenders benefit because a sentence of treatment allows them to avoid jail time (Pitts, Givens, & McNeeley, 2009). Unfortunately, noncompliance is a major problem for the courts: as many as three-quarters of offenders may not comply with treatment-based court orders (Gondolf, 2009). Pitts, Givens, and McNeeley (2009) found that a domestic violence court with a holistic approach that includes offender counseling results in a 30 percent compliance rate. While they argue that this low compliance is reasonable given the severity of offender problems, this ignores the fact that the 70 percent of offenders who do not comply may be continuing their abuse. Most would argue that this is unreasonable.

Victims also benefit from the treatment of offenders. Since we know that many victims are financially dependent on their abusers, it does not necessarily serve these victims to incarcerate their abusers (though this is not an argument to avoid incarceration). Mandating treatment provides offenders with the knowledge that their behavior is criminal, unacceptable, and must be changed. Gondolf found that even if batterers do not undergo treatment, a mere evaluation for mental health needs can decrease a batterer's future offending (2009). On the other hand, given that noncompliance is so high and that many treatment programs fail to effect change in batterer behavior, the emphasis on treatment gives victims false hope and can result in subsequent violence, which could have been avoided with a harsher sanction. These harsher sanctions include electronic monitoring, probation, and jail or prison time.

Probation

Policy changes concerning probation to supervise intimate partner violence offenders have followed a time line similar to that of changes to police policies. In the 1970s and 1980s, legislation was enacted across the nation that enabled prosecutors to handle intimate partner violence cases in a similar fashion to stranger crimes (Canales-Portalatin, 2000). As intimate partner violence was exposed as a serious social problem and mandatory arrest and no-drop policies became the law of the land in the mid- to late 1990s, judges began to impose sentences of probation for these offenses. Because intimate partner violence tends to be treated as isolated events, offenders are not likely to have extensive criminal histories, and probation seems the appropriate sanction in most cases. This follows the traditional sentencing logic. However, if victim safety is considered as an equal factor in sentence contemplation, probation for a repeat abuser may very well be an inappropriate sentence. Further research reveals that the cumulative intervention strategies of arrest, prosecution, and court sanctioning of probation do not necessarily have a positive outcome on reducing recidivism (Murphy, Musser, & Maton, 1998). However, since probation is the custodial sanction given to most misdemeanors (as intimate partner violence events are most commonly charged), probation remains a popular sanction.

Similar to police and prosecutors' offices, where specialized units were formed to address the growing issue of intimate partner violence, probation and parole organizations began to formulate policies and procedures for specialized caseloads for intimate partner violence probationers. These caseloads were much smaller than traditional caseloads. Due to a lack of financial resources, these caseloads quickly grew, and soon probation officers found themselves overwhelmed.

The reality of specialized caseloads for intimate partner violence probationers was that they were not often given special attention (Klein, 2004). Additionally, as probation is offender-oriented, past activity is not so much the focus. Instead, an emphasis is placed on future behaviors while under supervision. As has been found in probation research, probation officers frequently do not engage in the required presentencing investigation, unless the judge mandates such activity (Neubauer, 2005). Examining the conditions of probation in Rhode Island, Klein, Wilson, Crowe, and DeMichele (2008) found that counseling is either not mandated as a condition or probation officers do not enforce the conditions. Because intimate partner violence is most often treated as a misdemeanor, probation officers are less concerned with the safety of victims and are less likely to violate the probationers (i.e., revoke probation) if further allegations are made, unless accompanied by a conviction.

As demonstrated in the Rhode Island model, Klein, et al. (2008) found that a model of specialized domestic violence units (DVU) can achieve lower recidivism rates and safety for victims. Rhode Island's probation agency policies and implementation reveal that:

1. DVU cases are seen more frequently.
2. DVU victims are more likely to be contacted by their abusers' probation officers.
3. DVU probation officers are more likely to return probationers to court for technical violations (Klein, et al., 2008, p. 2).

Klein et al. conclude that while many probation officers do not coordinate or follow through with their cases, as does the Rhode Island model, this in fact can be accomplished. As is often the case, probation officers reserve the more serious sanction of revocation for offenders who demonstrate a total disregard for the law or for those who commit serious violations indicative of possible future criminal conduct. In other words, when probation officers are confronted with technical violations of the conditions of probation, they often attempt to address the transgression outside of the formal legal process and require the offender to adhere to additional conditions for a period of time. This may have cataclysmic effects for the victim.

Ignoring the severity of batterers' crimes can result in injury to the victim. In 2002, 7 percent of all probationers were convicted of intimate partner violence (Glaze, 2003). By 2008 these offenders represented 18 percent of all probationers, federal and state (Glaze & Bonczar, 2009). In 1998,

> 4 in 10 jail inmates convicted of a violent crime against an intimate had a criminal justice status at the time of the crime: about 20 percent were on probation, 9 percent were under a restraining order, and just under 10 percent were on parole, pretrial release, or other status.

(Greenfeld, et al., 1998) Furthermore, Lagan found that 43 percent of probationers were rearrested within three years (1994, as cited in Klein, et al., 2008, p. 20). In 2000, 21 percent of those arrested for intimate partner violence in Rhode Island were already on probation, and in Tennessee two-thirds of those arrested for intimate partner violence were on probation (Klein, 2004).

While we see that custodial sanctions, such as probation, have increasingly been applied to batterers, probation is ill-equipped to provide protection for victims in its current form. In large cities it is not uncommon to find that the court is unaware of pending cases for criminal defendants. It is possible for an offender to be sentenced to probation by more than one judge at the same time. The obvious potential for offenders to fall through the cracks is greater in these larger areas; however, the courts place the responsibility for monitoring offenders on the probation department. Klein et al. (2008) stress that community and system collaboration is the only method that allows probation departments to successfully manage their cases. The case of Kristin Lardner exemplifies the true lack of protection for intimate partner violence victims whose abusers are sentenced to probation in large cities.

Kristen Lardner was a twenty-one-year-old college student who was stalked and eventually killed by her former boyfriend, Michael Cartier, in 1992 (Klein, 2004; Rosenburg, 1995). After a violent attack, Kristin filed a restraining order against Michael Cartier and refused to see him. Kristin had learned that Cartier had prior convictions and was serving probation for his abuse of his previous girlfriend. Cartier reacted as many abusers do, by threatening and stalking Kristin. Though Cartier had violated his probation and Kristin's order of protection, the court decided to keep him out of jail, not knowing about his previous violence. Shortly after she obtained a permanent restraining order, Cartier accosted Kristin and demanded that she go out with him. When Kristin refused and walked away, Cartier shot her in the head. He ran as she fell to the sidewalk, but later returned to fire two more shots into her. Cartier went to his apartment and took his own life.

Cartier, who had been convicted of multiple offenses and four felonies, had repeatedly assaulted and battered women, and violated restraining orders and his conditions of probation. He had been reported to several agencies as being in violation of probation and should have been placed in jail. Instead, he fell through the cracks of an overworked and resource-depleted probation system. The probation system's compartmentalization, isolation, and failure to share information led to this unfortunate death.

Probation lacked the resources to effectively supervise all probationers. In fact, probation depended on the cooperation of the offender. The common practice of charging batterers with misdemeanor or low-level felony offenses created little, if any, documented criminal history, leaving many batterers under-supervised. As probation departments began to realize the gravity of intimate partner violence, much the same as the courts and the police, their efforts began to focus on improved supervision and victim safety.

One alternative used to enhance the supervision of probationers convicted of intimate partner violence is electronic monitoring. Electronic monitoring concentrating solely on the offender is known as unilateral electronic monitoring. When used in intimate partner violence cases, and assuming the additional function of victim protection, it is known as bilateral electronic monitoring (Erez, Ibarra, & Laurie, 2004). The use electronic monitoring provides several benefits. It:

1. protects the victim within the context of enforcing protective orders;

2. enforces the offender's liberty restrictions and monitors observance of exclusion zones;
3. provides the victim with an alert if the offender moves within a personal space restriction prohibited by no-contact orders; and
4. widens the net for offenders who may otherwise not have punitive sanctions (Ibarra & Erez, 2005).

Traditional electronic monitoring is viewed as an intermediate sanction in lieu of incarceration. The technology is based on radio frequency. Under the unilateral design, a tamper-resistant transmitter is placed on the offender's ankle and a receiver is placed in his home. Except during agreed-upon times for the offender to be away from his residence (employment, therapy, and personal exemptions approved by the court), the offender must remain within five hundred to one thousand feet of the receiver. When an offender is outside of the acceptable radius (presumably absconding from electronic monitoring), a central monitoring station is notified and probation authorities are also advised of the violation. The bilateral nature of electronic monitoring allows a receiver to be located at the victim's home or place of employment, or on the victim's person, in order to alert her that the offender is close. The victim is given the opportunity to notify authorities of the offender's close proximity (Erez, et al., 2004).

The Global Positioning System (GPS), a more technologically advanced system, is also used to monitor intimate partner violence offenders. The system requires an offender to wear a transmitting device that sends signals to a satellite. The offender's location can be determined in real time and precisely pinpointed, and the offender's whereabouts during an entire day can be recorded. This allows the probation department to examine the offender's habits and study location patterns to ensure compliance with no-contact orders. The system may permit victims to be notified when an offender is in close proximity. Yet electronic monitoring is not without its problems. For example, the radio frequency design utilizing telephone lines may fail. Power failures are not uncommon. Secondly, victims often rely too heavily on technology, and not on their own vigilance, to ensure their safety. Third, the devices can be tampered with and disabled. Finally, courts may be inclined to place offenders on electronic monitoring who are likely to re-offend, compromising the safety of the victims unnecessarily (Erez, et al., 2004; Klein, 2004).

The definitive success of electronic monitoring in intimate partner violence cases is limited, mixed, and inconclusive. Although states continue to be added to the growing list of those using electronic monitoring in both forms to combat intimate partner violence, more research is needed into its efficacy. The overall success of probation to address intimate partner violence is mixed. However, one unintended consequence of probation as a sentence for intimate partner violence is that victims may be more likely to stay with their abusers and, as a result, are exposed to continued abuse. Box 7.1 demonstrates the frequent use of probation and treatment in intimate partner violence cases, even with substantial injury and irrefutable evidence.

Incarcerating Offenders

Prison and jail classification has a more difficult time distinguishing intimate partner violence offenders from offenders sentenced for non-intimate offenses. Batterers confined to correctional facilities are not charged specifically with intimate partner violence crimes, and even in cases where it is obvious that intimates were the victims, the percentages are relatively small. In a study of eleven large counties, Durose et al. (2005) found that batterers made up 22 percent of the violent offenders in local jails in 2002. Sixty percent of these offenders were incarcerated for aggravated assault, while 18 percent were under an active order of protection when sentenced. They also found that a third of felony assaults within these counties were intimate partner violence offenses, and 73 percent of the offenders who committed these particular felony assaults had a previous felony or misdemeanor conviction of any crime type. Sixty-eight percent of these felony batterers were sentenced to jail, while 62 percent were sentenced to *prison*. Durose et al.'s study reveals that today felony offenders are treated with more severity.

On December 19, 2008, New York State senator Hiram Monserrate smashed a glass into the face of his girlfriend, Karla Giraldo, who then required twenty stitches (Long, 2009). Security video caught Monserrate as he dragged Giraldo down the stairs, across the lobby of the apartment building, and out of the door. The attending doctor and nurse at the hospital where Karla Giraldo was treated described the injury as relatively serious, involving a lot of blood. They testified that Giraldo described a violent attack, and soon after an order of protection was issued in order to keep Monserrate away from Giraldo.

In subsequent court testimony and in a later newspaper interview, Giraldo denied the testimony of the hospital staff (Gonzalez, 2009). She claimed that the injury was an accident and that Monserrate had tried to take her to the hospital against her wishes. Giraldo complained that the police had tricked her into going to the police department and had questioned her as if she were a criminal. She also complained that the media had harassed her to the point that she had to escape to her home country of Guatemala. In October of 2009, Giraldo asked the judge to lift the order of protection so that she could marry Monserrate. The judge refused, with the stipulation that the couple obtain counseling first in order to demonstrate that no conflict existed.

Monserrate, also a former police officer, waived his right to a jury, opting for a bench trial, in which a judge determines guilt or innocence. Although the attack was caught on camera, Senator Monserrate was convicted in October of 2009 on one misdemeanor assault charge but was acquitted of any felony charges. Monserrate's sentence included three years' probation, 250 hours of community service, one year of batterer counseling based in the power and control model and a fine of over one thousand dollars. According to the law, a senator cannot be stripped of his or her position unless convicted of a felony. On February 9, 2010, Monserrate was removed from office by the New York state legislature as a result of his conviction. In a March attempt to regain his seat, voters rejected Monserrate.

In the last decade, corrections departments have made efforts to become more sensitive to the victims' needs, concluding that *victim-centered policies* are part of the public safety mission of the agencies (Klein, 2004). Many state corrections departments and many local jails utilize the Victim Information and Notification Everyday (VINE) system. This is a computerized database that provides the location of inmates, and it is available to anyone who calls a centralized number. The system is operational twenty-four hours a day, seven days a week. Callers may also request that the system notify them when the offender is moved or released. The system will call the victim every thirty minutes for up to twenty-four hours until contact is made when an offender is moved, released, or escapes. Victims are given a code that they must punch into the system to verify their identity. Additionally, victim notification laws have been enacted in many states requiring that victims and prosecutors be notified when offenders are released or escape from custody, including when the release is a bail release or a preconviction release from local jails.

Incidents of inmates contacting victims from prison or jail led to jails and prisons enacting policies and procedures to prohibit phone contact. There are a variety of telephone systems used in correctional facilities that prevent inmates from calling victims. Victims can request that their telephone numbers be blocked, and the system will prevent any calls to that number; otherwise, specific blocks can be put on the call lists of individual inmates. Correctional officials can also monitor telephone conversations by directly listening in on inmate calls. Victims who complain of phone harassment can have prison or jail telephone records subpoenaed as evidence in future litigation.

Departments of correction and jails realize that there is a need for some sort of treatment for intimate partner violence offenders. Many local jails use anger management classes as programmatic solutions. It is understood that batterers are in need of more than just anger management to address their abusive and violent conduct. However, having moved away from the rehabilitation emphasis in the 1980s, corrections facilities do not offer or fund needed programs.

CRIMINALIZING INTIMATE PARTNER VIOLENCE VICTIMIZATION

Much attention in the area of criminalizing victim responses to intimate partner violence centers on the juvenile who is the victim of physical, emotional, and sexual abuse. Status offense convictions for incorrigibility and running away are disproportionately the purview of female delinquents. Data from the Office of Juvenile

Justice and Delinquency Prevention (OJJDP), the National Youth Survey, and the Uniform Crime Reports consistently reveal that girls are underrepresented in the majority of offense categories but disproportionally overrepresented in the status offenses, which are indicative of targeting practices toward female offenders (Belknap, 2007; Canter, 1982). The importance of this fact relates to the criminalization of female victims. Abused girls are twice as likely to be arrested as adult women, often for violent crimes (Chesney-Lind & Pasko, 2004).

There is little dispute over the fact that historically, women have been the victims of intimate partner violence. However, not all women are treated equally. There is mounting evidence that African-American women are more likely to call the police, and the police are more likely to make an arrest of African-American male batterers (Chesney-Lind, 2002). Chesney-Lind argues that this seems counterintuitive; however, women of higher means can afford to seek private medical assistance and safe shelters, and they are better able to keep the incident(s) of intimate partner violence out of official records.

Police involvement triggers mandatory arrest policies. The collateral consequences of those policies have taken a dramatic turn against the very groups they were designed to protect: girls and women, and more strikingly women and girls of color. Again, not all women are treated equally. Empirical evidence demonstrates that African-American women are more likely than white women to have their behaviors criminalized. In many instances these women are the sole providers for their children, and when imprisoned, they suffer serious depression, adding to the indignities they endured at the hands of their abusers.

Female perpetrators of intimate partner violence are at a minimum likely to be arrested at a rate comparable to their male counterparts. More insidious is the dual-arrest scenario, where the identity of the true aggressor cannot be determined and both parties are arrested and jailed. Arrests of women increased over the last decade. In Wichita, Kansas, women accounted for more than one-quarter of the intimate partner violence arrests in 2001. In

Prince William County, Virginia, the number of females arrested for intimate partner violence almost doubled between 1992 and 1996, and a Canadian study showed an increase of 35 percent in the six-year period ending in 1995 (see Chesney-Lind, 2002). The Bureau of Criminal Information and Analysis of the California Department of Justice (1999) reported that African-American females had arrest rates nearly three times the rate of white women and girls for intimate partner violence offenses.

Greenfield and Snell (1999, as cited in Chesney-Lind, 2002) found a substantial increase in violent crimes for females, growing about 2.5 times the male rate of increase over the same period. Archer (2000) argues that the evidence reveals that women are engaging in physical aggression in interpersonal relationships at roughly the same rate as men. The feminist community explains this increased use of aggression as a self-defense mechanism against continuing abuse in an intimate relationship (Belknap, 2007). It is estimated that as much as 25 percent of all arrests of women indicate that the woman is either the primary aggressor or is arrested in a dual-arrest situation. Chesney-Lind (2002) argues that the increase is not the result of women increasingly becoming the aggressors. Rather, female victims' responses to violence is changing. Women are using knives, guns, and other weapons at higher rates to defend themselves. Additionally, the reported rise in violence among women, as measured by the crime "assault," does not follow the general trend among women who commit other crimes of violence, including lethal violence. For many person-to-person crimes, the number of women offenders actually dropped during the same period. Only women's assault arrests are higher, and this is likely due to the criminalization of intimate partner violence victims' efforts to defend themselves. Thus, it is the criminal justice response that has changed more dramatically than the behavior of women.

Whatever the explanation, the collateral consequences of conviction for women have not received the necessary and appropriate attention. Bureau of Justice statistics show that the prosecution, conviction, and incarceration of women for intimate partner violence aggravated assault is higher than for nondomestic violence aggravated assault. Furthermore, Greene and Pranis (2004) found that female incarceration has increased by 757 percent since 1977. Women are now the fastest-growing segment of the prison population, surpassing the male prison population in terms of growth.

The removal of female offenders from society is more dramatic because women are the primary caregivers for their children. Women who have their victimization criminalized thus suffer further trauma: separation from their children. Nearly 65 percent of female prisoners in state facilities had minor children living with them at the time of their arrest. When women enter the prison system, less than 30 percent of their children live with the male parent (Glaze, 2008).

Many of these women suffer depression and other emotional hardships because their children are living with relatives, and are often divided up among several relatives. Many female inmates are from socially disorganized neighborhoods entrenched in drugs and poverty, with virtually no system of social support. Many are plagued by drug abuse problems combined with long histories of physical and mental abuse. These women are far more likely to be the sole caregivers to their children, who are now living with relatives. In approximately 15 percent of the cases, their children are surrendered to social services as a result of the conviction (Greene & Pranis, 2004).

As it relates to correctional supervision, the criminalization of intimate partner violence has had an impact on both the housing of female offenders and the treatment they receive while in custody. Within the prison system women find themselves subjected to physical and emotional abuse at the hands of correctional officers. Although the extent of this harassment and criminal conduct is not truly known, this is a growing concern within modern correctional environments.

The criminalization of intimate partner violence victims does not conclude with the conviction and sentence. Rather, women who defend themselves from abuse continue to suffer from the correctional system's inadequate and patriarchal mindset. This theme runs through all aspects of the criminal justice system and not just correctional institutions. However, one need only consider the societal structure described earlier in this text to place the correctional attempts at batterer treatment, the sentencing of abusers, and the correctional treatment of female victim-offenders of intimate partner violence in perspective.

CONCLUSION

In the approach to the correction of intimate partner violence, judges are the first responders. Sentences given batterers have often been based on social constructs that do not define intimate partner violence as a crime. Initially, the most common approaches were to ignore the problem and then to mandate counseling that treated offenders as pathological individuals. As social constructs changed, sentencing became more punitive. Today offenders are commonly sentenced to probation. However, the treatment mandate continues to reign. Judges tend to believe that it is their responsibility to ensure that batterers receive behavior modification and mental health treatment when necessary.

Increasingly common is the incarceration of intimate partner violence offenders in jails. Research shows that incarceration is commonly used in some jurisdictions. We can also see patterns of prison sentences for felony offenders. Unfortunately, most intimate partner violence offenses are still treated as misdemeanors, eliminating prison sentences, even for severe violence. Furthermore, since few studies indicate that probation enhancement and technology tracking can safeguard victims, many practitioners recommend incarceration as the only true form of protection. However, victimization can occur even when the perpetrator is in jail or prison. More vigilance on the part of correctional administrators is needed, especially in monitoring mail and phone calls, to prevent revictimization from prison and jail.

Social constructs among practitioners have also been expanded to include women as increasingly violent in intimate relationships. Although official statistics and self-report data do not reflect this increase in convictions, females are convicted and incarcerated at a higher rate than male batterers. This trend points to a definite back-lash, as has been the case in dual arrests of females who engage in self-defense. We find that the criminal justice response is the determining factor for this increase in convictions and not the actual behaviors of women. The continuation of criminal justice policies that fail to protect women from aggressive males will place more women under correctional supervision, because they must take their safety and protection into their own hands.

ESCAPING INTIMATE PARTNER VIOLENCE

The Shelter Movement

Social constructions of intimate partner violence enabled the justice system to ignore this social problem for centuries. The changing constructs during the 1960s and 1970s required a social response but still allowed for a predominantly do-nothing response. As constructs further changed, the criminal justice system started to impose mandatory arrest, pro-arrest and no-drop policies. Judges started to mandate batterer treatment and award protection orders to victims. Further, researchers, medical and mental health care professionals, and social service providers began a serious effort to fight intimate partner violence. Still, these social institutions definitely have a long road ahead in the continued fight.

The victim still faces many barriers. The economic strain that victims face may be a part of the abuse they are forced to endure, or it may be a result of the income lost when they leave their abusers, who might have been the financial providers. Victims may attempt to leave but are stalked by their abusers. They may ask for criminal justice help but may hit a wall of intimate partner violence myths, hindering their attempts. Many victims also face a lack of social support. They may be isolated from their family, friendships, and religious support networks or told to work things out. As Sullivan (1997, p. 109) points out, with all the barriers women face, we should not ask, "Why doesn't she stay?" but "How is she able to leave?"

Research has found that advocacy in the fight to end violence against women has been widely led by the victims themselves. As a result, we must recognize that victims, as powerless as they become in abusive relationships, do have agency. Researchers have found a lack of support for learned helplessness, PTSD, battered woman syndrome, and any long-term psychological disability in most victims of intimate partner violence (Belknap, 2007; Campbell, Miller, Cardwell, & Belknap, 1994; Outlaw, 2009; Schram & Koons-Witt, 2004). What we have found is that women who fall victim to abusive men often make several attempts to leave these abusive relationships before they finally succeed (Sullivan, 1997). In many cases, initial attempts failed because of a lack of justice support and community resources. In response to the lack of support and community services, there emerged the shelter movement to fill this void.

THE SHELTER MOVEMENT

As a creation of the feminist- and victim-led advocacy movement, the battered women's shelter was based on the "private is political" campaign. Consciousness-raising efforts of victims and advocate groups taught that violence against women was the inevitable product of a patriarchal society in which women were kept silent within the home. The feminist liberal philosophy that guided the battered women's movement and the anti-rape movement proclaimed that women have agency and would no longer silently accept their domestic cages. In order to encourage women's agency, early shelters taught empowerment and self-help, in addition to providing social and service support.

A Brief Overview of the History and Organizing Ideologies of the Battered Women's Shelter

The shelter movement started in the 1970s as an attempt to provide intimate partner violence victims the refuge and emotional support needed to escape their abusers. The battered women's shelter is a temporary haven that female intimate partner violence victims and their children are able to escape to and where they receive help in obtaining the financial, health care, child care, and social resources needed to start a stable, independent, violence-free life. Prior to the shelter movement, intimate partner violence victims had few resources available to them. However, through predominantly grassroots efforts and the influence of the anti-rape movement, shelters for battered women quickly spread across the nation. The shelter movement, like the anti-rape and battered women's movements, was premised on the belief that intimate partner violence was not a private trouble but a widespread social problem that needed to be addressed by the community as well as by the justice system. In fact, the feminist slant to this movement could be found in Great Britain, as well as in the United States.

Great Britain was the first to address the need for refuge of intimate partner violence victims. Chiswick Women's Aid was the first battered women's shelter and was established in 1972 (Schneider, 2000). Chiswick Women's Aid was developed as a consciousness-raising support group, but it quickly became a shelter when women revealed that they had nowhere to go. Within a year Chiswick was an overcrowded licensed shelter. The crowdedness required that the shelter be moved to a larger house, and it also demonstrated the dire need to develop more of the same.

Women's Advocates, founded in 1972 in St. Paul, Minnesota, was the first to establish a women's shelter in the United States. Similar to Chiswick Women's Aid in Great Britain, Women's Advocates was a consciousness-raising group. The organization learned from the county legal aid telephone service that most of the calls for aid were received from female intimate partner violence victims. In response, volunteers from Women's Advocates initially opened their homes as temporary shelters, then rented a one-bedroom apartment as a temporary shelter in 1973. Women's House was established in October of 1974, when Women's Advocates was evicted from the shelter apartment.

Advocates recognized that the lack of shelters was the primary obstacle to escaping male violence. By 1977 over 114 shelters had been established in England and Wales, and over 130 shelters had opened their doors in the United States. By the late 1990s, Great Britain had over 164 shelters, housing over 20,000 women and children, and in the United States over 1,200 shelters housed over 300,000 women and children. A lack of funding, overcrowding, and understaffing plagued battered women's shelters, and these are still issues today. Shelters were predominantly funded through rent, Social Security, and temporary government funding.

Overcrowding has remained a problem over time as more women learn that men are not entitled to abuse them. A 1979 survey in Minnesota found that 70 percent of intimate partner violence victims are turned away from shelters due to overcrowding (Schetcher, 1982). With overcrowding a major concern, shelters often place time limitations on the length of stay. The average shelter stay in England and Wales is five and a half months, while in the United States intimate partner violence victims and their children stay in battered women's shelters, on average, two weeks.

Battered women's shelters have faced many problems over the years. Some problems can be traced to financial and legal constraints, while others can be linked to organizing ideologies. Many of the early battered women's shelters were organized along feminist ideologies. In Great Britain hierarchical patriarchy was deemed to be a major contributor to intimate partner violence, and so shelters were organized along more informal, nonhierarchical lines. In the United States, however, shelters were organized along more structured and hierarchical lines. The structure, along with the specific feminist ideology adopted by the shelter, determined the shelter's approach to its residents.

Along with varying structures, feminist ideologies adopted by shelter staff differed. Among the most common were radical feminism, liberal feminism, and socialist feminism. *Radical feminist ideology*, a common framework adopted by shelter advocates in the United States, focused on the politics of the mind and the body (Jaggar, 1988). Radical feminists are concerned primarily with the sexual oppression of women within a male-dominated society. They argue that violence against women is the ultimate form of male dominance and that it is internalized by men and women and deemed acceptable. Since the various institutions within society, that is, the polity and institutions related to medicine, education, religion, media, and the family, tend either to be organized around this form of oppression or to be silent about this oppression, women internalize male entitlement to the use of violence. Radical feminists tended to focus on therapy as the remedy to improve female psychology and develop independent and empowered women within safer communities (Schetcher, 1982).

Also common within the United States was the *liberal feminist ideology*. Liberal feminism is among the most conservative of feminist ideologies. According to liberal feminists, inequality is caused by the rules within a given society; but males and females can coexist as equals within the current social structure (Jaggar, 1988). These feminists do not wish to change the social structure; instead, they attempt to change the system by which women are oppressed. Since many of the shelter advocates in the United States came from a legal or social work background, these feminists emphasized changing the legal system to ensure equality for women under the law and the enforcement of the law. Specific to intimate partner violence, liberal feminists fought to require the criminal justice system to give equal emphasis to crimes against women. In the shelters with a liberal feminist bent, hierarchy was the most common structure (Schetcher, 1982).

Socialist feminist ideology was most commonly practiced in Great Britain, though American shelters were known to adopt this ideology. Bridging radical feminism and Marxist feminism, which defines male dominance within a capitalist structure and which is the overarching cause of women's oppression, socialist feminists argue that capitalistic economic inequality and patriarchy are at the core of women's oppression (Jaggar, 1988). Thus, they argue that there is a connection between the class structure and women's oppression, laying the groundwork for a theory of intersectionality. Power and oppression are accomplished through the acquisition of material goods. Furthermore, since society is divided along class and gender lines, as well as racial lines, in order to eliminate oppressions, we must eliminate economic, gender, and race distinctions. Not surprisingly, socialist feminists within the shelter movement were organized along nonhierarchical lines (Schetcher, 1982). In addition, in order to work toward equalizing society, these shelters focused their efforts on obtaining economic independence via state-provided housing, health, and welfare benefits and services.

Financial Backing and Changing Ideologies

Private funding has been the most common form of financial backing received by shelters since resident turnover is relatively quick and government funding of shelters is temporary, highly competitive, and subject to renewal. As a result, local community fund-raisers, donations, private foundations, and corporations have provided most of the financial backing for shelters. Additionally, it is common for public and private community service providers to contribute goods or services, such as materials, transportation, office space, and professional services.

In the 1970s, the most stable government funding in the United States was obtained through the Department of Housing and Urban Development's (HUD) Community Development Block Grants. In 1978, HUD included shelter housing among those organizations eligible to receive these Block Grants. Additionally, by the late 1970s fifteen states were providing funds to shelter operators. Many states allocated money collected from marriage licenses, tax credit programs, and civil and criminal court fines to shelter funding. Yet, even with the great need for refuge, by 1981 less than half of all shelters in the United States were receiving state or federal funding, with only 30 percent of Great Britain's shelters receiving government funds. And, by 1982 HUD's Community Development Block Grants were given local control, which made these grants even more difficult to obtain.

The distinction between shelters and other more traditional services provided to battered women was a grassroots approach that was for the most part guided by feminist ideology. Early in the shelter movement, we can identify most of the *activist shelters*. Activist shelters, such as Women's Aid in Great Britain and Bradley-Angle House in Portland, Oregon, operated with a nonhierarchical style, bringing the clients into the fold of operations; encouraging resident self-governance, and resident and community consciousness-raising about violence against women; and fostering empowerment, mutual support, and system change. Initially, these shelters were predominantly administered through volunteer time, funds, and facilities, as well as resident rent, obtained through government benefits, such as Social Security and welfare. However, shelter operators soon learned that financial backing often determined the ideology and organizational structure of the shelter.

Another common type of shelter is known as the *philanthropic shelter*. These shelters do not operate on feminist ideology. The House of Ruth, established in 1977, for example, was not so much concerned with social change as it was with providing intimate partner violence victims with the immediate resources needed to live a safe and independent life. Shelters such as the House of Ruth placed some focus on resident counseling in order to ensure residents' mental and emotional functioning. Also common among the initial battered women's shelters, as well as today, *therapeutic shelters* utilized the medical model, focusing on the victims' emotional and psychological shortcomings. Rainbow Retreat in Phoenix, Arizona, was such as shelter. While Chiswick Women's Aid in Great Britain started out as an activist shelter, it quickly took on a therapeutic model. Therapeutic shelters attempt to aid victims in managing their personal problems, not focusing too much on intimate partner violence as a larger social problem. Many shelters find that adopting this model at least in part will enable them to secure funding.

Finally, there are *organizational or bureaucratic shelters*. These shelters focus on community-government collaboration in providing needed services to victims. Shelters such as Community Effort for Abused Spouses (CEASE) in Alexandra, Virginia, have adopted a more hierarchical structure and have attempted to utilize already existing community resources.

Morash describes the change in activism as a result of the change in the feminist movement (Morash, 2006). The second wave of the feminist movement, from the 1960s to the early 1980s, focused on equality in the workplace, valuing women's work, and women's right to control their bodies, and was dominated by grassroots activists, labor feminists, and victims of violence. By the late 1970s, liberal and radical feminism became blurred as both feminist and mainstream advocates worked toward eliminating gender oppression (Reinelt, 1995). Additionally, many of the feminist advocates moved into bureaucratic positions. In the early 1980s, the third wave of the feminist movement was increasingly focused on the intersections of gender oppression and backlash, and in its ranks were more bureaucrats than in the second wave of the feminist movement. Add to this the bureaucratic or medical model mandated by funding agencies, and the result was that many of the existing shelters moved in this direction, with newly established shelters using the bureaucratic model to establish themselves. Though those shelters have been criticized for alienating their residents and ignoring the structural and systemic basis for violence against women, this shelter structure enabled financial backing, which made it possible to give refuge to female victims of intimate partner violence.

By 2005 the primary federal funding source was the Department of Health and Human Services (HHS) and the Department of Justice. Trujillo and Test (2005) provide a detailed report on public and private funding sources available within the United States. And while funding is competitive and unsure, what shelter operators have learned is that the funding agencies tend to impose their own goals, which alters the shelter's ideology and structure. For example, Title IV-A: Temporary Assistance to Needy Families (TANF) has been an excellent source of funding for domestic violence shelters. The goals of TANF include providing assistance to needy families; promoting independence through job preparation, work, and marriage; preventing out-of-wedlock pregnancies; and encouraging the formation and maintenance of two-parent families. A bureaucratic shelter may take these goals to the extreme in counseling victims to work out their marital problems. Additionally, TANF requirements include having a trained domestic violence staff member develop program plans and demonstrating reasonable completion, and providing funding for victim and child short-term shelters and counseling. While these are all very noble services and goals, shelters may alter their ideologies to take on a bureaucratic or therapeutic model. TANF also requires the disclosure of the father's identity, which may or may not be waived by states but which can increase the danger to the victim and her children or keep her from applying for TANF.

Two other federal funding programs, Title IV-E: Foster Care and Adoption Assistance Programs and Title IV-B: Child Welfare Services Programs, provide funds for shelters as long as children are aided as well. Title XIX: Medicaid Program provides shelters with medical or mental health staff, and the Family Violence Prevention and Services Act stresses collaboration between child welfare agencies and domestic violence providers. Again, these are all incredible opportunities to fund shelters that will provide safe environments for intimate partner violence victims and their children; however, they also minimize the empowerment of victims, move advocates away from social structure or system change, and demand that they work within the existing structure, which requires victims to adapt to an oppressive system.

Funding within the U.S. Department of Justice is provided through the Office for Victims of Crime (OVC); the Office on Violence Against Women (OVW), developed through the Violence Against Women Act (VAWA); and the Office of Juvenile Justice and Delinquency Prevention (OJJDP). OVC's Crime Victims Fund was established by the Victims of Crime Act (VOCA). The VOCA provides various formulas and discretionary grants for the federal crime victims division, promising practices, and Indian country. For example, the Victim Assistance in Indian Country (VAIC) and the Children's Justice Act Partnerships for Indian Communities (CJA) aid in funding domestic violence shelters within tribal communities. The OJJDP provides the Title V, Community Prevention Grant Program. OVW grants include STOP Violence Against Women Formula Grants Program, STOP Violence Against Indian Women Discretionary Grants Programs, Grants to Encourage Arrest Policies and Enforcement of Protection Orders, and Education and Technical Assistance Grants to End Violence Against Women with Disabilities. Many of these grants require that victims work cooperatively with criminal justice and that there is a coordinated community-justice response to intimate partner violence. While these funding programs do not intend to undermine the feminist agenda, they do nevertheless require an organizational or bureaucratic model for shelters, one that places a greater emphasis on individual counseling and a lesser emphasis on social change.

Empowerment

The initial goal of shelter advocates, in addition to providing a safe environment, was to foster the empowerment of victims through consciousness-raising, education, and services. Empowerment increases a woman's agency, or self-direction. According to Schechter, "*[e]mpowerment* combines ideas about internalizing personal and collective power and validating women's personal experiences as politically oppressive rather than self-caused or 'crazy'" (1982, p. 109, italics added). Empowerment means working as a community to provide intimate partner violence victims the tools to take control of their lives. Self-help and self-direction are key goals. Within the domestic violence and shelter movements, feminist advocates provided support and connected victims to the needed resources. However, as professionals became more involved with the movement, the construction of self-help changed from one that incorporated advocates as organizers to one that replaced advocates with professionals as providers. The tension increased between professionals and advocates when they waged a debate about "politics versus expediency" (Schetcher, 1982, p. 108). The debate was settled primarily by the need for funding. Ultimately, feminist ideologies that stressed forcing systemic change were replaced by funding needs and funding agency preferences to support organized hierarchical structures.

Intimate partner violence victims were still perceived to experience severe psychological and emotional problems that either caused or were caused by intimate partner violence, and professionals determined that victims could be empowered without receiving needed treatment. Feminist advocates, on the other hand, maintained that victims needed to be politicized, which would then decrease self-blaming and end the violence against women. In the long run, professional ideologies became the dominant mode for most shelter operations. A shelter study conducted during the early 2000s suggests that there was a potential for shelters to become total institutions with rigid rules and policies of control (Moe, 2010). Many victims found it difficult to manage their immediate survival with strict rules that mandated counseling and required them to ask permission for everything.

No matter the philosophy, shelters have always aimed to help intimate partner violence victims. Their differences were reflected in their social constructs of the causes of this violence and the best way to end the violence. Advocates argued that the causes were rooted in male and class domination, while professionals argued that the causes were rooted in a lack of resources or mental functioning. Stark argues that the shift in ideology has resulted in shelters that are "active players in the shelter game that employs restrictive definitions of victims, highlights individual service rather than collective empowerment, utilizes stereotypes of worthy victims to discourage utilization, and marginalizes battered women" (2007, p. 79). However, while ideologies differed, common concerns plagued all shelters. Shelters were overcrowded, underfunded, and understaffed.

Shelter Services

Services provided to shelter residents vary according to the shelter's ideology, funding, resident needs, and community service availability. Since the average shelter stay within the United States is two weeks, shelters must maximize that time to meet victims' immediate needs. This typically includes providing emergency medical care and crisis intervention, and obtaining long-term housing, government aid, and legal aid, if needed. Transitional living programs involve long-term housing, from a few months to a year, and aid in moving intimate partner violence victims and their children from trauma to recovery.

Whether in an emergency shelter or a transitional living program, health services are very important, and not just emergency room care. Victims and their children often need ongoing medical treatment for injuries sustained at the hands of their abusers. Counseling is also important. Counseling can entail crisis intervention involving a social worker or psychologist or long-term individual and family counseling. In addition, many shelters provide or require group counseling intended to allow victims to understand the depth of intimate partner violence.

If the victim is pursuing civil or criminal justice in her case, legal services are also provided. The OVC provides states with funds for victim/witness assistance programs, designed to aid the victim in maneuvering through the criminal justice process, and victim compensation programs, designed to compensate victims of violent crimes for some of their losses. Unfortunately, due to lack of funding and large caseloads, these government programs are often so overwhelmed that victims are often not contacted when they should be or they do not receive the guidance required. Shelter staff often work with victims as advocates within the criminal and civil justice system, helping them maneuver through the system more easily. This may include educating victims on the justice process, assisting with complicated forms to obtain victim compensation and protection orders, or sitting with the victim in court simply as a support. Shelter staff also work to connect victims with legal aid services that will take on their cases for little or no money.

Since many shelter residents have custody of their children, shelter staff aid in finding day-to-day child care and recreation, education opportunities, and medical and counseling services. A major problem shelters face is the resident who has several children or who has teenage sons. Many shelters do not allow men within their walls under the belief that this will make the victims and their young children feel safe. However, a sixteen- or seventeen-year-old boy may be in as much need for shelter as an infant. These children are often turned away, thus breaking up families and further traumatizing children (Lyon, Lane, & Menard, 2008).

Along with child care, shelter staff aid residents in obtaining the needed social support. In addition to aiding residents in finding permanent housing, staff help residents obtain help paying their bills, including applying for government benefits, such as SSI, TANF, and Medicare. Staff may also help residents with résumés and job applications, or they may need to connect residents to educational or vocation training that will help them obtain jobs. Many staff duties involve making sure that residents are connected with the appropriate community services. As mentioned earlier, shelters work in collaboration with community social service agencies, which may donate their services. As a result, shelters within communities that do not have the needed services are unable to help their residents.

A seemingly conflicting issue within shelters is the victims' need to escape violence and their need for a respite. A *respite* is the process of taking a break from an abusive relationship that the victim is not ready to end. Research has found that some victims make several attempts to leave abusive relationships before they are successful (Dobash & Dobash, 1992; Gondolf & Fisher, 1988/2001; Krishnan, Hilbert, McNeil, & Newman, 2004; Moe, 2010; Stark, 2007). In some cases, the victim still loves her abuser and believes that she can change or that she change him. In other cases, the victim may have been emotionally battered and may not have the financial ability or the self-confidence to make it on her own or believe that she can. In still other cases, the victim may be too afraid to stay away from the abuser for very long, believing that he will eventually find her. There is a myriad of reasons why victims return to their abusers, all of them complex. However, in most cases the victims eventually leave.

The process of empowerment provides victims with the mental and political tools to enable them to eventually take control of their lives. If the victim goes to a shelter for a respite, she may not intend to use the services that may be mandated. If the shelter is strictly organized on a professional model, it may mandate that all victims attend one or more counseling sessions per week, as was the policy of the shelter studied by Moe (2010). Respite residents may be more harmed than helped if they are turned away from a shelter for violating these policies. On the other hand, victims who are residing at a shelter for emergency and transitional purposes may also feel a lack of agency in being forced to attend counseling sessions that they believe they may not need.

An additional problem for all intimate partner violence victims when discussing respites is the social constructs that intimate partner violence victims like to be abused, that they have control over their situations, and that they manipulate the system in order to make their abusers pay. These social constructs, which paint the intimate partner violence victim as undeserving, do not allow us to truly understand the dynamics involved when victims take a respite. That a victim is simply not emotionally, financially, or socially prepared to make the final break from her abuser does not mean that she shares responsibility for the violence. To ignore the fact that victims experience complex strains exasperates their situation and further diminishes their agency. We tend to define respite shelter residents as problematic and not serious about escaping violence, instead of accepting the fact that a respite gives the victim a bit more empowerment, a bit more support, and moves them a bit closer to leaving the abuser for good (Stark, 2007). Krishnan et al. (2004) stress that we should not see respite residents and transitional residents as mutually exclusive. Instead, we must understand that respite residents can be helped through the available shelter services to become transitional residents. Further, Krishnan et al. stress that shelter ideologies can address the needs of both respite and transitional residents, since their purposes are to provide a safe environment and to provide needed services.

Serving Diverse Communities

As third-wave feminists have stressed, shelters have learned that intimate partner violence victims have diverse backgrounds. Cultural and language barriers can lessen shelters' effectiveness and minimize victim recovery. While most shelter residents view their experiences positively, many victims complain about the cultural insensitivity they experience in shelters, as well as within the criminal justice system and among health and social service providers.

Funding and staffing issues and a shortage of space require shelters to turn away a lot of women and their children. However, cultural differences can often keep victims from seeking help. For example, lesbians and women of color fear that they will experience rejection, unfair scrutiny, or victim blaming by shelter staff. Many of these victims do not turn to shelters.

Lesbian intimate partner violence victims have the added complexity that their abusers are also women and, as a result, have a greater ability to access shelters (Sullivan, 1997). Lesbian intimate partner violence victims suffer multiple marginality because society constructs their sexual relationships as deviant. The heterosexism that lesbians face is experienced in all segments of society. Further, the domestic violence and shelter movements embraced a feminist ideology that identified male dominance and patriarchy as the root causes of intimate partner violence. The relationship structure for lesbian victims does not fit this into the neat explanation. Additionally, gay and lesbian intimate partner violence includes the added threat of "outing" the victim should he or she try to seek help or escape the violence (Renzetti, 1997). Responding to these added concerns, the first lesbian shelter was developed in Seattle, Washington, in 1985.

As was the case in the initial waves of the feminist movement, shelters have been predominantly operated by an all-white, often heterosexual staff, and since much of this work is done by volunteers, the staff enjoy economic stability. Intimate partner violence victims, however, tend to be from diverse backgrounds. Research has uncovered culture clashes, cultural insensitivity, and language barriers experienced by shelter residents. The language barriers may hinder victims from finding refuge from the violence. And, like lesbian intimate partner violence victims, many victims fear that shelter staff will not readily accept them. An added issue for many of the immigrant intimate partner violence victims is the clear anti-immigration ideology of the nation. As the Korean Women's Hotline in California found, anti-immigration laws severely limit resources for immigrants, such as health, educational, and social services (Park, 2005). Deportation laws and dual-arrest practices also place immigrant intimate partner violence victims in danger of being deported (Coker, 2005). This tends to complicate victims' situations, and as a result, immigrant victims often hesitate to seek help.

Racial, ethnic, and religious minority women with nonimmigrant status often experience or fear cultural insensitivity. Horsburgh (2005) points out that the Orthodox Jewish community makes it difficult for intimate partner violence victims to simply define their relationships as abusive. Secondly, Jewish law forbids intimate partner violence victims from divulging their experiences—to do so is to engage in "lies, gossip, and defamatory speech" (Horsburgh, 2005, p. 220)—and from escaping the abuse, since divorce is strictly forbidden. Third, many of these women have limited contact with non-Orthodox communities. Finally, the very intricacies of the Orthodox Jewish religion are not well understood by the non-Jewish community. Thus, even if Orthodox Jewish intimate partner violence victims seek refuge, unless the shelter is organized to abide by various religious mandates, these victims cannot use its services. Hassouneh-Phillips (1998) reveals similar findings among Muslim women in the United States. Muslim women are accused of rejecting their religion when they consider leaving their abusive husbands.

Examining ethnic diversity, West (2005) found that acculturation is associated with intimate partner violence. Among some Hispanic ethnic subgroups, those with medium levels of acculturation have lost the connection with their country of origin but have not yet adopted the values and networks of the U.S. culture and, as a result, have higher rates of intimate partner violence. Cultural pressures to maintain the ties to family and religion tend to be very strong among victims with low to medium acculturation, increasing pressure for women to stay within abusive relationships. In order to effectively help those who do seek refuge within shelters, however, staff must be in tune to the various pressures these women are facing. As a result, specific services have been developed to aid these victims, such as the Korean Women's Hotline, Everywomens Shelter for Asian women, Asian Women's Shelter, and Casa de las Madres, all in California; Casa de Esperanza in Minnesota; Hebrew Shelter Home in Ohio; and Apna Ghar, a Muslim shelter in Chicago. Con-

Rosalina Lopez-Umanzor entered the United States in 1989 as an undocumented immigrant and married permanent resident Luis Calzadillas. Luis Calzadillas was a very violent man, and upon entry into the United States, Rosalina was drugged and raped by Calzadillas. Rosalina became pregnant from this attack, and during her marriage she endured two more pregnancies. Unfortunately, as a result of the physical abuse Rosalina experienced, she miscarried one of her babies. Rosalina endured extreme violence and tried to escape Calzadillas, but he followed her from Texas to California, then from California to Alaska. While living in Anchorage, Alaska, Calzadillas arrived at Rosalina's apartment drunk and attacked her with a knife. In the emergency room Rosalina lied about the cause of her injury, fearing Calzadillas's threats of retaliation. Rosalina eventually sought refuge at a domestic violence shelter in Anchorage, unable to escape her husband.

In 1999, Rosalina was arrested and charged with a third-degree drug trafficking offense while riding as a passenger with Jose Armando Gomez-Mendoza, her daughter's boyfriend. Testimony from an informant was entered as to Rosalina's involvement with crack cocaine trafficking, though no evidence was ever found on her person or in her apartment. Furthermore, there was no documentation about or witness to the interviews with the informant. However, the U.S. government sought her removal from the country. At her court hearing Rosalina applied for cancellation of removal under 8 U.S.C. SS1228b(b)(2) of the Immigration and Nationality Act. Under this law, "[t]he Attorney General may cancel removal of, and adjust the status of an alien lawfully admitted for permanent residence, an alien who is inadmissible or deportable from the United States if the alien demonstrates that (i) . . . (II) the alien has been battered or subjected to extreme cruelty by a spouse or parent who is or was a lawful permanent resident. . . ."

Rosalina testified that she was a victim of intimate partner violence and requested to enter evidence and expert testimony to present her case, including emergency medical records and statements from social service workers and a psychologist. The immigration judge denied her request, claiming that the drug trafficking charge called into question her moral character and therefore undermined the credibility of her claim of domestic violence and noting that she had not been in the United States for ten years (though three years was the minimum requirement as provided by the Violence Against Women Act of 1994). Rosalina's hearing resulted in a ruling of removal.

The case of *Lopez-Umanzor v. Gonzales* was an appeal to the United States Court of Appeals for the Ninth Circuit requesting another hearing on the basis that Rosalina Lopez-Umanzor's due process rights had been violated. Rosalina's lawyers had to demonstrate that she was not deportable due to criminal activity because of her victimization. Rosalina argued that the immigration judge had also allowed false testimony. The immigration judge wrote that even before hearing the informant's testimony, he had doubted Rosalina's credibility. The appellate court ruled that

> [t]o answer that question, the IJ had to weigh Petitioner's credibility against the credibility of the detective and the credibility of the absent informant. We rarely disturb the result of that kind of balancing. But here, the IJ's assessment of Petitioner's credibility was skewed by prejudgment, personal speculation, bias, and conjecture; and his refusal to allow Petitioner to challenge those views by presenting expert testimony violated Petitioner's right to due process. We cannot assume that the IJ would have struck the same balance had the weighing begun on an even plane (*Lopez-Umanzor v. Gonzales*, 2005).

sider the case of Rosalina Lopez-Umanzor (Box 8.1), an immigrant and a victim of intimate partner violence.

Lopez-Umanzor v. Gonzales signifies the many problems faced by immigrant victims of intimate partner violence. First, as research has uncovered, immigrants with low levels of acculturation have weaker ties to U.S. culture, weak social supports, and little understanding of the criminal justice system and community services and, as a result, may experience higher levels of intimate partner violence (West, 2005). Rosalina experienced extreme violence at the hands of Luis Calzadillas from the onset. However, due to her undocumented status, she did not understand the legal options and social support services available to her. Secondly, since she was a recent immigrant from Honduras, a language barrier and cultural differences likely impeded her ability to escape the violence. Thirdly, social constructs of immigrants as criminals, and especially of Latino/a immigrants as drug dealers, likely engendered the detectives' and immigrant judge's hasty accusations and beliefs that Rosalina was lying and was a drug trafficker, even though no evidence of this was found.

Addressing Male Victims of Intimate Partner Violence

The battered women's movement was very successful in defining intimate partner violence as violence against women that results from male entitlement and power and control. Researchers have expanded our knowledge of the causes of and responses to intimate partner violence, including same-sex intimate partner violence. Advocates have institutionalized funding opportunities and services for female victims and their children. Unfortunately, these efforts have widely ignored male victims of intimate partner violence. While females tend to represent the larger portion of intimate partner violence victims worldwide, male are also victims of female-on-male and male-on-male intimate partner violence. Yet, our social constructs deny male victims. When dual arrests are made, it is still assumed that the male partner is violent in some way.

As mentioned previously, older male children tend to be turned away from shelters, separating them from their mothers. The rationale behind this decision is twofold. First, it is believed that the female residents will feel unsafe living with almost grown men, fearing violence from all men. Second, it is believed that these teenage males, having witnessed male violence, will become violent as well in the process of the intergenerational transmission of violence (Widom, 1989). As a result, when male victims of intimate partner violence and their children seek refuge in shelters, they are often turned away. Montgomeryshire Family Crisis Centre was the first exclusively male domestic violence shelter in southwest England. In the United States, while many shelters provide services to male victims, Valley Oasis Family Violence Shelter is one of the few shelters that house battered men.

CONCLUSION

While shelter research is increasing, this area of intimate partner violence has been largely ignored. Shelters are given low priority by criminal justice. They also tend to be few and far between. Furthermore, short stays in shelters and the small resident numbers tend to mask the vital importance of shelters for intimate partner violence victims. It has long been know that many women are under the greatest danger when they attempt to escape from an abusive relationship. Without the refuge provided by shelters, many of these women surely would fall victim to further violence, possibly even fatal violence. However, there appears to be a need to further understand the causes of and solutions to intimate partner violence, especially when considering the diverse backgrounds of intimate partner violence victims. Shelter conditions are far from ideal. Funding, the amount of space, services, and cultural understanding must be improved. Regardless of the ideology practiced by the shelter, the services available to shelter residents have proven to aid in recovery and transitional living.

9

REALITY RECONSIDERED

Female Intimate Partner
Violence Victim Images in Society

The social construction of reality is a powerful determinant in how victims of intimate partner violence experience victimization, justice, and healing. As we have seen in our discussion of the history of constructing and naming intimate partner violence, society moved from defining the rights of men to physically chastise their wives to requiring restraint in chastisement to criminalizing violence against wives. Our social constructs initially included only men's violence against their wives and then evolved to include male violence against any intimate partner and then to criminalize any intimate partner violence within any current or former intimate relationship.

Society has progressed in recognizing the oppression women face as victims of violence. Our social constructs have incorporated not only the physical violence but the sexual, emotional, financial, and stalking abuse as well. Research has uncovered the fact that intersections of sex, race, income, age, religion, and sexuality hold different experiences of abuse and social and justice responses (Potter, 2010; Richie, 2000). However, as with any change, social constructs have undergone an evolution of thought, not a revolution of thought. The result is that existing constructs can continue to be utilized in part or in whole. In other words, myths of intimate partner violence causation and solutions may continue to negatively influence victims and the criminal justice response.

SOCIAL CONSTRUCTS, MYTHOLOGY, AND SELF-BLAMING

As we saw in Chapter 3, victim blaming based on widely accepted myths still persists within society and is currently practiced in much of the criminal justice response. The notion of the ideal victim particularly has a powerful impact on victims themselves. We have argued that criminal justice officials are members of the larger society. These myths are produced and reproduced within society, and so it is logical to see their acceptance and utilization within criminal justice. However, we must also recognize that victims are also members of this same society and often internalize some blame in their victimization as well.

One well-documented phenomenon of self-blame, self-blame among rape victims, was examined in a study conducted by Peterson and Muehlenhard (2004). Peterson and Muehlenhard found that victims who did not identify themselves as the ideal rape victim (i.e., raped violently by a stranger) were less likely to acknowledge that they had been raped. Ideal rapes tend to construct the victim as the good girl who does not tease, dress provocatively, drink excessively, or date too much, who is not promiscuous, and who does not frequent bars. Women who engage in these behaviors are viewed as having "asked for it" or "enticed the offender."

The phenomenon of the *unacknowledged rape victim* applies to intimate partner violence, as sexual assault is a common form of intimate partner violence. Research finds that between 14 percent and 25 percent of women are sexually assaulted by intimate partners, with 68 percent of physically abused victims also reporting sexual assault (McFarlane & Malecha, 2005). Only 6 percent of these victims report the first sexual assault to the police. We know that many intimate partner violence victims fear calling the police or are unable to do so due to financial instability. However, we can also speculate that many of these women represent a portion of the 68 percent of unacknowledged rape victims identified by Peterson and Muehlenhard.

Accepting sexual assault within marriage seems to be foreign, since the criminal justice system often does not give these accusations much merit (Belknap, 2007). Consider the comment of a criminal justice student in a class held by one of the authors of this book. When discussing the extent and frequency of marital rape, one perplexed young woman declared that she could not see how rape could occur, because even if the woman does not want sex, "she should just take one for the team." The idea that women have an obligation to provide sex to their intimates places them in situations where they know they have been violated but do not believe that they have grounds to complain. If we examine this further, then we can begin to understand research that shows a drastic difference between self-reported sexual assaults and intimate partner violence and official statistics on these cases. Since criminal justice and the larger society tend to overlook or reject sexual assault as a common form of intimate partner violence, this problem of the unacknowledged rape victim can only further reinforce myths, victim blaming, and self-blaming.

We can apply this concept to intimate partner violence victims who do not define their relationships as abusive if the violence is occasional and/or minor. Victims may also deny abuse if there is only evidence of emotional or financial abuse. Victims holding to victim-blaming myths may take on some blame if they perceive that they might have pushed the abuser too far (i.e., the nagging woman myth) or if they believe that their abusers cannot control their tempers (i.e., the aggressive woman/man out of control myth). Victims who fight back may see that they are not victims, since they refuse to lie down and be beaten; hence they may not see the need to call the police. These victims may also internalize the mutual combat myth that women who fight back are equally aggressive. When society does not correct its mythology, victims can internalize the self-blaming, trapping themselves in abusive relationships. Why doesn't she leave? Perhaps because she does not realize that she should.

STRUCTURAL CONSEQUENCES OF THE SOCIAL CONSTRUCTION OF REALITY

Constructing Reality in the Social and Behavioral Sciences

Much of the discourse of naming and stopping intimate partner violence emerges from social and behavioral science discourse (De-

Keseredy & Dragiewicz, 2005). As discussed in previous chapters, scientists are members of the larger society and often tend to further develop the sciences within the current social constructs. At a time when intimate partner violence was constructed as a private family matter, much of it was ignored by the social and behavioral sciences. When social constructs of this behavior started to change, behavioral scientists utilized current constructs of the mentally unstable abuser. As was common, typologies of personality disorders were developed. When behavioral scientists started to recognize the psychological trauma that victims of severe abuse experience, these same scientists led the criminal justice response in identifying many of these victims as mentally unstable.

There seems to be no easy answer in addressing intimate partner violence. We must recognize that very violent abusers may have very real mental health problems. We must also recognize the mental trauma that many victims experience. However, the behavioral scientists must work in collaboration with the criminal justice system to educate practitioners in how to identify when an abuser is not mentally competent to warrant criminal responsibility. As the experts, behavioral scientists lead the criminal justice response of mandating treatment for many batterers. Intimate partner violence is the only crime for which the offender may very well not be held responsible when extreme violence occurs. With stranger crimes, society hesitates to declare violent offenders mentally incompetent for fear that they will not be held criminally responsible. Behavioral scientists must be responsible for educating criminal justice practitioners on this very complex field. However, models of treatment are not fully examined for their effectiveness. Nor is it made clear which batterers would be better served by which treatment model. Even more important is the responsibility that criminal justice has to ensure compliance with treatment mandates. Behavioral scientists cannot be expected to require compliance, as they have no legal authority to do so. Criminal justice practitioners must take the lead in these efforts as treatment is often part of the criminal justice response.

Social scientists are also guilty of reproducing victim-blaming constructs. In fact, the discipline of victimology was founded on the victim-blaming ideology, having borrowed directly from criminology. Over the course of decades, social scientists sought to further refine the degree of shared responsibility. Sociologists similarly sought to refine their explanations within a systems framework and came up with a structural-functional explanation (i.e., society is structured adequately, but dysfunction within the family leads to violence).

It was not until feminist social scientists and activists successfully called into question victim blaming and myths of violence against women that real progress was made in identifying the real social problem. Feminists have been largely successful in reconstructing intimate partner violence; however, old constructs still persist, making their work ongoing. Some feminists have worked to reinforce myths—such as the mentally unstable woman suffering from battered woman syndrome, and intimate partner violence as a personal trouble—when encouraging the police to allow victims to determine if an arrest is made. Feminists have been successful in creating new myths, such as males are abusers and not victims. With their continued focus on the female victim, feminists have in some ways ignored and sometimes denied the male victim of female violence within our society.

As with behavioral scientists, social scientists need to take responsibility for the harm they may do to the social construction of intimate partner violence. While their work is not as directly linked to offender treatment, there are very real consequences when the social sciences perpetuate myths. It must be stressed, however, that this work must continue. Theories must be examined and reexamined. Methodologies must be refined. And, most especially, scientists must recognize that science is not value neutral in its practice.

Policing Intimate Partner Violence

There is no shortage of case studies into the frequency of intimate partner violence. One need only look at the headlines in newspapers. Charlie Sheen was arrested for intimate partner violence on Christmas Day. Tiger Woods' wife smashed his car window, and his numerous affairs were publicized. Governor Paterson of New

York experienced tremendous pressure as a result of his involvement in a case of intimate partner violence against a member of his staff. Television star Gary Dourdan, of *CSI*, was assaulted by his girlfriend.

The criminal justice system's response to intimate partner violence has improved, especially in the judicial arena. There seems to be a proliferation of violence among intimates, and legislatures are responding around the country by adding new behaviors to intimate partner violence statutes. The criminal justice system needs to adjust to these changing times. Our courts are the final arbiter of such legislation. Let's hope they continue making adjustments in a positive direction.

Implications for the Victim

The most significant change in the police response to intimate partner violence has been the institution of mandatory arrest or pro-arrest statutes. As discussed in detail, the social construct of the ideal victim was of a female who suffered physical abuse at the hands of her partner. Often that abuse was repetitive and severe. However, the law evolved, and to some extent the social construction of victims evolved to include gay and lesbian partners and, to a lesser extent, male victims. Police were reluctant to involve themselves in intimate partner violence cases until mandated and then only to the extent of protecting traditional victims. The police saw mandatory arrest policies as a means to protect themselves and the department from litigation, and to a lesser degree, to provide the victim with protection.

The victims' rights movement conflicts with the arrest policy. Research demonstrates that many intimate partner violence victims do not necessarily want their abusers arrested (Hirschel & Hutchison, 2003). Instead victims want control of a situation that has spiraled out of control. Stopping the immediate violence is paramount, but arrest depends on the individual circumstances of the relationship. There is no statistical difference between traditional victims and nontraditional victims. Mandatory arrest often does not make the victim safer (in the long term) and could have a deteriorating effect on the victim's ability to manage her life.

Consideration of the victim's desire for arrest can work to empower the victim and possibly speed her recovery. However, placing this decision in the hands of the victim maintains the social construct that intimate partner violence is a private affair to be handled by the victim. We have seen that victims are often too intimidated to request that an arrest be made, an order of protection be issued, or a criminal trial proceed (Holt, Kernic, Lumley, Wolf, & Rivara, 2002). The system's response seems to be at a critical point in affecting real change. However, advocacy groups and varying feminist camps calling on one end of the equation for empowerment tend to collide with the demand to treat intimate partner violence as a crime on the other end of the equation. There seems to be a paradox here, in that the form of empowerment many people want, the choice to affect an arrest, tends to further the victimization. Crime victims and their advocates are not exempt from responsibility in the police–victim encounters.

Implications for the Criminal Justice System

Pro-arrest or mandatory arrest polices serve as a form of social control for police conduct. Police are no longer able to ignore intimate partner violence cases. In spite of objections by police, the police have increased the number of arrests of intimate partner violence offenders. As social constructs of the ideal victim evolve to include gay, lesbian, and male victims, the police are confronted with further policy shifts to treat all intimate partner violence as a serious crime.

Despite attempts by the police to improve their relationships with crime victims in general, and with intimate partner violence victims specifically, much work needs to be done in this area. A one-size-fits-all approach to police intervention is unworkable, especially considering the changing definition of who constitutes a true victim. Police training academies are responsible for improving police-victim services. Research demonstrates the distrust of the police in minority communities, and many speculate that, as a result, the volume of intimate partner violence incidents in these communities is not truly known (Potter, 2010). The police need to attend to these communities with increased awareness and empathy.

Unfortunately, the police are moved by politics, and just as victims face the dilemma of becoming empowered through arrest decisions or allowing the police to have this sole power, the police are influenced by this discourse. While research reveals that the police have a very long road to travel to ensure equal and fair justice in their responses, this road remains rocky when the discourse of the best course of action has not yet been decided. Research has revealed that in the long run, arrest does not always deter the violence (Sherman, 1992). Does this mean, however, that the police should not make arrests? Since the discourse continues to evolve, the only solution is for the police to enforce the law as they are empowered to do. This means that when any relatively violent crime occurs where there is probable cause to make an arrest, whether the parties involved are strangers or intimates, an arrest should be made. In sum, until we can know the final solution, then the police must simply do their jobs, that is, enforce the law.

Implications for Society

Mandatory arrest polices elevated intimate partner violence offenses to a special category of criminal conduct. They acknowledged the dehumanization of women while addressing society's interests in social control. With the changing construct of the ideal victim and the opposition of many to the designation of gays and lesbians as worthy victims, the social control mechanisms will grapple with this issue. Improvement in the police–victim encounter in intimate partner violence cases will allow society to continue to place a special emphasis on these crimes and will increase the reporting of incidents. The eradication of intimate partner violence is an important goal of society, and better relations between the police and the communities in which victimization is widespread is an important step forward in these efforts.

Changes to the police organization to combat intimate partner violence is a positive step for social control. Clearly, society has identified intimate partner violence as a crime in need of special attention. It is the only misdemeanor offense requiring mandatory arrest. This sends a clear signal that intimate partner violence is outside the bounds of social order. As the definition of the intimate partner violence victim continues to evolve to include gays, lesbians, and heterosexual men, society demonstrates the evolution of inclusion for these minority groups.

The Court Processing of Intimate Partner Violence

Implications for the Victim

The court processing of intimate partner violence underwent significant changes, as well. Prosecutors instituted no-drop policies and evidence-based prosecutions presumably to protect victims. Under these polices victims do not have to face their abusers. Victims benefit from these policies as their offenders are more likely to plea-bargain when they know they cannot intimidate their victims. Many offenders are sentenced to jail terms and/or to terms of probation. Under supervision they are often forced to undergo treatment. Victims also benefit in that jail terms allow them time to plan their future. While the prosecution of intimate partner violence cases met uncertainty with recent court rulings regarding the definitions of the Confrontation Clause (of the Sixth Amendment), excited utterances, and testimonial evidence (Jaros, 2005), we still see the forward movement to protect victims of intimate partner violence.

Civil remedies for intimate partner violence victims include orders of protection. These orders have proved to be ineffective in many cases because courts have been unable to enforce them. The protection requires police involvement. However, these are civil orders and police reluctance is well documented. Without the willingness of the police to enforce the orders, these orders are not worth the paper they are written on. With the construction of the ideal victim somewhat intact, police are hesitant to get involved in the enforcement. Only lawsuits by victims or their estates have moved the police to take these orders of protection seriously. On the other hand, we find that the very process of filing for orders of protection tends to empower many victims to demand freedom from violence and become survivors, instead of remaining victims (Keilitz, Davis, Efkeman, Flango, & Hannaford, 1998).

Courts are slow in changing their evidentiary rules. Battered woman syndrome never gained traction as a viable defense despite psychological expertise legitimizing the syndrome as a reasonable response to repeated victimization (Huss, Tomkins, Garbin, Schopp, & Kilian, 2006). The male-centered court system accepted a similar defense, post-traumatic stress disorder, which is a well-known psychological disorder in individuals during wartime. Courts must take a more active role in examining their rules of evidence to remain current with modern social science. Failure to adapt will render the courts ineffective in protecting victims of intimate partner violence, especially in light of the changing construction of "victims." On the other hand, we recognize the harm these constructs do to victims in reinforcing the myth that most, if not all, victims suffered extreme psychological trauma and damage before the intimate partner violence or as a result of it. This focus tends to disempower victims, denying their agency in defending themselves when the system fails them.

Implications for the Criminal Justice System

The no-drop and evidence-based prosecution policies increased the courts' workload and the workload of the police. Police officers are no longer responsible only for making an arrest. Under these policies, the police are also responsible for evidence gathering (Jaros, 2005). As misdemeanor offenses rarely warrant the involvement of detectives, the investigation function is the responsibility of the uniformed police officer. This increases the time involved in these incidents. Additionally, the police are often reluctant to get involved, seeing their primary concern as "crime fighting." While this construct of real police work excluding "family problems" has evolved for many officers, we still see a lingering reluctance of the police to involve themselves in issues where victims are believed to hold some responsibility. The bottom line, however, is that police are tasked with enforcing the law and not their personal opinions (even if those opinions are supported by a large portion of society). Continued resistance to do their jobs fairly and equitably only works to decrease police officers' legitimacy, as victims are left to provide for their own protection.

There is a need to have orders of protection enforced. Taking these orders seriously on the part of law enforcement will require more time and person hours. Police departments can expect continued litigation from those victims who are injured because the police failed to take the enforcement of protection orders seriously. We should also expect that "nontraditional" intimate partner violence victims will face barriers to enforcement similar to those women confronted. Enforcement will mean increased court dockets and judicial involvement in intimate partner violence cases. However, it is important for judges to stay engaged and to require police agencies to enforce these orders.

The failure of the courts to recognize that traditional definitions of defenses are changing as the social and behavioral sciences become more sophisticated can only hurt the credibility of the courts in the eyes of the public. Courts are social institutions that are relied upon to mete out justice and fairness. When the courts lose credibility and the faith of the people, they are no longer an effective institution.

Implications for Society

Society has a vested interest in the courts' ability to promote justice for all. Although courts made progress in the no-drop and evidenced-based prosecution of intimate partner violence cases, there remains uncertainty in minority communities about the courts' ability and willingness to mete out justice. Males seem to be able to avoid the courts' full power through the use of technicalities in the laws. Orders of protection are examples of well-intentioned efforts being ineffective. Society has invested a great deal of its social control responsibilities in the courts. To date, the courts have not fully embraced the post-traumatic stress disorder defense. Instead, they hide behind antiquated rules of evidence that are not interested in the courts' truth-finding function. The courts remain a male-dominated and male-oriented institution. As such, traditional perpetrators of intimate partner violence benefit from the courts' reluctance to administer justice. The social order is compromised by these actions. The courts serve as the final arbiter of social boundaries and acceptable behavior. In the instance of intimate partner violence, the courts have a long way to go in order to gain and retain the confidence of the public.

Correcting Intimate Partner Violence

Implications for the Victim

Correctional agencies are not victim-centered. They are offender-oriented. Correctional agencies in today's crime-control ideology are also focused on custodial punishment, not on treatment. As a result, the immediate needs of the victim tend to be overlooked. While incarceration definitely eliminates direct offender–victim intimate partner violence, corrections facilities are unsuccessful in curtailing continued harassment via telephone and mail (Ibarra & Erez, 2005). Efforts to work with victims in reporting offender harassment, as well as to inform victims when offenders are no longer incarcerated, constitute a big step toward ensuring safety. These technologies and policies must be implemented nationwide and must be made available to all victims.

Yet, most offenders are not incarcerated, so they pose a possible threat to the victim. Whether the batterer is mandated solely to treatment or treatment is part of the offender's conditions of probation, treatment programs tend to have limited effectiveness (Hansen & Harway, 1997; Ventura & Davis, 2005). Noncompliance with treatment mandates is also a major problem, owing to very little enforcement. Courts do not have enforcement power, and corrections officials often do not follow through with the treatment conditions of probation, whether as a consequence of large caseloads or of the nonfeasance of staff. So while the treatment of the offender can be a powerful tool to eliminating battering, the effects are not able to be realized. The added problem with treatment is the lack of consensus as to which treatment works. Many treatment models still hold to myths of the batterer who lacks self-control; however, there is the reality that many abusers possess mental health problems that must be treated, lest we welcome future violence.

Victims must be able to rely on probation departments for the enforcement of treatment conditions and the enforcement of orders of protection. The use of various forms of electronic monitoring also can provide victims with some sense of protection. When electronic monitoring programs utilize victim alert systems, intimate partner violence victims are made aware that the offender is close to them and can employ the proper care (Ibarra & Erez, 2005). However, probation agencies are not good at immediate reaction, and therefore victims are left on their own to seek police intervention for immediate protection. GPS can tell probation officers where offenders are at any given time and can track their daily movements to ensure that they are not harassing the victims physically. However, this protection is more likely to be reactionary rather than preventive, and victims may have a false sense of security with these programs.

Implications for the Criminal Justice System

The changes in the social constructs of intimate partner violence and the criminal justice response can have far-reaching implications for corrections agencies. However, these agencies cannot affect change if the two previous subsystems, the police and the courts, do not fulfill their responsibilities. The police must enforce the laws in investigating allegations of intimate partner violence and making arrests of the true primary aggressors. The courts must afford these cases fair and equal treatment, comparable to the way they treat similar stranger crimes, and sentences must be meted out that will serve to hold the offenders criminally responsible, as well as aid in behavior modification. Until those sentences are handed down, corrections agencies cannot act. If treatment is mandated without probation, then corrections does not become involved. However, once probation or incarceration becomes a factor, then these agencies must take their responsibilities seriously, or they perpetuate the problem, giving batterers the message that their behaviors are acceptable. While corrections remains punishment and offender oriented, there is increased awareness of victim safety. The victim notification policies discussed earlier are a start to recognizing corrections' responsibility to this segment of the public.

Implications for Society

One surprising element of society's efforts to control intimate partner violence is that, unlike most other crimes, intimate partner violence has remained free from increased sentencing polices. The social order for the better part of the last twenty-five years has been the retribution ideology. Deserved punishment implies that society considers criminal behavior to be far outside the boundaries of civility. Yet, for the most part, intimate partner violence has remained a misdemeanor offense. With all the focus on policing and processing intimate partner violence, and on expanding the definition of intimate partner violence, and with the discourse about ways to eradicate this social problem, it is surprising that punishments have remained somewhat soft.

Society has been given the false hope that the current efforts on the part of the police and the courts are sufficient to control intimate partner violence. The problem of intimate partner violence continues despite the efforts discussed in this book. The missing piece of the puzzle may be an increase in sanctions to include mandatory jail time or perhaps prison time for repeat offenders. These are certainly worth exploring.

CONCLUSION

Victim Empowerment Versus Disempowerment

What does this all mean for the victim and the fight against intimate partner violence? First, we must recognize that intimate partner violence is a very complex problem. It has its roots in historical ideologies as well as current ideologies. It encompasses various victims and offenders and various forms of abuse. Second, it requires various methods of redress. We cannot simply conclude that all victims experience psychological trauma or a cycle of violence, or that all victims need is consciousness-raising. We must examine what works best for various situations. Third, we must recognize that our explanations for this social problem are laden with social constructions of reality. Until we can recognize our own ideologies and prejudices, we will continue to add to the problem in some way. Finally, we must revise our definitions of victim empowerment.

Much of activist work has centered on the empowerment of victims. Victims lack agency when they are abused and oppressed by their intimate partners, and again when criminal justice does not recognize these crimes. It is further argued that strengthening agency requires empowering victims. Together, these allow victims to recognize their oppressions and actively work toward healing, freedom, and equality. This cannot be further from the truth, and we agree with this. What we fail to recognize is that placing the "choice" of criminal justice sanctioning in the hands of victims *disempowers* victims, because it perpetuates intimate partner violence as a personal trouble and treats these victims as unequal and unworthy.

Crimes are wrongs committed against society, hence the judicial determination of *People v. Smith*. Prosecutors represent the people, and victims become witnesses in the crime against society. Activists stress empowerment in victim choices of police arrest, prosecution charging, and judicial sentencing. However, this is often examined by *malestream* social scientists and the criminal justice system in relation to deterrence. On the one hand, recognizing victim choice is empowering. On the other hand, by allowing intimate partner violence to be processed in this manner, we devalue and demote the newly defined social problem to an individual problem that is assigned to civil court or kept in the family.

The continued focus on women's experiences as different often works to enable positive social change; however, this focus simultaneously works to keep women in an oppressed state (Garcia, 2003). Until criminal justice officially mandates that all crimes be processed according to individual desires, intimate partner violence will be mandated to the private realm. Criminal justice has never determined that arrest should not be made in any stranger violent situation until deterrence can be proven. Mandates of treatment as the sole form of punishment are not common among stranger violent offenders. It has not been official policy to charge serious, violent stranger felonies as misdemeanors. This has not been done, because these crimes are viewed as crimes against the people and as representing real social problems. Until intimate partner violence crimes are treated in a similar fashion, victims will be disempowered.

APPENDIX

RELATED INTERNET SITES

American Public Human Services Association www.aphsa.org /Home/home_news.asp

An Abuse, Rape and Domestic Violence Aid and Resource Collection: Domestic Violence in Popular Films www.aardvarc.org/dv /dvfilms.shtml

Bureau of Justice Statistics, *Female Victims of Violence* http://bjs .ojp.usdoj.gov/content/pub/pdf/fvv.pdf

Bureau of Labor Statistics www.bls.gov/cps/cpsaat11.pdf

Cambridge Encyclopedia: Postmodernism, Poststructuralism and Deconstruction http://encyclopedia.stateuniversity.com /pages/17766/Postmodernism.html

Casa de las Madres www.lacasadelasmadres.org/index.html

Centers for Disease Prevention and Control www.cdc.gov/ violenceprevention

Corporate Alliance to End Partner Violence www.caepv.org/

Domestic Abuse Intervention Program: The Duluth Model www .theduluthmodel.org/duluthmodel.php

Easy Access to NIBRS: Victims of Domestic Violence, 2005 http://ojjdp.ncjrs.gov/ojstatbb/ezanibrsdv/

Family Violence Prevention Fund http://endabuse.org/

Federal Bureau of Investigation, *Uniformed Crime Reports* www.fbi.gov/ucr/cius2008/index.html

Herstory of Domestic Violence: A Timeline of the Battered Women's Movement www.mincava.umn.edu/documents/herstory /herstory.html

House of Ruth www.hruth.org/

National Center for Victims of Crime www.ncvc.org/ncvc/main .aspx?dbName=DocumentViewer&DocumentID=32369

National Criminal Justice Resource Services www.ncjrs.gov

National Domestic Violence Hotline www.ndvh.org/

National Institute of Justice: *Stalking* www.ojp.usdoj.gov/nij/ topics/crime/stalking/welcome.htm

National Online Resource Center on Violence Against Women www.vawnet.org/

Office of Crime Victims www.ovc.gov/

Office of Justice Programs www.ojp.usdoj.gov./flash.htm

Office of Violence Against Women www.ovw.usdoj.gov/index.html

United States Department of Justice Statistics /www.govtech.com /gt/95569?id=95569&full=1&story_pg=2

Women's Prison Association www.wpaonline.org/

NOTES

CHAPTER 1

1. Age minorities and homosexuals were not part of the discourse in early American history. In fact, homosexual individuals were condemned as ungodly.

2. However, social constructs of gender proscribe homosexuality, so the focus is inherent to the analysis. Furthermore, non-Christians and non-U.S. citizens tend to be ignored by society, unless the focus is on the cause of social problems.

REFERENCES

Abbott, Pamela, and Claire Wallace. 1990. *An introduction to sociology: Feminist perspectives*. New York: Routledge.

Acker, Joan. 1992. Gender institutions: From sex roles to gendered institutions. *Contemporary Sociology* 21 (5):565–69.

Adams, B., C. Puzzanchera, and W. Kang. 2008. Easy access to NIBRS: Victims of domestic violence, 2005.

Agger, Ben. 1991. *A critical theory of public life: Knowledge, discourse and politics in an age of decline*. London: Famer Press.

Allen, H. 1980. *Homicide: Perspectives on prevention*. New York: Human Sciences Press.

Alpert, Adrienne. 2009. Celebrity-stalking has common threads. KABC-TV/DT.

Altheide, D. L. 2002. *Creating fear: News and the construction of crisis*. New York: Aldine De Gruyter.

American Psychiatric Association. 1980. Post-traumatic stress disorder. In *Diagnostic and statistical manual of mental disorders (DSM-III-R)*. Washington, D.C.: American Psychiatric Association.

———. 1994. *Diagnostic and statistical manual of mental disorders (DMS-IV)*. Washington, D.C.: American Psychiatric Association.

Amir, M. 1971. *Patterns in forcible rape*. Chicago: University of Chicago Press.

Anderson, E. 1999. *The code of the streets*. New York: W. W. Norton.

Anderson, M. 2002. From chastity requirement to sexuality license: Sexual consent and a new rape shield law. *George Washington Law Review* 70:51–165.

Archer, J. 2000. Sex differences in aggression between heterosexual partners: A meta-analytic review. *Psychological Bulletin* 126 (5):651–80.

Archives of Family Medicine. 1998. How do you define abuse? *Archives of Family Medicine* 7:31–32.

Barden, J. C. 1981. Rape in marriage defined. *New York Times*, April 19, 1981.

Barsky, Hillary. 2009. Is Rihanna going back? *Good Morning America Radio*, March 2, 2009.

Bauman, B., S. Messner, and R. Felson. 2000. The role of victim characteristics in the disposition of murder cases. *Justice Quarterly* 17:281–308.

Belknap, J. 1992. Perceptions of woman battering. In *The changing roles of women in the criminal justice system: Offenders, victims and professionals.* Edited by I. Moyer. Prospect Heights, IL: Waveland Press, 151–202.

———. 2007. *The invisible woman: gender, crime, and justice.* 3rd ed. Belmont, CA: Thomson Wadsworth.

Belknap, J., D. Graham, V. Lippen, and J. Sutherland. 1999. Predicting court outcomes in intimate partner violence cases: Preliminary findings. *Domestic Violence Report* 5:1–10.

Belknap, J., J. L. Hartman, and V. L. Lippen. 2010. Misdemeanor domestic violence cases in the courts: A detailed description of the cases. In *Female victims of crime: Reality reconsidered.* Edited by V. Garcia and J. E. Clifford. Upper River Saddle, NJ: Pearson Education, 259–78.

Bennett, L., L. Goodman, and M. A. Dutton. 1999. Systematic obstacles to criminal prosecution of battering partner. *Journal of Interpersonal Violence* 14:761–72.

Bennice, J. A., and P. A. Resick. 2003. Marital rape: History, research and practice. *Trauma, Violence, and Abuse* 4 (3):228–46.

Berger, P. L., and T. Luckmann. 1966. *The social construction of reality: A treatise in the sociology of knowledge.* New York: Anchor Books.

Berk, Richard A., Donileen R. Loseke, Sarah Fenstermaker Berk, and David Rauma. 1980. Bringing the cops back in: A study of efforts to make the criminal justice system more responsive to incidents of family violence. *Social Science Research* 9 (3):195–215.

Boston Public Health Commission. 2010. *Chris Brown-Rihanna survey results to be discussed Thursday.* 2009 [cited March 17 2010]. Available from www.bphc.org/Newsroom/Pages/TopStoriesView.aspx?ID=63.

Botec Analysis Corporation. 2001. *Rhode Island victim's needs assessment.* Cambridge, MA: Botec Analysis Corporation.

Boyd-Jackson, Sharon. 2010. Domestic violence: Overview of theoretical etiology, psychological impact and interventions. In *Female victims of crime: Reality reconsidered.* Edited by V. Garcia and J. E. Clifford. Upper Saddle River, NJ: Prentice Hall, 128–44.

Browne, Angela, and Shari S. Bassuk. 1997. Intimate violence in the lives of homeless and poor housed women: Prevalence and patterns in an ethnically diverse sample. *American Journal of Orthopsychiatry* 67 (2):261–78.

Bureau of Criminal Information and Analysis. 1999. Report on arrests for domestic violence in California, 1998. Sacramento, CA: Office of the Attorney General.

Bureau of Labor Statisics. 2009. Labor force statistics from the current population survey. Edited by U.S. Department of Labor. Washington, D.C.: U.S. Bureau of Labor Statistics Division of Labor Force Statistics.

Buttell, F. P. , and M. M. Carney. 2005. Do batterer intervention programs serve African-American and Caucasian batterers equally well? An investigation of a 26-week program. *Research on Social Work Practice* 15:19–28.

Buzawa, Eve S., and C. G. Buzawa. 2003. *Domestic violence: The criminal justice response.* 3 ed. Thousand Oaks, CA: Sage Publications.

Buzawa, Eve S., G. T. Hotaling, Andrew Klein, and J. Byrne. 1999. *Response to domestic violence in a pro-active court setting: Final report.* Lowell: University of Massachusetts.

Cadsky, O., R. K. Hanson, M. Crawford, and C. Lalonde. 1996. Attrition from a male batterer treatment program: Client treatment congruence and lifestyle instability. *Violence and Victims* 11:51–64.

Campbell, Jacquelyn C., Paul Miller, Mary M. Cardwell, and Ruth Ann Belknap. 1994. Relationship status of battered women over time. *Journal of Family Violence* 9 (2):99–111.

Canales-Portalatin, David. 2000. Intimate-partner assailants: Comparison of cases referred to a probation department. *Journal of Interpersonal Violence* 15 (8):843–54.

Canter, R. 1982. Sex differences in self-report delinquency. *Criminology* 20:373–93.

Catalano, Shannan , Erica Smith, Howard Snyder, and Michael Rand. 2009. Female victims of violence. In *National Crime Victimization Survey.* Bureau of Justice Statistics. Washington, D.C.: U.S. Department of Justice, Office of Justice Programs.

Centers for Disease Control and Prevention. 2009. *Understanding intimate partner violence fact sheet, 2009.* National Center for Injury Prevention and Control. Atlanta: Centers for Disease Control and Prevention.

Chambliss, William J. 1964. A sociological analysis of the law of vagrancy. *Social Problems* 12 (1):67–77.

———. 1994. Policing the ghetto underclass: The politics of law and law enforcement. *Social Problems* 41 (2):177–94.

Chermack, S. 1995. *Victims in the news.* Boulder, CO: Westview Press.

Chesney-Lind, Meda. 2002. Criminalizing victimization: The unintended consequences of pro-arrest policies for girls and women. *Criminology and Public Policy* 2 (1):81–90.

Chesney-Lind, Meda, and Lisa J. Pasko. 2004. *The female offender: Girls, women, and crime.* 2nd ed. London: Sage Publications.

Clear, T., G. Cole, and M. Reisig. 2010. *American corrections.* 9 ed. Belmont, CA: Wadsworth.

Coker, Donna. 2005. Shifting power for battered women: Law, material resources, and poor women of color. In *Domestic violence at the margins: Readings on race, class, gender and culture.* Edited by N. J. Sokoloff and C. Pratt. New Brunswick, NJ: Rutgers University Press, 369–85.

Comstock, Gary D. 1991. *Violence against lesbians and gay men.* New York: Columbia University Press.

Connor, T. 2004. She made eyes at me. *Daily News,* September 1.

Coulter, M., A. Alexander, and V. Harrison. 2005. Specialized domestic violence courts: Improvement for women victims? *Women and Criminal Justice* 16 (3):91–106.

CourtTV. 2004. *Bryant attorneys hint at strategy of focusing on accuser* [cited September 24, 2004]. Available from http://courttv.com/trials/bryant/090803_strategy_ap.html.

Curtis, L. 1974. Victim precipitation and violent crime. *Social Problems* 21:594–605.

Davis, R., and B. Taylor. 1999. Does batterer treatment reduce violence? A synthesis of the literature. *Women and Criminal Justice* 10:69–93.

Davis, R., B. Taylor, and C. Maxwell. 1998. *Does batterer treatment reduce violence? A randomized experiment in Brooklyn.* Washington, D.C.: National Institute of Justice/NCJRS.

DeKeseredy, Walter S., and Molly Dragiewicz. 2005. *Shifting public policy direction: Gender-focused versus bi-directional intimate partner violence.* Oshawa, Canada: University of Ontario Institute of Technology.

DeKeseredy, Walter S., and Linda MacLeod. 1997. *Woman abuse: A sociological story.* Toronto: Harcourt Brace & Company, Inc.

DeKeseredy, Walter S., and Marty Schwartz. 1998. *Measuring the extent of women abuse in intimate heterosexual relationships: A critique of the conflict tactics scales*. Available from http://new.vawnet.org/Assoc_files_ VAWnet/AR_ctscnt.pdf.

Della Giustina, Jo-Ann. 2010. The impact of gender, race, and class discrimination on femicide rates. In *Female victims of crime: Reality reconsidered*. Edited by V. Garcia and J. E. Clifford. Upper River Saddle, NJ: Pearson Education, 95–112.

Dobash, R. Emerson, and Russell Dobash. 1992. *Women, violence and social change*. New York: Routledge.

Domestic Abuse Intervention Program. 2010. *The Duluth Model*. Domestic Abuse Intervention Program 2008 [cited March 15 2010]. Available from www.theduluthmodel.org/duluthmodel.php.

Donovan, Brian. 2005. Gender inequality and criminal seduction: Prosecuting sexual coercion in the early 20th century. *Law and Social Inquiry* 30 (1):61–88.

Doob, Christopher Bates. 2005. *Race, ethnicity, and the American urban mainstream*. Boston: Allyn & Bacon.

Dugan, L. 2003. Domestic violence legislation: Exploring its impact on the likelihood of domestic violence police involvement and arrest. *Criminology & Public Policy* 2 (2):283–312.

Durfee, Alesha. 2010. The gendered paradox of victimization and agency in protection order filings. In *Female victims of crime: Reality reconsidered*. Edited by V. Garcia and J. E. Clifford. Upper Saddle River, NJ: Pearson Education, 243–58.

Durose, Matthew R., Caroline Wolf Harlow, Patrick A. Langan, Mark Motivans, Ramona R. Rantala, and Erica L. Smith. 2005. *Family violence statistics: Including statistics on strangers and acquaintances*. Edited by U.S. Department of Justice. Washington, D.C.: Bureau of Justice Statistics.

Eigenberg, H. M. 2003. Victim blaming. In *Controversies in victimology*. Edited by L. J. Moriarty. Cincinnati, OH: Anderson, 15–24.

Elbow, M. 1977. Theoretical considerations of violent marriages. *Social Casework* 58:515–526.

Ephesians 5. *The New American Bible*. Edited by S. J. Edition, *The New American Bible*. New York: Catholic Book Publishing.

Erez, E., P. R. Ibarra, and N. A. Laurie. 2004. Applying electronic monitoring to domestic violence cases: A comparison of two bilateral programs. *Federal Probation* 68:15–20.

Erez, Edna. 1986. Intimacy, violence, and the police. *Human Relations* 39:265–81.

Erez, Edna, and Joanne Belknap. 1998. In their own words: Battered women's assessment of systemic responses. *Violence and Victims* 13:3–20.

Ewing, C. P., and M. Aubrey. 1987. Battered woman and public opinion: Some realities about the myths. *Journal of Family Violence* 2:257–64.

Fagan, J. 1996. *The criminalization of domestic violence: Promises and limits.* U.S. Department of Justice. Washington, D.C.: National Institute of Justice.

Faulk, M. 1974. Men who assault their wives. *Medicine, Science, and the Law* 14 (3):180–83.

Feder, L., and D. Forde. 2000. *A test of the efficacy of court-mandated counseling for domestic violence offenders: The Broward Experiment.* Washington, D.C.: National Institute of Justice/NCJRS.

Federal Bureau of Investigation. 2010. *Crime in the United States, 2008.* Department of Justice, U.S. Government Printing Office 2008 [cited March 17 2010]. Available from www.fbi.gov/ucr/cius2008/index.html.

Feinman, Clarice. 1986. *Women in the Criminal Justice System.* 2 ed. New York: Praeger.

Fernandez, L. A., and A. Alverez. 2009. Unwelcome citizens: Latinos and the criminal justice system. In *Investigating difference: Human and cultural relations in criminal justice.* Edited by The Criminology & Criminal Justice Collective of Northern Arizona University. Upper Saddle River, NJ: Prentice Hall, 114–25.

Finkel, N. 1995. *Commonsense justice: Jurors notions of the law.* Cambridge, MA: Harvard University Press.

Finn, P., and S. Colson. 1990. Civil protection orders: Legislation, current court practice, and enforcement. National Institute of Justice (U.S.). Washington, DC: Office of Justice Programs.

Fowler, Glenn. Democrats support bills for protection of battered wives. *New York Times*, February 17, 1977

Fry, Melissa S. 2010. Becoming victims, becoming citizens: A brief history of gender-motivated violence in U.S. law. In *Female victims of crime: Reality reconsidered.* Edited by V. Garcia and J. E. Clifford. Upper Saddle River, NJ: Pearson Education, 20–44

Frye, V., M. Haviland, and V. Rajah. 2007. Dual arrest and other unintended consequences of mandatory arrest in New York City: A brief report. *Journal of Family Violence* 22:397–405.

Furedi, F. 1997. Princess Diana and the new cult of victimhood. *Wall Street Journal: Eastern Edition* September 10, 1997:A22.

Garcia, Venessa. 1994. Police response to domestic violence: An organizational analysis. Buffalo: State University of New York University at Buffalo.

————. 1995. Police response to domestic violence: Social change or the presence of the past?

————. 2003. "Difference" in the police department: Women, policing and "doing gender." *Journal of Contemporary Criminal Justice* 19 (3):330–44.

————. 2008. Constructing the other within police culture: Analysis of a deviant unit within a police organization. *Contemporary Issues in Law Enforcement and Policing* 6 (1):65–80.

Garcia, Venessa, and Erica J. Schweikert. 2010. Cultural images–media images: "Doing culture" and victim blaming of female crime victims. In *Female victims of crime: Reality reconsidered.* Edited by V. Garcia and J. E. Clifford. Upper Saddle River, NJ: Pearson Education, 3–39.

Garner, Joel, and Elizabeth Clemmer. 1986. *Danger to police in domestic disturbances: A new look.* U.S. Department of Justice. Washington, D.C.: National Institute of Justice.

Gelles, Richard J. 1983. An exchange/social control theory. In *The dark side of families: Current family violence research.* Edited by D. Finkelhor, R. J. Gelles and G. T. Hotaling. Beverly Hills, CA: Sage Publications.

Gerstenfeld, Phyllis B. 2010. *Hate crime: Causes, control and controversies.* 2 ed. Thousand Oaks, CA: Sage Publications, 151–65

Gerstenfeld, Phyllis B. . 2004. *Hate crimes: Causes, controls, and controversies.* Thousand, Oaks, CA: Sage Publications, 151–65.

Glaze, Lauren E. 2003. *Probation and parole in the United States, 2002.* U.S. Department of Justice. Washington, D.C.: Bureau of Justice Statistics.

————. 2008. *Parents in prison and their minor children.* U.S. Department of Justice. Washington, D.C.: Bureau of Justice Statistics.

Glaze, Lauren E., and Thomas P. Bonczar. 2009. *Probation and parole in the United States, 2008.* U.S. Department of Justice. Washington, D.C.: Bureau of Justice Statistics.

Gondolf, E. W., and Ellen Fisher. 1988/2001. Battered women as survivors: An alternative to treatin learned helplessness. In *Battered women and the law.* Edited by C. Dalton and E. M. Schneider. New York: Foundation Press, 107–17.

Gondolf, E. W., J. McWilliams, B. Hart, and J. Stuehling. 1994. Court response to petitions for civil protection orders. *Journal of Interpersonal Violence* 9:503–17.

Gondolf, Edward W. 1997. Patterns of re-assault in batterer programs. *Violence and Victims* 12: 373–87.

————. 2009. Outcomes from referring batterer program participants to mental health treatment. *Journal of Family Violence* 24:577–88.

Gonzalez, Juan. 2009. Karla Giraldo anxious to be reunited with man who assaulted her, Sen. Hiram Monserrate. *New York Daily News*, October 18, 2009.

Gosselin, D. 2000. *Heavy hands: An introduction to crimes of domestic violence*. Upper Saddle River, NJ: Prentice Hall.

Graber, D. 2002. *Crime news and the public*. New York: Praeger.

Grady, A. 2002. Female-on-male domestic violence: Uncommon or ignored? In *New visions of crime victims*. Edited by C. Hoyle and R. Young. Portland, OR: Hart Publishing, 71–96.

Grau, J., J. Fagan, and S. Wexler. 1985. Restraining orders for battered women: Issues of access and efficacy. In *Criminal justice politics and women: The aftermath of legally mandated change*. Edited by C. Schweber and C. Feinman. New York, NY: Haworth Press, 13–28.

Greene, J., and K. Pranis. 2010. *The punitiveness report-HARD HIT: The growth in the imprisonment of women 1977–2004*. Institute on Women and Criminal Justice 2004 [cited March 2 2010]. Available from www.wpaonline.org/institute/hardhit/index.htm.

Greenfeld, L. A., M. R. Rand, D. Craven, P. A. Klaus, C. A. Perkins, C. Ringel, G. Warchol, C. Maston, and J. A. Fox. 1998. *Violence by intimates: Analysis of data on crimes by current or former spouses, boyfriends, and girlfriends*. U.S. Department of Justice. Washington, D.C.: Bureau of Justice Statistics.

Greenwald, Robert. 1985. *The Burning Bed*. [Movie]

Grossberg, L., E. Wartella, and D.C. Whitney. 1998. *MediaMaking: Mass media in a popular culture*. Thousand Oaks, CA: Sage Publications.

Hansen, Marsali, and Michelle Harway. 1997. Theory and therapy: A feminist perspective on intimate violence. In *Violence between intimate partners: Patterns, causes and effects*. Edited by A. P. Cardarelli. Needham Heights, MA: Allyn & Bacon.

Harrell, A., and B. E. Smith. 1996. Effects of restraining orders on domestic violence victims. In *Do arrests and restraining orders work?* Edited by E. S. B. & and C. G. Buzawa. Thousand Oaks, CA: Sage Publications, 214–42.

Hart, B. J. 1992. State codes on domestic violence: Analysis, commentary, and recommendations. *Juvenile and Family Court Journal* 43 (4):1–81.

Hassouneh-Phillips, Dena Sadat. 1998. Culture and systems of oppression in abused women's lives. *Journal of Obstetric, Gynecological, and Neonatal Nursing*, 27 (6):678–83.

Hawkesworth, M. E. 1990. *Beyond oppression: Feminist theory and political strategy*. New York: Continuum Publishing Co.

Henning, K., B. Renauer, and R. Holdford. 2006. Victim or offender? Heterogeneity among women arrested for intimate partner violence. *Journal of Family Violence* 21:351–68.

Hirschel, David. 2008. *Domestic violence cases: What research shows about arrest and dual arrest rates.* National Institute of Justice. Washington, D.C.: U.S. Office of Justice Programs.

Hirschel, David, and Ira W. Hutchison. 2003. The voices of domestic violence victims: Predictors of victim preference for arrest and the relationship between preference for arrest and revictimization. *Crime Delinquency* 49 (2):313–36.

Hockett, Jericho M., Donald A. Saucier, Bethany H. Hoffman, Sara J. Smith, and Adam W. Craig. 2009. Oppression through acceptance? Predicting rape myth acceptance and attitudes toward rape victims. *Violence Against Women* 15 (8):877–97.

Holt, Victoria L., Mary A. Kernic, Thomas Lumley, Marsha E. Wolf, and Frederick P. Rivara. 2002. Civil protection orders and risk of subsequent police-reported violence. *Journal of the American Medical Association* 288:589–94.

Holtzworth-Munroe, Amy, and Gregory L. Stuart. 1994. Typologies of male batterers: Three subtypes and the differences among them. *Psychological Bulletin* 116 (3):476–97.

Horne, Charles F. *Ancient history sourcebook: Code of Hammurabi, c. 1780 BCE* 1915 [cited March 22. Available from www.fordham.edu/halsall /ancient/hamcode.html#horne.

Horsburgh, Beverly. 2005. Lifting the veil of secrecy: Domestic violence in the Jewish Community. In *Domestic violence at the margins: Readings on race, class, gender and culture.* Edited by N. J. Sokoloff and C. Pratt. New Brunswick, NJ: Rutgers University Press, 206–26.

Houskamp, B., and D. Foy. 1991. The assessment of posttraumatic stress disorder in battered women. *Journal of Interpersonal Violence* 6:367–75.

Hunter, Ronald D., and Mark L. Dantzker. 2005. *Crime and criminality: Causes and consequences.* Monsey, NY: Criminal Justice Press.

Huss, M., A. Tomkins, C. Garbin, R. Schopp, and A. Kilian. 2006. Battered women who kill their abusers: An examination of commonsense notions, cognitions, and judgments. *Journal of Interpersonal Violence* 21:1060–83.

Hust, Stacey J. T., Jane D. Brown, and Kelly Ladin L'Engle. 2008. Boys will be boys and girls better be prepared: An analysis of the rare sexual health messages in young adolescents' media. *Mass Communication & Society* 11 (1):3–23.

Ibarra, P.R., and Edna Erez. 2005. Victim-centric diversion: The electronic monitoring of domestic violence cases. *Behavior Sciences and the Law* 23:259–76.

Jaggar, A. M. 1988. *Feminist politics and human nature.* Lanham, MD: Rowman & Littlefield.

Jaros, David. 2005. The lessons of *People v. Muscat*: Confronting judicial bias in domestic violence cases interpretating *Crawford v. Washington. The American Criminal Law Review* 42 (3):995–1009.

Jhally, Sut. 1994. *Data rape backlash: Media and denial of rape.* [Movie]

Johnson, I. 2007. Victims' perceptions of police response to domestic violence incidents. *Journal of Criminal Justice* 35:495–510.

Johnson, J., Y. Luna, and J. Stein. 2003. Victim protection orders and the stake in conformity thesis. *Journal of Family Violence* 18 (6):317–23.

Johnson, Marilou, and Barbara A. Elliott. 1997. Domestic violence among family practice patients in midsized and rural communities. *The Journal of Family Practice* 44 (4):391–400.

Josephson, Jyl. 2005. The intersectionality of domestic violence and welfare in the lives of poor women. In *Domestic violence at the margins: Readings on race, class, and culture.* Edited by N. J. Sokoloff. New Brunswick, NJ: Rutgers University Press, 53–101.

Kappeler, Victor E., Mark Blumberg, and Gary W. Potter. 2000. *The mythology of crime and criminal justice.* 3 ed. Prospect Heights, IL: Waveland Press, Inc.

Karan, A., S. Keilitz, and S. Denard. 1999. Domestic violence courts: What are they and how should we manage them? *Juvenile and Family Court Journal* 71:75–86.

Karmen, Andrew. 2010. *Crime victims: An introduction to victimology.* Belmont, CA: Wadsworth Cengage Learning.

Keilitz, S., R. Guerrero, A. M. Jones, D. M. Rubio, S. Keilib, H. Efkeman, V. Garcia, V. Hansford, and S. Denaro. 2001/2003. *Specialization of domestic violence case management in the courts: A national survey.* Washington, D.C.: National Criminal Justice Reference Center.

Keilitz, Susan L., Courtenay Davis, Hillery S. Efkeman, Carol Flango, and Paula L. Hannaford. 1998. *Civil protection orders: Victims' views on effectiveness.* U.S. Department of Justice. Washington, D.C.: National Institute of Justice.

Keitner, Chimene I. 2002. Victim or vamp? Images of violent women in the criminal justice system. *Columbia Journal of Gender and the Law* 11:38–72.

Klein, A. R. 2004. *The criminal justice response to domestic violence.* Belmont, CA: Thomson/Wadsworth.

Klein, Andrew R., Douglas Wilson, Ann H. Crowe, and Matthew DeMichele. 2008. *Evaluation of the Rhode Island Probation Specialized Domestic Violence Supervision Unit.* U.S. Department of Justice. Washington, D.C.: National Institute of Justice.

Krishnan, Satya P., Judith C. Hilbert, Keith McNeil, and Isadore Newman. 2004. From respite to transition: Women's use of domestic violence shelters in rural New Mexico. *Journal of Family Violence* 19 (3):165–73.

Kukkonen, Karin. 2008. Popular cultural memory: Comics, communities and context knowledge. *NORDICOM Review* 29 (2):261–73.

Lee, M.Y., A. Uken, and J. Sebold. 2007. Role of self-determined goals in predicting recidivism in domestic violence offenders. *Research on Social Work Practice* 17:30–41.

Lefkowitz, Mary R., and Maureen B. Fant. 2005. *Women's life in Greece and Rome: A source book in translation.* 3 ed. Baltimore: The John Hopkins University Press.

Lemon, Nancy. 1996. *Domestic violence law: A comprehensive overview of cases and sources.* San Francisco, CA: Austin and Winfield.

Leonard, Elizabeth. 2009. Rihanna and Chris Brown are back together. *People Magazine,* Friday February 27, 2009.

Lilith, R. 2001. Reconsidering the abuse that dare not speak its name: A criticism of recent legal scholarship regarding same-gender domestic violence. *Michigan Journal of Gender & Law* 7:181–219.

Logan, T. K., Robert Walker, and Carl G. Leukefeld. 2001. Rural, urban influenced and urban differences among domestic violence arrestees. *Journal of Interpersonal Violence* 16 (3):266–83.

Long, Colleen. 2009. NY senator sentenced to probation, counseling. *The Associated Press,* December 4, 2009.

Loseke, D. R. 1999. *Thinking about social problems: An introduction to constructionist perspectives.* New York: Aldine de Gruyter.

Lyon, Eleanor, Shannon Lane, and Anne Menard. 2008. *Meeting survivors' needs: A multi-state study of domestic violence shelter experiences, final report.* Washington, D.C.: U.S. Department of Justice.

Mann, C. 1988. Getting even: Women who kill in domestic encounters. *Justice Quarterly,* 5 (1):33–51.

Marsh, Ian, and Gaynor Melville. 2009. *Crime, justice and the media.* New York: Routledge.

Martin, Del. 1983. *Battered wives.* New York: Pocket Books.

Martin, M. E. 1994. Mandatory arrest for domestic violence: The court's response. *Criminal Justice Review* 19:212–27.

Mason, Mary Ann. 1994. *From father's property to children's rights: The history of child custody in the United States.* New York: Columbia University Press.

Maxwell, Christopher D., Joel H. Garner, and Jeffrey A. Fagan. 2001. *The effects of arrest on intimate partner violence: New evidence from the Spousal Assault Replication Program,* Department of Justice. Washington, D.C.: National Institute of Justice.

McFadden, Robert D. 1982. New law cited in dropping rape charge. *New York Times,* November 15.

McFarlane, Judith, and Ann Malecha. 2005. *Sexual assault among intimates: Frequency, consequences and treatments.* Washington, D.C.: Office of Justice Programs.

McFarlane, Judith, Ann Malecha, Julia Gist, Kathy Watson, Elizabeth Batten, Iva Hall, and Sheila Smith. 2004. Protection orders and intimate partner violence: An 18-month study of 150 black, hispanic, and white women. *American Journal of Public Health* 94:613–18.

McManimon, Patrick. 2010. Criminalization of victimization in female offenders: Emerging correctional responses. In *Female victims of crime: Reality reconsidered.* Edited by V. Garcia and J. E. Clifford. Upper Saddle River, NJ: Prentice Hall, 292–307.

McNulty, Faith. 1980. *The burning bed: The true story of an abused wife.* New York: Harcourt Brace Jovanovich.

Melton, Heather. 1999. Police response to domestic violence. *Journal of Offender Rehabilitation* 29 (1/2):1–12.

Melvin, Tessa. 1983. Rape laws, "myths" assailed. *New York Times,* November 27.

Meyer, J.W., J. Boli, and G. M. Thomas. 1994. Ontology and rationalization in western cultural account. In *Institutional environments and organizations: Structural complexity and individualism.* Edited by W. R. Scott and J. W. Meyer. Thousand Oaks, CA: Sage Publications, 9–27.

Meyer, John, and Brian Rowan. 1977. Institutionalized organizations: Formal structure as myth and ceremony. *American Journal of Sociology* 83:340–63.

Meyerowitz, Joanne Jay. 1994. *Not June Cleaver: Women and gender in postwar America, 1945–1960.* Philadelphia: Temple University Press.

Michalowski, R. J. 2009. Social class, crime, and justice. In *Investigating difference: Human and cultural relations in criminal justice.* Edited by The Criminology & Criminal Justice Collective of Northern Arizona University. Upper Saddle River, NJ: Prentice Hall, 55–73.

Miller, Neal. 2002. *Stalking laws and implementation practices: A national review for policymakers and practitioners.* U.S. Department of Justice. Washington, D.C.

Mills, C. Wright. 1959/1976. *The sociological imagination.* New York: Oxford University Press.

Mills, C. Wright. 1959/2008. The promise. In *Rethinking society in the 21st century: Critical readings in sociology.* Edited by M. Webber. Toronto, Ontario: Canadians Scholars Press, Inc. Original edition, 1959, 16–19.

Moe, Angela M. 2010. A sheltered life: Observations on a domestic violence shelter. In *Female victims of crime: Reality reconsidered.* Edited by V. Garcia and J. E. Clifford. Upper Saddle River, NJ: Prentice Hall, 180–99.

Morash, Merry. 2006. *Understanding gender, crime, and justice.* Thousand Oaks, CA: Sage Publications.

Moylan, C., T. Herrenkohl, C. Sousa, E. Tajima, R. Herrenkohl, and M. Russo. 2010. The effects of child abuse and exposure to domestic violence on adolescent internalizing and externalizing behavior problems. *Journal of Family Violence* 25 (1):53–63.

Murphy, C. M., and V. A. Baxter. 1997. Motivating batterers to change in the treatment context. *Journal of Interpersonal Violence* 12:607–19.

Murphy, M., P. H. Musser, and K. I. Maton. 1998. Coordinated community intervention for domestic batterers: Interventions, system involvement, and criminal recidivisim. *Journal of Family Violence* 13:263–83.

Murray, Susan B. 1988. The unhappy marriage of theory and practice: An analysis of a battered women's shelter. *National Women's Studies Association Journal* 1 (1):75–92.

Naffine, Ngaire. 1987. *Female crime: The construction of women in criminology.* Sydney; Boston: Allen & Unwin.

National Center for State Courts. 2010. *Court Statistics Project.* National Center for State Courts 2006 [cited April 9 2010]. Available from www .ncsonline.org/D_Research/Ct_Struct/Index.html.

National Center for Victims of Crime. 2010. *Sexual Assault.* National center for Victims of Crime 2008 [cited March 2 2010]. Available from www.ncvc.org/ncvc/main.aspx?dbName=DocumentViewer&Documen tID=32369.

National Institute of Justice. 2010. *Stalking.* 2007 [cited January 2, 2010]. Available from www.ojp.usdoj.gov/nij/topics/crime/stalking/welcome .htm.

Neubauer, David W. 2005. *America's courts and the criminal justice system.* 8 ed. Belmont, CA: Wadsworth.

Office on Violence Against Women. 2010. *Facts about Violence Against Women Act.* 2000 [cited March 22 2010]. Available from www.ovw.usdoj .gov/ovw-fs.htm#fs-act.

Outlaw, Maureen. 2009. No one type of intimate partner abuse: Exploring physical and non-physical abuse among intimate partners. *Journal of Family Violence* 24 (4):263–72.

Pagelow, Mildred D. 1981. *Woman-battering: Victims and their experiences.* Beverly Hills, CA: Sage Publications.

Park, Lisa Sun-Hee. 2005. Navigating the anti-immigration wave: The Korean Women's Hotline and the politics of community. In *Domestic violence at the margins: Readings on race, class, gender and culture.* Edited by N. J. Sokoloff and C. Pratt. New Brunswick, NJ: Rutgers University Press, 350–68.

Pascale, Celine-Marie. 2001. All in a day's work: a feminist analysis of class formation and social identity. *Race, Gender & Class* 8 (2):34.

Pate, Anthony M., and Edwin E. Hamilton. 1992. Formal and informal deterrents to domestic violence: The Dade County spouse assault experiment. *American Sociological Review* 57 (5):691–97.

Pattavina, April, David Hirschel, Eve Buzawa, Don Faggiani, and Helen Bentley. 2007. A comparison of the police response to heterosexual versus same-sex intimate partner violence. *Violence Against Women* 13 (4):374–94.

Perry, Barbara. 2009. Perpetual outsiders: Criminal justice and the Asian American experience. In *Investigating difference: Human and cultural relations in criminal justice.* Edited by The Criminology & Criminal Justice Collective of Northern Arizona University. Upper Saddle River, NJ: Prentice Hall, 126–38.

Perry, Barbara, L. A. Fernandez, and M. Costelloe. 2009. Exclusion, inclusion, and violence: Immigrants and criminal justice. In *Investigating difference: Human and cultural relations in criminal justice.* Edited by The Criminology & Criminal Justice Collective of Northern Arizona University. Upper Saddle River, NJ: Prentice Hall, 88–101.

Peterson, Zoe D., and Charlene L. Muehlenhard. 2004. Was it rape? The function of women's rape myth acceptance and definitions of sex in labeling their own experiences. *Sex Roles* 51 (3/4):129–44.

Pincus, Fred. 2008. *Understanding diversity: An introduction to class, race, gender, and sexual orientation.* Boulder, CO: Lynne Rienner Publishers, Inc.

Pitts, Wayne, J., Eugena Givens, and Susan McNeeley. 2009. The need for a holistic approach to specialized domestic violence court programming:

Evaluating offender rehabilitation needs and recidivism. *Juvenile and Family Court Journal* 60 (3):1–21.

Postmus, Judy L. 2007. Challenging the negative assumptions surrounding civil protection orders: A guide for advocates. *Affilia: Journal of Women and Social Work* 22:347–56.

Potter, Hillary. 2010. "I don't think a cop has ever asked me if I was ok": Battered women's experience with police intervention. In *Female victims of crime: Reality reconsidered*, edited by V. Garcia and J. E. Clifford. Upper Saddle River, NJ: Prentice Hall, 219–420.

Pyles, Loretta. 2007. The complexities of the religious response to domestic violence: Implications for faith-based initiatives. *Affilia: Journal of Women and Social Work* 22 (3):281–91.

Rand, Michael R. 2009. *Criminal victimization, 2008*. Bureau of Justice Statistics. Washington, D.C.: U.S. Department of Justice.

Reiman, J. H. 1995. *The rich get richer and the poor get prison: Ideology, class, and criminal justice*. Hoboken, NJ: John Wiley.

Reinelt, Claire. 1995. Moving into the terrain of the state: The battered women's movement and the politics of engagement. In *Feminist organizations: Harvest on the new women's movement*. Edited by M. M. Ferree and P. Y. Martin. Philadelphia: Temple University Press.

Rennison, Callie Marie. 2002. *Rape and sexual assault: Reporting to police and medical attention, 1992–2000*. Bureau of Justice Statistics. Washington, D.C.: Office of Justice Programs.

Renzetti, Claire M. 1992. *Victim betrayal: Partner abuse in lesbian relationships*. Newbury Park, CA: Sage Publications.

———. 1997. Violence and abuse among same-sex couples. In *Violence between intimate partners*. Edited by A. P. Cardarelli. Boston, MA: Allyn & Bacon, 70–89.

Richie, Beth E. 1996. *Compelled to crime: The gender entrapment of black battered women*. New York: Routledge.

———. 2000. A black feminist reflection on the antiviolence movement. *Signs* 25 (4):1133–37.

Roberts, Albert R. 1988. Substance abuse among men who batter their mates. *Journal of Substance Abuse and Treatment* 5:83–87.

Robinson, Matthew B. 2009. *Justice blind? Ideals and realities of American criminal justice*. 3 ed. Upper Saddle River, NJ: Prentice Hall.

Rock, Paul. 2002. On becoming a victim. In *New visions of crime victims.*, Edited by C. Hoyle and R. Young. Portland, OR: Hart Publishing, 1–22.

Rosenblum, K. E., and T.-M. C. Travis. 1996. *The meaning of difference: American constructions of race, sex and gender, social class, and sexual orientation*. New York: McGraw-Hill.

Rosenburg, Tina. 1995. Fatal attraction. *New York Times*, December 10, 1995.

Ruben, Joseph. 1991. *Sleeping with the enemy*. [Movie]

Russell, B. L., and L. S. Melillo. 2006. Attitudes toward battered women who kill: Defendant typicality and judgment culpability. *Criminal Justice and Behavior* 33:219–41.

Ryan, W. 1976. *Blaming the victim*. New York: Vintage Books.

Sack, Emily. 2002. *Creating a domestic violence court: Guidelines and best practices*. San Francisco: Family Violence Prevention Fund.

Schechter, Susan. 1982. *Women and male violence: The visions and struggles of the Battered Women's Movement*. Boston: South End Press.

Schenone, Laura 2003. *A thousand years over a hot stove: A history of American women told through food, recipes and remembrances*. New York: W. W. Norton & Co.

Schetcher, Susan. 1982. *Women and male violence: The visions and struggles of the battered women's movement*. Cambridge, MA: South End Press.

Schneider, Elizabeth M. 2000. *Battered women and feminist lawmaking*. New Haven, CT: Yale University Press.

Schram, Pamela J., and Barbara Koons-Witt. 2004. *Gendered (in)justice: Theory and practice in feminist criminology*. Long Grove, IL.: Waveland Press.

Schuller, Regina A. 1992. The impact of battered woman syndrome evidence on jury decision processes. *Law and Human Behavior* 16 (6):597–620.

Scott, Ridley. 1991. *Thelma and Louise*. [Movie].

Sherman, L. W., and R. A. Berk. 1984. The specific deterrent effects of arrest for domestic assault. *American Sociological Review* 49 (2):261–72.

Sherman, Lawrence. 1992. *Policing domestic violence: Experiments and dilemmas*. New York: Free Press.

Sigler, R., and C. Shook. 1997. Judicial acceptance of battered women's syndrome. *Criminal Justice Policy Review* 8 (497):365–82.

Smith, Brian J. 2009. The significance of race: African Americans and criminal justice. In *Investigating difference: Human and cultural relations in criminal justice*. Edited by The Criminology & Criminal Justice Collective of Northern Arizona University. Upper Saddle River, NJ: Prentice Hall, 102–13.

Sokoloff, Natalie J., and Christina Pratt, eds. 2005. *Domestic violence at the margins: Readings on race, class, gender, and culture*. New Brunswick, NJ: Rutgers University Press.

Stark, Evan. 1993. Mandatory arrest of batterers: A reply to critics. *American Behavioral Scientist* 36 (5):651–79.

———. 2007. *Coercive control: How men entrap women in personal life.* New York: Oxford University Press.

Straus, M. A. 1979. Measuring intrafamily conflict and violence: The Conflict Tactics (CT) Scales. *Journal of Marriage and Family* 41 (1):75–88.

———. 1990. *Physical violence in American families.* New Brunswick, NJ: Transaction Publishers.

Straus, M. A., and R. J. Gelles. 1986. Societal change and change in family violence from 1975 to 1985 as revealed by two national surveys. *Journal of Marriage and the Family* 48 (3):465–79.

Sullivan, Cris M. 1997. Societal collusion and culpability in intimate male violence: The impact on community response toward women with abusive partners. In *Violence between intimate partners: Patterns, causes, and effects.* Edited by A. P. Cardarelli. Boston: Allyn & Bacon, 154–64.

Surette, R. 1998. *Media, crime and criminal justice: Images and realities.* Belmont, CA: Wadsworth.

Tjaden, Patricia, and Nancy Thoennes. 1998. *Stalking in America: Findings from the National Violence Against Women Survey.* Centers for Disease Control and Prevention, National Institute of Justice. Washington, D.C.: U.S. Department of Justice.

———. 2000. *Extent, nature and consequences of intimate partner violence: Findings from the national violence against women survey.* Washington, D.C.: National Institute of Justice.

Tolman, R., and L. Bennett. 1992. *Intervention for men who batter: An ecological approach.* Newbury Park, CA: Sage Publications.

Trujillo, Olga R., and Gretchen Test. *Funding the work: Community efforts to end domestic violence and child abuse.* American Public Human Services Association 2005. Available from www.thegreenbook.info/documents/fundingstreams.pdf.

U.S. Attorney General. 1999. *Cyberstalking: A new challenge for law enforcement and industry.* Washington, D.C.: Department of Justice.

van Wormer, Katherine Stuart, and Clemens Bartollas. 2007. *Women and the criminal justice system.* Boston, MA: Allyn & Bacon.

Ventura, Lois A., and Gabrielle Davis. 2005. Domestic violence: Court case conviction and recidivism. *Violence Against Women* 11 (2):255–77.

Vyas, Pami. 2006. Reconceptualizing domestic violence in India: Economic abuse and the need for broad statutory interpretation to promote women's fundamental rights. *Michigan Journal of Gender & Law* 13 (1):177–206.

Walker, Lenore E. 1977. Who are the battered women? *Frontiers: A Journal of Women Studies* 2 (1):52–57.

———. 1978. Battered women and learned helplessness. *Victimology* 2 (3–4):525–34.

———. 1989. *Terrifying love: Why battered women kill and how society responds.* New York, NY: HarperCollins Publishers.

———. 2000. *The battered woman syndrome.* New York: Springer Publishing Company.

———. 2001. The battered women syndrome is a psychological consequence of abuse. In *Battered women and the law.* Edited by C. Dalton and E. M. Schneider. New York: Foundation Press, 117–22.

Wallace, Harvey. 1999. *Family violence: Legal, medical, and social perspectives.* Boston: Allyn & Bacon.

Weiss, Karen G. 2009. "Boys will be boys" and other gendered accounts: An exploration of victims' excuses and justifications for unwanted sexual contact and coercion. *Violence Against Women* 15 (7):810–34.

West, Angelique, and Mary L. Wandrei. 2002. Intimate partner violence: A model for predicting interventions by informal helpers. *Journal of Interpersonal Violence* 17 (9):972–86.

West, C., and S. Fenstermaker. 1993. Power, inequality, and the accomplishment of gender: An ethnomethodological view. In *Theory on gender/feminism on theory.* Edited by P. England. New York: Aldine, 151–74.

West, Carolyn M. 2005. Domestic violence in ethnically and racially diverse families. In *Domestic violence at the margins: Readings on race, class, gender and culture.* Edited by N. J. Sokoloff and C. Pratt. New Brunswick, NJ: Rutgers University Press, 157–73.

White, Robert J., and Edward W. Gondolf. 2000. Implications of personality profiles for battered treatment. *Journal of Interpersonal Violence* 15 (5):467–88.

Widom, Cathy Spatz. 1989. The cycle of violence. *Science* 244:160–66.

Winick, B. J. 2000. Applying the law therapeutically in domestic violence cases. *University of Missouri at Kansas City Law Review* 69:33.

Winter, J. 2002. The trial of Rose West: Contesting notions of victimhood. In *New visions of crime victims.* Edited by C. Hoyle and R. Young. Portland, OR: Hart Publishing, 173–96.

Wolf, Marsha E., Uyen Ly, Margaret A. Hobart, and Mary A. Kernic. 2003. Barriers to seeking police help for intimate partner violence. *Journal of Family Violence* 18 (2):121–29.

Wolfgang, Marvin E. 1958. *Patterns in criminal homicide*. Philadelphia: University of Pennsylvania Press.

Wolfgang, Marvin E., and F. Ferracuti. 1967. *The subculture of violence: Towards an integrated theory in criminology*. London: Tavistock.

Wolfgang, Marvin E., and F. Ferracuti. 1982. *The subculture of violence*. 2 ed. London: Tavistock.

Yamawaki, Niwako, Joseph Ostenson, and C. Ryan Brown. 2009. The functions of gender role traditionality, ambivalent sexism, injury, and frequency of assault on domest violence perception. *Violence Against Women* 15 (9):1126–42.

Yellin, Emily. 2004. *Our mother's war: American women at home and at the front during World War II*. New York: Free Press.

Young, Vernetta D. 1986. Gender expectations and their impact on black female offenders and victims. *Justice Quarterly* 3:305–27.

LEGAL CASES

Bradley v. State. 1824. 1 Miss. 156.

Bradwell v. Illinois. 1872. 83 U.S. 130.

Commonwealth v. Fogerty. 1857. 74 Mass. (8 Gray) 489, 491.

Crawford v. Washington. 2004. 541 U.S. 36.

Frazier v. State. 1905. 86 S.W. 754 Tex. Crim. App.

Fulgham v. State. 1871. 46 Ala. 143.

Harris v. State. 1894. 71 Miss. 462.

Leser v. Garnett. 1922. 258 U.S. 130.

Lopez-Umanzor v. Gonzales. 2005. In *405 F. 3d 1049, 05 Cal. Daily Op. Serv.* 3798: United States Court of Appeals for the Ninth Circuit.

Navarro v. Block. 1995. In *72 F.3d 712,* : 9th Cir.

People v. Liberta. 1984. 64 N.Y.2d 152.

People v. Moscat. 2004. 777 N.Y.S. 2d 875, N.Y. Crim. Ct.

State v. Barnes. 1996. 680 A. 2d. 449, Me.

State v. Dowell. 1890. 106 N.C. 722, 11 S.E. 525.

State v. Oliver. 1879. In *70 N.C. 60, 61-62*.

State v. Sims. 1995. 890 P.2d 521, Wash.

Thurman v. City of Torrington. 1984. In *595 F.Supp 1521 (D.Conn. 1984)*.

United States v. Morrison. 2000. 529 U.S. 598.

INDEX

Abbott, P., 46
Acker, J., 8, 10, 46, 55
Adams, B., 35–37
Agger, B., 45–46
Aid to Families with Dependent
  Children (AFDC), 36
agency, 4, 39, 44, 49, 128, 137, 148,
  162, 170, 174, 190, 195
alcohol use and abuse:
arrests and, 100; murder of victims
  and, 125; offenders and, 37;
  posttraumatic stress disorder
  (PTSD) and, 129; precipitative
  victims and, 51; victims and, 104
Alexander, A., 134–35
Allen, H., 51
Alpert, A., 24
Altheide, D. L., 16
Alverez, A., 13
ambivalent sexism, 59
American legal history, 69–72
American Psychiatric Association,
  129
Amir, M., 52–53

ancient legal tradition, 66
Anderson, E., 51
Anderson, M., 81–83
anti-rape movement, 22, 24,
  162–63
anti-stalking legislation, 24, 30–31,
  80, 107
Archer, J., 156
Archives of Family Medicine, 20,
  25–26, 54
arrest, 23, 29, 41;
accountability and, 98;
age and, 36–37; crime type and, 61;
  deterrence and, 41, 75, 92, 94–
  99, 145, 188; discretion and, 106;
  dual arrest, 41, 58, 61, 99–102,
  106, 156, 175, 179; female perpetrators and, 155–59; mandatory arrest policies and, 41, 61,
  74–75, 89–90, 93–102, 106, 115,
  155, 186–87; myths and, 18, 23,
  61, 92, 185; presumptive arrest
  policies and, 61, 95–96; politics
  and, 188; pro-arrest policies and,

61, 75, 78, 95, 97–98, 187; probation and, 147, 149; race and, 36,
42, 99–100, 155; same-sex partners and, 101–2; statistics and,
36, 61, 112, 149; victim desires
and, 187, 195; victim/offender relationship and, 37; victim-police
encounter and, 103–4; warrant-
less arrests and, 31, 90, 96
Aubrey, M., 127–28
Augustine, Aurelius, 21–22

backlash, 41, 56, 60, 90, 99, 159,
168
Barden, J. C., 56, 60
Barsky, H., 5
Bartollas, C., 63
Bassuk, S., 36, 41–42
Batten, E., 122
batterer treatment: benefits of,
146; compliance of, 146–47;
court mandated, 141, 144,
145–46; Deluth Model and,
143; effectiveness of, 144–47;
feminist models of, 142–44;
race and, 144–45; therapeutic
jurisprudence and, 145; victim
blaming and, 142
batterer typologies, 38–39, 57–58,
141, 184
battered woman syndrome, 39–40,
48, 58, 62, 76, 111, 125–32, 137,
162, 185, 190
battered women's movement, 22,
24, 41, 61, 74–75, 110, 162–63,
170, 175, 178
Bauman, B., 114
Baxter, V. A., 144
Bradley v. State, 3, 70

Bradwell v. Illinois, 71
Belknap, J., 2, 8, 10, 13, 15, 17,
23–24, 27, 29, 32, 37, 40–41, 56,
58–59, 61–62, 71, 99, 111–12,
114–15, 118, 121–23, 134, 140,
155–56, 162, 182
Belknap, R. A., 39, 40, 58, 162
Bennett, L., 115, 126
Bennice, J. A., 29
Bentley, H., 102
Berger, P. L., 8–9, 16, 18
Berk R. A., 41, 75, 90–91, 95–96,
188
Blumberg, M., 54
Boli, J., 16
Bonczar, T. P., 149
Boston Public Health Commission,
3, 5
Botec Analysis Corporation, 112,
121
Boyd-Jackson, S., 26
Brown, Chris, 5
Brown, C. R., 59
Brown, J. D. 2, 9
Browne, A., 36, 41–42
Bureau of Criminal Information
and Analysis, 156
Bureau of Justice Statistics, 156,
197
Bureau of Labor Statistics, 15, 197
Buttell, F. P., 145
Buzawa, C. G., 22, 37, 40, 42, 62,
90–92, 112–14
Buzawa, E. S., 22, 37, 40, 42, 56, 62,
90–92, 102, 112–14
Byrne, J., 56

Cadsky, O., 144
Campbell, J. C., 39–40, 58, 162

Canales-Portalatin, D., 140–41, 147
Canter, R., 155
Cardwell, M. M., 39–40, 58, 162
Carney, M. M., 145
Cartier, Michael, 149–50
Casa de las Madres, 176, 197
Catalano, S., 1, 24, 26, 35, 61
Centers for Disease Prevention and
    Control, 26–27
Chambliss, W. J., 17
Chermack, S., 59
Chesney-Lind, M., 61, 98–100,
    155–56
Christian doctrine, 53, 55, 59,
    67–68
Clear, T., 141
Clemmer, E., 91
Code of Hammurabi, 65–66
Coker, D., 176
Cole, G., 141
Colson, S., 124
Commonwealth v. Fogerty, 70
Comstock, G. D., 101
Conflict Tactic Scale (CTS), 41
Connor, T., 60
consent, 2, 69, 75–76, 80–83
consent decree, 110
corrections response: abuse by
    officers, 157; implications of,
    192–94; jail and, 62, 152; myths
    and, 63; prison and, 62, 152;
    statistics and, 152; treatment
    and, 62–63
Costelloe, M., 13, 17
costs of victimization, 27
Coulter, M., 134–35
CourtTV, 60
Craig, A. W., 56
Craven, D., 149

Crawford v. Washington, 116, 118
Crawford, M., 144
Crime Bill, 77–78, 120
criminalization of victims, 140–41,
    154–58; dual arrest and, 155–57;
    mandatory arrest and, 155; race
    and, 155
Crowe, A. H., 148–49
cult of domesticity/ true woman-
    hood, 12, 16
cultural defects theory, 13
Curtis, L., 51
cyberstalking, 30
cycle of violence, 39, 40, 76–77,
    130–31, 195. See also Walker, L.

Dantzker, M. L., 50
date rape, 24 28–29, 52, 56–57, 60
Davis, C., 122–23, 190
Davis, G., 141, 192
Davis, R., 144
deconstruction, 6, 42, 45–63
DeKeseredy, W. S., 22–23, 111, 184
deliberate indifference, 20
Della Giustina, J., 13, 43
DeMichele, M., 148–49
Denard, S., 133–34
Denaro, S., 133–34
Derridean method, 46
deserving victim: defined, 3, 111;
    constructs and, 16, 93; media
    and, 48–49, 60
discrimination, 6, 8, 89, 99–100,
    104
disempower, 190, 194–96
divorce rights, 67
Dobash, R., 173
Dobash, R. E., 173
doing culture, 46, 63

doing gender, 10, 46, 55
Domestic Abuse Intervention Program, 32, 143
domestic cages, 14, 162
domestic violence courts: court reform and, 62, 111; models of, 133–36; purpose of, 76; therapeutic jurisprudence and, 145–46; victim satisfaction and, 136
Donovan, B., 28–29, 80
Doob, C. B., 13
Dragiewicz, M., 184
drugs: arrests and, 100; criminalization of victimization and, 157; divorce and, 67; murder of victims, 125; offenders and, 37; posttraumatic stress disorder (PTSD) and, 129; precipitative victims and, 51; victims and police encounters and, 104
Dugan, L., 98
Duluth Model: Equality Wheel and, 32–34, 143; Power and Control Wheel and, 32–33, 143
Durfee, A., 121, 124
Durose, M. R., 152
Dutton, M. A., 115

Easy Access to NIBRS: Victims of Domestic Violence, 35, 197
economic abuse, 25, 31–32, 174, 181, 183
Efkeman, H., 122–23, 133–34, 190
Eigenberg, H., 47, 50
Elbow, M., 53, 142
electronic monitoring, 150–52, 193
Elliott, B. A., 42
empowerment: arrest and, 187–88; courts and, 134; orders of

protection and, 122, 124, 190; shelters and, 170–71, 173–74
English common law, 66, 68–69
Ephesians 5, 67
Equal Employment Opportunity Act of 1972, 15
equal protection, 20, 75–76, 89, 94, 99
Erez, E., 24, 122, 134, 150–52, 192–93
essentialism, 9
Ewing, C. P., 127–28
excited utterance, 116–17, 189

Fagan, J. A., 77, 92, 98, 122, 134–35
Faggiani, D., 102
family ideal, 72
Faulk, M., 53, 142
fear of retaliation, 96–97
Feder, L., 144
Federal Bureau of Investigation (FBI), 1, 35–36, 91
Feinman, C., 55
Felson, R., 114
femicide, 43
feminist movement, 8, 22, 94, 175; second-wave and, 22, 167–68; third-wave and, 168, 174
feminist theory, 10, 42–44
Fenstermaker Berk, S., 10, 90–91
Fernandez, L. A., 13, 17
Ferracuti, F., 42, 51, 54
financial abuse. See also economic abuse
Finkel, N., 127
Finn, P., 124
Fisher, E., 39, 58, 123–24, 173
Flango, C., 122–23, 190
Forde, D., 144

Fourteenth Amendment, 79, 89, 94.
 See also equal protection
Fowler, G., 23
Fox, J. A., 149
Foy, D., 129
Frazier v. State, 71
French law, 68
Fry, M. S., 27–28
Frye, V., 100
Fulgham v. State, 4, 71
Furedi, F., 16

Garbin, C., 125–27, 129, 190
Garcia, V., 8–10, 12, 16–17, 26, 37,
 46, 53, 56, 59–60, 91–92, 119,
 123, 134, 195
Garner, J., 91, 98
Garland, T., 50
Gaynor, M., 60
Gelles, R. J., 2, 40–41, 63
gender discrimination, 104. *See also*
 equal protection
gender ideologies, 2, 7–8, 13, 19
gender neutral, 8
gender role expectations, 3, 10, 15,
 55, 59, 100
gender specific, 7–8
gendered justice, 4–8
gendered victimization, 1, 27
Gerstendfeld, P. B., 13, 84
Gist, J., 122
Givens, E., 146
Glaze, L. E., 149, 157
Global Positioning System (GPS),
 151–52
Gondolf, E. W., 39, 57–58, 63, 141,
 145–46, 173
Gonzalez, J., 153
Goodman, L., 115

Gosselin, D., 68–70, 72, 74
Graber, D., 60
Grady, A., 2
Graham, D., 118
Grau, J., 122
Greene, J., 157
Greenfeld, L. A., 149
Greenwald, R., 130
Grossberg, L., 8, 10
Guerrero, R., 133–34
Gun Control Act, 78

Hall, I., 122
Hamilton, E. E., 95–96
Hannaford, P. L., 122–23, 190
Hansen, M., 142, 192
Hansford, V., 133–34
Hanson, R. K., 144
Harlow, C. W., 152
Harrell, A., 123–24
Harris v. State, 71
Harrison, V., 134–35
Hart, B., 123–24
Hartman, J. L., 23, 61, 112, 114
Harway, M., 142, 192
Hassouneh-Phillips, D. S., 176
hate crime, 83–85
Haviland, M., 100
Hawkesworth, M. E., 21
hegemonic ideology, 6–7, 12, 109
Henning, K., 101
Herrenkohl, R., 42
Herrenkohl, T., 42
hierarchies, 11
Hilbert, J. C., 173–74
Hirschel, D., 61, 102–3, 186
Hobart, M. A., 103
Hockett, J. M., 56
Hoffman, B. H., 56

Holdford, R., 101
Holt, V. L., 121–23, 187
Holtzworth-Munroe, A., 38, 57, 63, 141
homeless victims, 36, 41
Horne, C. F., 66
Horsburgh, B., 176
Hotaling, G. T., 56
House of Ruth, 167, 198
Houskamp, B., 129
Hughes, Francine, 76, 110, 130–31
Hunter, R. D., 50
husbands' rights, 75–76, 90; conjugal rights and, 24; right to chastise and, 181
Huss, M., 125–27, 129, 190
Hust, S. J., 2, 9
Hutchison, I. W., 103, 186
hypermasculine men, 43, 59

Ibarra, P. R., 150–52, 192–93
ideal victim, 2, 54–55, 58, 60, 81, 93, 109, 128, 182, 186; jury and, 62; race/ethnicity and, 17; rape and, 182; sexual orientation and, 17; shared responsibility and, 17
ideal woman, 72
ideology: age and, 7; anti-immigration and, 13, 175–78; crime control and, 139–40, 192–94; class and, 13; defined, 6–7; family and, 19, 21, 24, 72; feminist and, 140, 164–67, 170, 175; gender and, 2, 7–8, 11–12, 15, 19–21, 24, 42, 46, 51, 59; patriarchy and, 63; punishment and, 84, 139, 194; race/ethnic and, 7, 13; religious and, 7, 20, 65; sexist and, 59; shelters of,

162–68, 171, 174; social and, 65; structure and, 46; Victorian and, 14; victim blaming and, 47, 49, 51–52, 59, 136, 185; work and, 7
Immigration and Nationality Act, 177
inequality: gender, 5–6, 15, 43, 66, 94, 165; economic, 43, 165; racial, 43
innocent victims, 16–17, 51, 53–54
institutionalization, 16–17, 19, 45, 133–34, 179
International Association of Chiefs of Police (IACP), 91
intersections/intersectionality, 7, 11–17, 43–44, 52, 55, 62, 165–68, 181
intimate partner violence: criminalization of victims and, 140; historical perspective of, 3–5; spousal abuse and, 4; statistics of, 1–2

Jaggar, A. M., 164–65
Jaros, D., 116–17, 189–90
Jhally, S., 60
Johnson, I., 103–4
Johnson, J., 121–22, 124
Johnson, M., 42
Jones, A. M., 133–34
Josephson, J., 36, 41
judicial response: implications of, 189–92; lack of expertise and, 119; misdemeanor offenses and, 118–19
jury decisions: battered woman syndrome and, 62, 126–29; date rape and, 29; defendant typical-

ity and, 127; expert testimony and, 127
just world hypothesis, 47, 49–50, 55

Kang, W., 35–37
Kappeler, V. E., 54
Karan, A., 133–34
Karmen, A., 17, 23–24, 26–27, 29, 47, 49, 114
Keilib, S., 133–34
Keilitz, S., 122–23, 133–34, 190
Keitner, C. I., 10, 17, 55
Kernic, M. A., 103, 121–23, 187
Kilian, A., 125–127, 129, 190
Klein, A., 56, 58, 62–63, 89, 96, 101, 105, 110, 113–14, 117–18, 141–44, 148–49, 152–53
Klaus, P. A., 149
Koons-Witt, B., 40, 162
Krishnan, S. P., 173–74
Kukkonen, K., 9

L'Engle, K., 2, 9
Lalonde, C., 144
Lane, S., 172
Langan, P. A., 152
Larder, Kristen, 149–50
Laurie, N. A., 150–52
Law Enforcement Assistance Administration (LEAA), 94–95
laws of chastisement, 66–67, 71
learned helplessness, 39–40, 48, 58, 76, 128, 137, 162
Lee, M. Y., 144
Lefkowski, M. R., 67
legal reform, 4–6, 72–73, 76, 78–80
Lemon, N., 67
Leonard, E., 5
Leser v. Garnett, 72

Leukefeld, C. G., 42
Lilith, R., 93
Lippen, V., 23, 61, 112, 114, 118
Locke, John, 21–22
Logan, T. K., 42
Long, C., 153
Lopez-Umanzor v. Gonzales, 177–78
Loseke, D. R., 9, 18, 90–91
Luckmann, T., 8–9, 16, 18
Lumley, T., 121–23, 187
Luna, Y., 121–22, 124
Lyon, E., 172

MacLeod, L., 22–23
male domination, 22, 66, 171
male entitlement, 43, 52–53, 59, 82, 164–65, 178
Malecha, A., 29, 122, 182
Mann, C., 131
marital rape, 24; English common law and, 69; legal reform and, 28–29, 56–57, 74–76, 83; social constructs and, 50, 52, 60
Marsali, H., 8, 10
Marsh, I., 60
Martin, D., 23, 68–70, 74
Martin, M. E., 112
Mason, M. A., 12, 14
master status, 2, 10, 11
Maston, C., 149
Maton, K. I., 147
Maureen B. F., 67
Maxwell, C., 98, 144
McFadden, R. D. 60
McFarlane, J., 29, 122, 182
McManimon, P., 127, 131
McNeeley, S., 146
McNeil, K., 173–74
McNulty, F., 130

McWilliams, J., 123–24
media: celebrity cases and, 5, 24, 153; images of intimate partner violence and, 59–60;
myths and, 56; social constructs of women and, 14; victim blaming and, 50
Melillo, L. S., 125, 128
Melton, H., 90, 94–96
Melvin, T., 57
Menard A., 172
Messner, S., 114
Meyer, J. W., 16, 133
Meyerowitz, J. J., 14
Michalowski, R. J., 13
Miller, N., 30
Miller, P., 39–40, 58, 162
Mills, C. W., 22
Minneapolis Domestic Violence Experiment, 75, 95–100, 112
Moe, A. M., 171, 173
Morash, M., 24, 42–43, 59, 167
Motivans, M., 152
Moylan, C., 42
Muehlenhard, C. L., 182
multiple marginality, 11, 13, 44, 175
Murphy, C. M., 144
Murphy, M., 147
Murray, S. B., 22
Musser, P. H., 147
mutual combat, 2, 58; arrests and, 90, 100, 106; defined, 41; myth and, 183
myths: aggressive woman/man out of control and, 57–58, 61, 183; cultural and, 4, 46, 59–60; ideal rape and, 60; ideal victims and, 48, 54–55, 58, 63; male entitlement and, 59; manipulative/

nagging woman and, 55–56, 62, 123; masochistic woman and, 39, 56–57, 127, 142; mentally unstable/crazy woman and, 32, 58, 62, 128, 137, 184–85

Naffine, N., 8
naming violence against women, 22–25, 55, 181, 183
National Center for Crime Victims, 27, 198
National Center for Education Statistics, 15
National Center for State Courts, 119
National Coalition Against Domestic Violence, 23–24
National Counseling of Juvenile and Family Court Judges, 100
National Crime Victimization Survey (NCVS), 28, 31, 33, 61, 98, 145
National Incident-Based Reporting Center, 35–36
National Institute of Justice, 29–31, 34, 95, 198
National Youth Survey, 155
Navarro v. Block, 20, 26, 105
Navarro, Maria, 20, 26, 44
Neubauer, D. W., 114, 119, 148
New York seduction laws, 28
Newman, I., 173–74
Nineteenth Amendment, 14, 72
noninterference policy, 72, 74, 89
normative ambiguity, 26
normative assumptions, 66, 91, 141–42

Office of Domestic Violence, 74
Office of Juvenile Justice and Delinquency Prevention (OJJDP), 155

Office on Violence Against Women, 80, 169, 198

oppression: economic and, 43–44, 49; gender and, 20, 42–44, 49, 73, 94, 164–68, 181, 195; racial/ethnic, 43–44, 49; sexual orientation and, 43–44, 49; structural, 41, 47, 165; civil remedies and, 120, 136, 186; criminal recourse and, 136; effectiveness of, 122; enforcement of, 110, 122, 191; judicial resistance of, 121; myths and, 62, 119, 122–23; possession of firearms and, 79, 120; probation and, 193; provisions of, 76–77; purpose of, 120–24; service of, 121–22, 124; shelter victims and, 172; statistics and, 121, 152; victim blaming and, 136; victim requests and, 110, 137, 187; violations of, 78–79, 96, 150, 153. *See also* inequality orders of protection

Ostenson, J., 59

Outlaw, M., 31–34, 40, 162

Pagelow, M. D., 39, 58

paid labor. *See also* workforce

Park, L. S., 175

Pascale, C., 12

Pate, A. M., 95–96

patriarchy, 5–8, 11, 21–22, 42–43, 59, 63, 66–70, 140–42, 157, 162–65, 175

Pattavina, A., 102

People v. Liberta, 69, 75–76

People v. Moscat, 117–18

Perkins, C. A., 149

Perry, B., 13, 17

Peterson, Z. D., 182

physical violence, 20, 25–27, 31–32, 34, 126, 143, 181

Pincus, F., 6, 13, 15

Pitts, W. J., 146

police response: classic response and, 90–95; do nothing response and, 60–61, 90–92; ideal/deserving victim and, 93; implications of, 185–89; myths and, 60; police deaths and, 91; primary aggressor laws and, 100–1, 114, 193; promotional policy and, 92; race and, 103–4; real police work and, 90; reform and, 94–95; same-sex violence and, 93; training and, 104–5; victim encounter and, 102–4; zero-tolerance policy and, 99. *See also* arrest

Postmus, J. L., 56, 62, 123

posttraumatic stress disorder (PTSD): alcohol and substance abuse and, 129; cycle of violence and, 76; DSM-III-R and, 39–40; judicial acceptance and, 111, 131–32, 190, 192; rejection of, 162; self defense and, 130–32; social constructs and, 58

Potter, G. W., 54

Potter, H., 17, 54, 61, 97, 99, 103–4, 114, 188

power and control, 5, 27, 30, 32, 42–43, 142–44, 153, 178

Pranis, K., 157

Pratt, C., 44

prescribed gender roles, 10, 59, 100

private issue/trouble: corrections and, 63; defined, 19; family vio-

lence and, 20–23; implications
of, 187, 195; legal jurisprudence
and, 73;
policing and, 61, 87, 90–93, 97;
prosecution and courts and, 62,
112, 117; shelter movement and,
162–63; social and behavioral
sciences and, 184
probation, 140–41, 143; effectiveness of, 159–50; specialized
caseloads and, 147–48; statistics
of, 149
prosecution: cost and, 118; credibility of victim and, 114; domestic
violence prosecution unit, 77;
evidence-based prosecution, 77,
116–18, 136, 189, 190; felony
charges and, 112; implications of,
189–92; mandatory prosecution
policies and, 113; misdemeanor
charges and, 112; no-drop policies and, 61, 113, 115–18, 136,
161, 189–91; race and, 62; victim
cooperation and, 114–15; victim
obstacles and, 115
psychological abuse, 20, 32–35,
58–59, 111, 122, 170, 184, 190,
195
psychological coercion, 28
psychological counseling, 30, 133,
162, 172
psychological perspectives, 38–40, 57
punishment, 139–40
Puritan law, 69–70
Puzzanchera, C., 35–37
Pyles, L., 59

race: disproportionately and,
97–99; offenders and, 36;

recidivism and, 98–99; request
police service and, 97; victims
and, 35
Rajah, V., 100
Rand, M. R., 1, 24, 26, 28, 35, 61,
82, 149
Rantala, R., 152
rape. *See also* sexual assault/victim-
ization
rape laws, 26–29; corroboration
and, 28, 57, 116; exemptions
and, 29, 76, 82; rape shield law,
29, 80–83; reform and, 56, 60,
71; resistance test, 2, 28, 57
Rauma, D., 90–91
real victims, 16
rehabilitation, 140
Reiman, J. H., 17
Reinelt, C., 168
Reisig, M., 141
Renauer, B., 101
Rennison, C. M., 28
Renzetti, C. M., 93, 175
Resick, P. A., 29
restraining orders. *See also* orders
of protection
Rhianna, 5
Richie, B. E., 44, 181
Ringel, C., 149
Rivara, F. P., 121–23, 187
Roberts, A. R., 37
Robinson, M. B., 109
Rock, P., 16
Roman Empire, 66–67
Rosenblum, K. E., 10
Rosenburg, T., 149
Rowan, B., 133
Ruben, J., 48
Rubio, D. M., 133–34

rule of immunity, 71
rule of thumb, 3–4, 67–69
Russell, B. L., 125, 128
Russian laws, 68
Russo, M., 42
Ryan, W., 49

Sack, E., 133, 145
same-sex intimate partner violence,
    25, 83, 93–94, 101–2, 106, 179
Saucier, D. A., 56
Schechter, S., 23, 142, 170
Schenone, L., 12
Schneider, E. M., 163
Schopp, R., 125–27, 129, 190
Schram, P. J., 40, 162
Schuller, R. A., 127
Schwartz, M., 111
Scott, R., 48
Sebold, J., 144
self blaming, 182–83
self defense, 101, 111. *See also* bat-
    tered woman syndrome
sentencing batterers, 141–54
separate spheres ideology, 11;
    private sphere and, 7, 11, 14,
    42–43, 97; public sphere and, 7,
    11, 15, 42–43
sexual assault/victimization, 1, 2,
    27–29, 182–83; chastity and, 21,
    29, 80–82
sexuality, 10, 16, n199
shared responsibility, 47, 51, 54,
    185
shelters: acculturation and, 176–78;
    children and, 172, 179; diverse
    communities and, 174–78;
    feminist ideologies and, 164–66;
    financial backing and, 166–70;

immigrants and, 175–78; male
    victims and, 178–79; organizing
    ideologies and, 164–65; over-
    crowding of, 164; race and, 176;
    religion and, 176; respite and,
    173–74; services and, 171–74;
    types of, 166–68
shelter movement, 22, 161–80;
    consciousness-raising and, 163,
    170; defined, 162–63; history of,
    162–66
Sherman, L. W., 41, 75, 95–96, 188
Shook, C., 132
Sigler, R., 132
Sir Francis Buller, 3, 69
Sixth Amendment, 116, 189
Smith, B. E., 123–24
Smith, B. J., 13, 17
Smith, E., 1, 24, 26, 35, 61, 152
Smith, S., 122
Smith, S. J., 56
Snyder, H., 1, 24, 26, 35, 61
social construction: arrests and,
    23, 29; categorization and, 9,
    17; consequences of, 183–85;
    defined, 8–9; *doing* and, 8–11,
    37–44; economic abuse and,
    31–32; female victims and, 2;
    feminism and, 42–44, 97; gender
    and, 4, 199; husbands rights and,
    3–4, 75; ideal type and, 26–27,
    42, 48, 110–11, 119, 123, 186–89;
    ideal woman and, 72; *making*
    and, 8–10; manhood and, 13;
    norms and, 9–10; *other* and,
    10–11; physical violence and,
    25–26; psychology and, 38–40;
    psychological abuse and, 32–35;
    sexual violence and, 2, 27–29;

sociology and, 40–42; stalking and, 30; victimhood and, 16–17, 19–20, 29, 51, 54, 60; womanhood and, 11–16
sociological imagination, 22, 46
sociological perspectives, 40–42; exchange/social control theory and, 40–41, 63; family-oriented approach and, 40–41; intergenerational transmission of violence and, 42, 179; sociocultural theories and, 41; structural–functional paradigm and, 40–41, 46; subculture of violence and, 41, 51. *See also* Widom, C. S.
Sokoloff, N. J., 44
Sousa, C., 42
stalking, 24, 29–31
Stark, E., 97, 171, 173–74
State v. Barnes, 116
State v. Dowell, 71
State v. Oliver, 4, 71
State v. Sims, 116
statistics: alcohol use and abuse and, 37; drugs and, 37; economic abuse and, 31; offenders and, 36–37; officer death and, 91; physical violence and, 26; psychological violence and, 34; sexual violence and, 28–29; stalking and, 30; victims and, 1–2, 26–27, 35–36; women in paid labor and, 15
Stein, J., 121–22, 124
Straus, M. A., 2, 41, 58
Stuart, G. L., 38, 57, 63, 141
Stuehling, J., 123–24
Sullivan, C. M., 161–62, 175

Surette, R., 9, 60
Sutherland, J., 118

Tajima, E., 42
Taylor, B., 144
Tertullian, Septimius Florens, 20–22
Test, G., 168
text, 45–46
therapeutic jurisprudence, 133, 145
Thoennes, N., 29–30, 121, 124
Thomas, G. M., 16
Thurman v. City of Torrington, 26, 74, 88
Thurman, Tracy, 26, 74–75, 88–89, 106, 121
Title IV, 15
Tjaden, P., 29–30, 121, 124
Tolman, R., 126
Tomkins, A., 125–27, 129, 190
Travis, T., 10
Trujillo, O. R., 168
typification, 9, 16

Uken, A., 144
unacknowledged rape victim, 182–83
undeserving: defined, 60; media and, 48–49; social constructs and, 174
Uniform Crime Reports (UCR), 61, 155
United States Attorney General, 30
United States v. Morrison, 79, 80
Uyen L., 103

van Wormer, K. S., 63
Ventura, L. A., 141, 192
victim assistance programs, 77

victim blaming: deconstruction and, 46; shared responsibility and, 47; typology and, 50–54; victim facilitation and, 52–53; victim precipitation and, 38, 49, 51–54; victim provocation and, 53–54

Victim Information and Notification Everyday (VINE), 153–54

victim notification laws, 154

victim/offender relationship, 17

victim-witness assistance programs, 114–15, 172

victimhood, 16–17, 19, 20, 29, 51, 54, 60

victims' rights movement, 112, 162, 186

Victorian era, 12–14; ideology and, 14; womanhood and, 12–13

Violence Against Women Act (VAWA), 77–80; Interstate Travel to Commit Domestic Violence, 78–80

Vyas, P., 31

Walker, L., 39, 58, 76, 110, 111, 125, 126, 129–31, 137

Walker, R., 42

Wallace, C., 46

Wallace, H., 58

Wandrei, M. L., 58

Warchol, G., 149

Wartella, E., 8, 10

Watson, K., 122

Weiss, K. G., 56

West, A., 58

West, C., 10, 176, 178

Wexler, S., 122

White, R. J., 57, 63

Whitney. D. C., 8, 10

Widom, C. S., 42, 179

Wilson, D., 148–49

Winick, B. J., 133

Winter, J., 16

Wolf, M. E., 103, 121–23, 187

Wolfgang, Marvin E., 42, 51, 54

women's rights, 8, 12–15, 68–69, 90; civil rights and, 88, 94, 97; due process rights and, 177

women's suffrage movement, 14

workforce/paid labor, 8–9, 12–15, 55, 73, 168; statistics of, 15

Yamawaki, N., 59

Yellin, E., 14

Young, V. D., 55

ABOUT THE AUTHORS

Venessa Garcia, Ph.D. is assistant professor of criminal justice at Kean University. She received her M.A. and Ph.D. in sociology at the State University of New York University at Buffalo. Her family court research resulted in a book *Domestic Violence and Child Custody Disputes: A Resource Handbook for Judges and Court Managers*. Her research in policing has been published in the *Journal of Contemporary Criminal Justice, Journal of Criminal Justice, Police Practice and Research: An International Journal, Handbook of Police Administration*, and *Contemporary Issues in Law Enforcement and Policing*. She also over twenty published reports, encyclopedia entries, professional articles, and book reviews. Her latest book, *Female Victims of Crime: Reality Reconsidered* (2010), was an anthology which examined the myths and realities of women crime victims. She served as editor of the *New Jersey Criminal Justice Educator* and deputy editor of *Feminist Criminology*. In 2005, she won the New Scholar of the Year award from the Division of Women and Crime of American Society of Criminology. She serviced as Chair of the Division of Women and Crime from 2007–2009.

Patrick McManimon, Ph.D. is assistant professor at the School of Criminal Justice and Public Policy at Kean University. He received his Ph.D. from Rutgers University in 2000. His research interests include rights of the offender, prison violence, hate crimes, and the criminal justice system response to intimate partner violence. He has published in the *Journal of Criminal Justice Education* and *American Jails*. His teaching concentration is corrections, research methods at the undergraduate level and corrections and theory at the graduate level. He was recently named coordinator of the Criminal Justice Program.